Mór Jókai

Black Diamonds

A Novel

Mór Jókai

Black Diamonds
A Novel

ISBN/EAN: 9783337039288

Printed in Europe, USA, Canada, Australia, Japan

Cover: Foto ©ninafisch / pixelio.de

More available books at **www.hansebooks.com**

MAURUS JOKAI

BLACK DIAMONDS

A Novel

TRANSLATED BY

FRANCES A. GERARD

NEW YORK AND LONDON
HARPER & BROTHERS PUBLISHERS
1898

CONTENTS

CHAPTER	PAGE
I. A Black Place	1
II. The Slave of the Black Diamonds	11
III. The Man-eater	27
IV. A Modern Alchemist	35
V. The Doctor	50
VI. Countess Theudelinde	63
VII. The Countess's Album	79
VIII. The Exorcist	95
IX. "An Obstinate Fellow"	132
X. The Higher Mathematics	146
XI. Soirées Amalgamantes	155
XII. Ritter Magnet	166
XIII. Only a Trifle	189
XIV. Thirty-three Parts	207
XV. Two Points	225
XVI. Good-bye	232
XVII. The Last Rehearsal	245
XVIII. Financial Wisdom	253
XIX. Filthy Lucre	259
XX. No, Eveline!	278
XXI. Respect for Halina Cloth	291
XXII. Two Suppliants	301

CHAPTER	PAGE
XXIII. Financial Intrigue	312
XXIV. The Bondavara Railway	317
XXV. The Poor Dear Prince	324
XXVI. Dies Iræ	327
XXVII. From the Sublime to the Ridiculous	348
XXVIII. Two Children	352
XXIX. Immaculate	357
XXX. Man and Wife	365
XXXI. Eva Dirkmal	373
XXXII. Crushed	378
XXXIII. Charcoal	387
XXXIV. Csanta's Last Will and Testament	395
XXXV. The Ground Burns under His Feet	401
XXXVI. Child's Play	406
XXXVII. Eureka	411
XXXVIII. At Par	419
XXXIX. The Underground World	428
XL. Angela is Even with Ivan	442
XLI. How Ivan Mourned	450
XLII. Evila	453
XLIII. The Diamond Remained always a Diamond	459

BLACK DIAMONDS

BLACK DIAMONDS

BLACK DIAMONDS

CHAPTER I

A BLACK PLACE

WE are in the depths of an underground cavern. It is bad enough to be underground, but here we are all enveloped in black as well: the ceiling is black, so are the walls; they are made of blocks of coal. The floor is one great black looking-glass. It is a sort of pond, polished as steel. Over this polished surface glistens the reflection of a solitary light, the light of a safety-lamp shining through a wire net.

A man guides himself over the pond in a narrow boat. By the doubtful light of the lamp he sees high pillars, which rise out of the depths below and reach to the very roof of the cavern—pillars slender, like the columns of a Moorish palace. These pillars are half white and half black; up to a certain point only are they coal black, beyond that they are light in color.

What are these pillars?

They are the stems of pines and palm-trees. These gigantic stems are quite at home in the layers over the coal-mine, but how have they descended here? They belong to another world—the world of light and air.

The coal layers overhead sometimes take fire of themselves, and the fire, being intense, has loosened the hold of these giants and sent them below.

Coal-pits kindle of themselves often, as every novice knows, but in this case who extinguished the flames? That is the question.

The solitary occupant of the rudely shaped boat or canoe goes restlessly here and there, up and down. He is a man of about thirty years, with a pale face and a dark beard. His firmly closed lips give him an expression of earnestness, or strong, decided will; while his forehead, which is broad, with large bumps over the eyes, shows that he is a deep thinker. His head is uncovered, for here in this vault the air is heavy, and his curly black hair is in thick masses, so that he needs no covering.

What is he doing here?

He drives his boat over the black looking-glass of the lake; round and round he goes, searching the black walls with anxiety, his lamp raised in his disengaged hand. Does he imagine that a secret is hidden there? Does he think that by touching a spring, and saying "Open Sesame," the treasure hidden there for hundreds of years will spring forth?

In truth, he does find treasures. Here and there from the black wall—weakly constructed in some places by Nature's hand—a piece of stone loosens itself—upon it the impression of a leaf belonging to a long-ago-extinct species. A wonderful treasure this! In other places he comes upon unknown crystals, to which science has not as yet given a name; or upon a new conglomeration of different quartz, metal, and stone—a silent testimony to a convulsion of Nature before this world was. All these witnesses speak.

The pillars, too; over them the water of the pond has by degrees formed a crustation of crystals, small, but visible even without a glass. This, too, gives testimony.

The pond is in itself wonderful. It has ebb and flow: twice in the day it empties itself; twice in the day it fills. The water rushes in leaps and bounds, joyously, tumultuously, into this dark, sullen vault; fills it higher, higher, until it reaches the point on the pillars where the color changes. There it remains, sometimes for two hours, stationary, smooth, and placid as a glass. Then it begins to sink, slowly, surely, until it vanishes away into the secret hiding-places from whence it has come. Curious, mysterious visitor! The man in the boat knows its ways; he has studied them. He waits patiently, until, with a sullen, gurgling sound, as if lamenting the necessity, the last current of water vanishes behind a projecting mass of coal. Then he hurriedly casts off his coat, his shoes, his stockings; he has nothing on but his shirt and trousers. He fastens round him a leather pocket, in which is a hammer and chisel; he takes his safety-lamp and fastens it to his belt; and, so equipped, he glides into one of the fissures in the black rock. He is following the vanishing stream. He is a courageous man to undertake such a task, for his way lies through the palace of death. It needs a heart of stone to be there alone in the awful silence. It is a strong motive that brings him. He is seeking the secret which lies under seven seals, the treasure which Nature has concealed for thousands of years. But this man knows not what fear is. He remains three hours seeking. If he had any one—a wife, a sister, even a faithful servant, who knew where he was, what danger he was in, how their souls would have gone out in agony of fear for what might happen!

But he has no one; he is alone—always alone. There is no one to weep for his absence or to be joyful at his coming; his life is solitary, in the clear air of daylight as well as in the depths of the cavern.

The vanished stream is as capricious as a coquettish maiden, as full of tricks and humors. Sometimes it does not show itself for three or four hours; at other moments it comes frolicking back in one, and woe to the unfortunate wight who is caught in its embrace in the narrow windings of the coal-vault! But this man knows the humors of the stream; he has studied them. He and it are old acquaintances; he knows the signs upon which he can depend, and he knows how long the pause will last. He can gauge its duration by the underground wind. When it whistles through the clefts and fissures, then he knows the stream is at hand. Should he wait until the shrill piping ceases, then he is a dead man.

In the darkness a ghostly sound is heard—it is like a long-drawn sigh, the far-away sobbing of an Æolian harp; and immediately the shimmer of the lamp is seen coming nearer and nearer, and in a minute the mysterious searcher of the hidden secret appears.

His countenance is paler than before—deathly; and drops of sweat course down his forehead and cheeks. Down below the air must be heavier in the cavern, or the nightmare of the abyss has caused this cold damp. He throws his well-filled wallet into the boat, and seats himself in it again.

It was time. Scarcely has he taken his place when a gurgling is heard, and out of the fissures of the rock comes a gush of black water, shooting forth with a loud, bubbling noise. Then follows a few minutes' pause, and again another gush of water. The cavern is filling rapidly. In a short time, over the smooth surface of the wall, the watermark shows itself. Clear as a looking-glass it rises, noiselessly, surely, until it has reached the black line upon the pillars.

The boat, with its silent, watchful occupant, floats upon the water like the ghost of the cavern. The water is not like ordinary water; it is heavy like metal. The boat moves slowly, only now the rower does not care to look into the depths of the black looking-glass; he pays no attention to the mysterious signs on the walls. He is occupied taking stock of the air about him, which is growing denser every moment, and he looks carefully at his safety-lamp, but it is closely shut. No escape there.

There is a great fog all round the lamp. The air in this underground abyss takes a blue shade. The man in the boat knows well what this means. The flame of the safety-lamp flares high, and the wick turns red—bad signs these! The angel of death is hovering near.

Two spirits dwell in these subterranean regions—two fearfully wicked spirits. The pitmen call one Stormy Weather, the other Bad Weather; and these two evil spirits haunt every coal-mine, under different names. Bad Weather steals upon its victim, lies like a thick vapor upon his chest, follows the miner step by step, takes away his breath and his speech, laughs at his alarm, and vanishes, when it has reached its height, just as suddenly as it came. Stormy Weather is far more cruel—fearful. It comes like a whirlwind; it sets everything in a flame, kindles the lumps of coal, shatters the vaults, destroys the shaft, burns the ground, and dashes human beings to pieces. Those who gain their livelihood by working underground can never tell when they may meet one or other of these evil spirits.

The secret of "stormy weather," whence it comes, when it may come, no man has yet discovered. It is believed that it arises from the contact of the hydrogen gases with the acid gases which are contained in the open air; and "bad weather" needs only a spark to turn into "stormy weather." The thoughtless opening of a safety-lamp, the striking of a match, is sufficient to fuse the two evil spirits into one.

The solitary man whom we have been shadowing sees, with an anxiety that increases every moment, how the air becomes more and more the color of an opal. Already it is enveloping him in a thin cloud. He does not wait for the flood to rise to its highest point, for, when he reaches a place in the wall where a sort of landing-stage has been made, he jumps upon it, draws the boat by its chain, and moors it fast, and then, ascending by some rude steps to a strong iron door, he opens it with a key, and, closing it behind him, finds himself in a passage which leads him straight into the pit.

Here he is in a busy world, very different from the solitude he has left. The streets, which are narrow and close, are full of miners hard at work with their hammers. The men are nearly naked, the boys who push the wagons are wholly so. There is no sound heard but that of the never-ceasing hammers. In the mine there are no jolly songs, no hearty laughter. Over the mouth of each miner a thick cloth is tied, through which he breathes.

Some of the passages are so narrow that the worker is obliged to lie upon his back, and in this position to reach the coal with his pick. When he has loosened it he drops it into the little wagon, which the naked boys, crawling upon their stomachs, push before them to the opening.

The man who has come out of the dark cavern does not differ in dress from any of the others. He is clothed, certainly, but his clothes are covered with coal-dust, his hands are just as coarse, and he carries a pick and a hammer on his shoulder. Nevertheless, they all know him; there is a rough civility in the tone of each man as he answers the other's greeting, "Good-evening. Bad Weather is coming."

The word is repeated all round.

It was true. Bad Weather *was* close at hand, and these men and boys, who quietly come and go, hammer, shove the wagons, lie on their backs, all know, as well as the convict who is awaiting the execution of his sentence, that death is near.

The heavy, damp fog which lies upon each man's chest, and which fills the mine with its unwholesome smell, needs only a spark, and those who now live and move are dead men, buried underground, while overhead a hundred widows and orphans weep and clamor for their lost ones.

And yet, knowing this, the miners continue calmly to work, as if quite unconscious that the dread Angel of Death is hovering about them.

The man who has just entered is Ivan Behrend, the owner of the mine. He unites in himself the office of overseer, director, surveyor, and bookkeeper. He has enough to do; but we all know the proverb, and, if we have lived long enough, have tested its truth, "If you want a thing well done, do it yourself." Moreover, it is an encouragement to the worker if he sees his employer go shoulder to shoulder with him in the work. Therefore, as we have just seen, the master greets all his workmen with the words, "Bad Weather is coming," and they all know that the master does not consider *his* life of more value than theirs; he does not fly and leave them all the danger, because he is the owner and gets all the profit. Quietly, with the most perfect composure, he gives his orders—the ventilators are to be opened—a charge of cool air at once to the heated coal; and the workers are to go off work after three instead of six hours. He gets into the pail, covered with buffalo-skin, and lets himself down to the bottom of the shaft, to see if the new openings are dangerous. He turns over carefully with an iron bar the coal-dust, to try if any of it is heated, or if gas is there concealed which might cause an explosion. Then, as the ventilators below and the air-pump above begin to work, he takes his place at the anometer. This is a tender little machine, something like the humming-top of children. Its axle turns upon a ruby, and the spring sets a wheel with a hundred teeth in motion; the velocity of this wheel shows the strength of the current of air in the shaft. It should neither be stronger nor weaker than the motion of the "bad weather."

He has now seen to everything; he has taken every precaution, he has left nothing to chance, and, when all the miners have quitted the pit, he is the last to ascend in the basket to the fresh air and the daylight.

Fresh air—daylight!

In Bondavara the sun never shines, the shadow of the smoke hangs like a thick cloud over the land; it is a black country, painted in chalk. The roads are black with coal-tracks; the houses are black from the coal-dust, which the wind carries here and there from the large coal warehouses; the men and the women are black. It is a wonder the birds over there in the woods are not black also.

The mouth of the Bondavara pit is on the slope of a hill, which, when you ascend it, gives you a fine view over the whole country. On the other side, in the valley, are the tall chimneys of the distilling-ovens. These chimneys are busy night and day, vomiting forth smoke, sometimes white, but generally coal-black; for here is distilled the sulphur which forms a component of the coal.

The metal can only be melted when in this condition. One of the principal customers of the coal-mine is the iron-foundry on the neighboring mountain, which has five chimneys from which the smoke issues. If the hammer throws up white smoke, then the oven distils black smoke, and so contrariwise. Both factories working together cast over the valley a continuous veil of cloud and smoke, through which even the beams of the sun look brown and dingy.

From the foundry flows a rusty-red stream, and out of the coal-mine another, which is as black as ink. In the valley both these streams unite and continue their course together. For a little the rusty-red tries to get the better of the inky-black, but it has to give up, and the black rivulet flows on triumphantly through the black meadow lands.

It is a most depressing landscape, and it is saddening to reflect that in such a place men have grown from childhood to middle age, from middle age to old age, and have never seen the green fields or the blue sky of God's heaven.

But Ivan Behrend, when he ascended from the pit into the open air, found little contrast between the upper and the under ground. Below, there was the stifling smell of gas; above, a suffocating fog: below, the black vault of the mine; above, the murky vault of the heavens: and the same men above and below.

It was then evening; the sun had gone down, and for the moment even the vile smoke could not rob it of its setting glory. The towers of the distant castle of Bondavara were touched with its gleam, and the chimneys of the distilling-houses were aglow with this crimson light. The miners were standing about idly; the women and the girls, who are employed in shoving the wheelbarrows, sat gossiping together, as is the manner of the sex. One of them, a young girl, began to sing—a simple little song, with simple words. It was a Slav volkslied—a sort of romance. A mother is taking leave of her daughter, a bride of a few hours; she recalls to the girl her childish days and her mother's care in these words:

> "Wenn ich das Haar dir strich,
> Zerr' ich am Haare dich?
> Wenn ich dich wusch, mein Kind,
> War ich je ungelind?"

The melody was touching, with the sad strain that all the Slav music has, as if composed with tears; and the voice of the one who sang was musical and full of feeling. Ivan stopped to listen to the song until the singer and her companions disappeared behind the houses.

At this moment it seemed to him that there was a great difference between life underground and life in the open.

The song still sounded in the distance; the clouds had passed over and extinguished the light of the setting sun, enveloping the landscape in total darkness. No star, no white house; only the light from the windows of the foundry lighted up the darkness of night; and the smoke of the distilling-factory rose from the chimneys and cast yellow circles upon the sky.

CHAPTER II

THE SLAVE OF THE BLACK DIAMONDS

THERE is nothing startling or new in the declaration that when we speak of "black diamonds" we mean *coal*. That beautiful, brilliant stone, the diamond, is made of carbon. So is your house-coal—the only difference being, the one is transparent, the other black; and the first is the demon, the last the angel.

Coal moves the world. The spirit of progress comes from it; railroads, steamboats borrow from it their wonderful strength. Every machine that is, and works, has its existence from coal. It makes the earth habitable; it gives to the great cities their mighty blaze and splendor. It is a treasure, the last gift presented by earth to extravagant man.

Therefore it is that we call coal "black diamonds."

Ivan Behrend, the owner of the Bondavara coal-mine, was not exactly in the condition of some of his pitmen. He had seen God's heaven, and knew how in happier lands life was bright, careless, sunny as the cloudless sky itself. But for an existence which was all play and no work, Ivan would not have cared. He had inherited the coal-mine from his father, who had left him also an inheritance of a strong will and inflexible perseverance. No trifle, nor even a great obstacle, could stand in the way of Ivan's wishes, and his wish and his pride was to work the Bondavara mine without any help but what his pitmen gave him. It was his ambition—perhaps a foolish one—to have no company at his back, no shareholders to find fault, no widows and orphans to be involved in possible ruin; the mine was his, and his it should be absolutely. Therefore it was a quiet business. The foundry and the inhabitants of the nearest town consumed the yearly output at an uncommonly low price. It never could be, unless with enormous outlay, a great money-making business, seeing that the mine was too far away from any of the great centres. Nevertheless, it brought in a steady income, especially as Ivan paid no useless expenses, and was, as we have said, his own overseer and accountant. He knew everything that went on, he understood his own business perfectly, and he took a pleasure in looking after his own affairs; and these three qualifications, as any business man knows, insure ultimate success.

It was well, however, that he enjoyed such good health, and that this superabundance of vital energy kept him always occupied, and, by a natural consequence, never dull. There was no denying that it was a solitary life for so young a man.

Ivan was very little over thirty, and when he opened the door of his small house with his key, and closed the door behind him, he was alone. He hadn't even a dog to come and greet him. He waited upon himself; and in this he was a great man. Eating he looked upon as an unnecessary waste of time; nevertheless, he ate a great deal, for his muscular and mental system needed food. He was not delicate in his appetite. He dined every day at the tavern. His food was very little better than that of his pitmen, the only difference being that he avoided the strong drinks they indulged in—for this reason, that they worked only with their bodies; he had to bring to his work a clear intellect, not a soddened one. His bed needed no making. It was a wooden plank, upon which a mattress was placed, covered with a sheep-skin. There was no use in brushing his clothes; they were always permeated with coal-dust.

Any one who would offer, by way of doing him a service, to clear out his room, would, in fact, have done him a deadly injury. It was full of every sort of thing —new books half cut, minerals, scientific instruments, plans, pictures, retorts. Not one of these should be moved from its place. There was order in the disorder, and in the heterogeneous mass Ivan could find what he wanted. In one corner was Lavoisier's pyrometer; in another Berard's gas food-warmer. Over there a wonderful sun-telescope; against the wall Bunsen's galvanic battery, together with every conceivable invention, every sort of chemical apparatus for analyzing and searching into the mysteries of Nature.

Amongst these things Ivan was wont to spend the long nights. Another man, tired as he must have been with his day's work, would have flung himself upon his bed, and have sought in sleep some compensation for the labors of the day, or if not weary enough for this, would have sat before his door and breathed the fresh air, which at night was free from smoke and coal-dust. But this student of the unseen withdrew into his inner chamber, lit his fire, made his lamp blaze, and busied himself breaking lumps of coal, cooking seeds, developing deadly gases, a breath of which was enough to send a man into eternity.

What was it he searched for? Was he seeking the secret of the philosopher's stone? Did he abandon sleep to find out how diamonds can be made out of coal? Did he strive to extract deadly poisons, or was he simply pursuing the *ignis fatuus* of knowledge—trying experiments, grubbing in the dark until, in the hopeless endeavor, the over-strained brain would give way, and there would be only the wreck of what was once a noble intellect?

Nothing of the sort. This man had a purpose; he wanted to learn a secret which would be of infinite benefit to mankind—at least, to those who are buried in the pits and caverns of the earth. He wanted to find out by what means it would be possible to extinguish fire in burning pits. To discover this he consumed his nights and the years of his youth and his manhood. It was no thought born of to-day or yesterday; it had been his one desire for many years. He had seen so much misery, such heartrending scenes enacted before these pit mouths—these monsters which swallow up human life like the Juggernauts of old. He wanted to prevent this amount of sacrifice—a sacrifice never thought of by those who profit from the labor of these victims, whose very blood is spilled to keep others warm. It is possible this one idea might drive him mad, or he might lose his life; but the knowledge, if he did gain it, would be, in his opinion, worth the loss. After all, what is the loss of one life against the saving of millions? This man had a fine nature; there was no tinge of self in Ivan Behrend. Also, he had a certain enjoyment in his search. Enjoyment is not the word. Whenever he got even a glimpse of what he wanted, his joy was something unearthly. Surely these moments were worth all the pleasures the world could offer him; and if we can bring our minds to understand this, then we shall comprehend how a young man preferred to be shut up in a cavern, in danger of losing his life, or in a stifling room, trying risky experiments, rather than spend the night with beautiful maidens or pleasant fellows, drinking, dancing, and love-making. There is a charm in Science to those who know her that far surpasses carnal joys.

To-night, however, it must be confessed, Ivan's experiments fell a little flat. Either he was tired, or some other cause was at work. Could it be possible that a girl's song— Yes, such was the humiliating condition of affairs. At the moment when he least expected it, this thing had unexpectedly seized upon him.

With an effort Ivan lit his lamp and lighted his furnace. His experiments, however, were a failure. That girl's song kept running in his head, and the words— how did they go?

> "Say when I smoothed thy hair,
> Showed I not tender care?
> Say when I dressed my child,
> Was I not fond and mild?"*

It was very pretty, and the voice wonderful—so sweet and clear and melodious. To-morrow evening she might be at the pit's mouth again, and then he would find out her name. Even if she were not there, the other girls would know; there were not so many singers among them.

> "Say when I smoothed thy hair"—

Oh, he could settle down to nothing with this tiresome song!—

> "Showed I not tender care?"

He wished he had seen her face, merely to know if it matched the voice. Very likely not. She would be

---

* These lines have been kindly translated from the original by Miss Troutbeck.

hard-featured, like the other girls—bold, unwomanly creatures; beauty and modesty were rare gifts in Bondavara.

The next day Ivan was early at the pit. The opening of the air-oven had done its work; there was only a fractional quantity of hydrogen mixed with the pit air. The ventilators could be shut, and Ivan was able to spend some time in the open.

At twelve o'clock the bell rang to leave off work. As the girls came from the wheelbarrows, he again heard the clear young voice singing the same song. He had not been wrong as to the voice; it was fresh and lovely, like the blackbird in the woods, uneducated and unspoiled, but full of natural charm, tender and joyous as the feathered songster. He could now see the singer—a very young girl, not more than sixteen. The common blue bodice she wore showed every undulation of her girlish figure, untrammelled by any fashionable stays. Her short red skirt, tucked up on one side, and fastened to her waist, disclosed her still shorter chemise, which only reached to her knees, so that her legs were uncovered. They might have been modelled for a statue of Hebe, so perfect were they in shape—the ankles small, and little feet beautifully rounded, like a child's. About her head the girl had wound a colored cloth, and under this she had tucked away her hair; her face, like those of her companions, was blackened by the coal-dust, but even this enemy to beauty could not disfigure her. You could see that her features were regular, her eyebrows thick and dark, her lips red. There was a mixture of earthly dirt and supernatural beauty about this child; besides, she had one thing that even coal-dust could not conceal or dim, her eyes—her large black eyes—shining like two diamonds, which lit up the darkness as two stars.

As these wonderful eyes met Ivan's glance, it seemed to that philosopher as if these diamonds cut away a portion of the glass phial in which he had preserved his heart, and so kept it untouched up to this. But he did not know that this was only the beginning; his glass protector will soon lie in fragments all round him.

The girl made a little curtsey to her employer, and accompanied this small act of duty with a smile which showed two rows of beautiful, pearly-white teeth.

Ivan felt like an enchanted knight in a fairy tale. He forgot what had brought him here, and what he wanted to say; he remained rooted to the spot, gazing blankly after the retreating figure of the girl and her companions. He hoped, without exactly defining what his hope was, that she would look back. That little action would have broken the charm under which he lay. But she did not look back, although one of her companions called her by her name, "Evila." Ivan could see them talking to her, whispering, no doubt, about him. This did not seem to rouse any curiosity in her. She and they had now come to an open shed. Here they seated themselves upon the ground, took out of their pockets pieces of black bread and wild apples, and ate their meal with as much zest as if it had been chicken and grapes.

Ivan returned to his house. For the first time in his life it struck him how lonely it was. It was his custom to keep a sort of log-book, in which he entered his personal notes upon all his work-people. He found this practice very necessary; he knew that a skilled workman of good conduct is far more useful at high wages than a lazy, good-for-nothing fellow of doubtful character who would come for half the wage. At the footnote by the name "Evila" he read—

"A young orphan; supports a crippled brother younger

than herself, who goes upon crutches, and whose tongue is paralyzed. She is very steady, and does not go to the town."

It was certain, therefore, that he must have seen this child before, but had given no attention to her. Every Saturday he paid every workman, every girl and lad in the pit; how, then, had he escaped noticing those wonderful eyes? He did not know, learned as he was, that there is an affinity between two souls destined for one another. It is like an electric shock, this sudden birth of love; but Ivan ridiculed such an idea. Love? Nonsense! He in love with a girl out of the pit? Ridiculous! It was compassion, merely pity for a pretty child, left without either father or mother to watch over her tender age, and, still worse, with a deformed brother to care for and provide with food and medicines. No doubt she gave him the best of everything, while she had to be content with black bread and wild apples, and all the time remained an honest, steady girl. She never even turned her head to look after him. There was nothing but pity in his heart for this coal-black Naiad; it was only pity made him wish to cover those tender little feet with proper shoes; it was only a proper regard for the weakest among his work-people which would cause him to make inquiries as to this poor forlorn child. Oh, self-deception, what a part you play in men's hearts!

The following Saturday the workers came to receive their weekly wages. Ivan, who always paid them himself, remained at his desk until the last one came. On this occasion Evila was the last. Ivan sat at a table, on which was placed the sum to be paid, which was regulated by the account of the work done, which was registered in the day-book.

When the girl, who was dressed as when we first saw

her, in her blue bodice and red skirt, presented herself, Ivan said to her kindly—

" My child, I have determined to increase your wages ; from this day you shall have double pay."

The girl opened her large eyes, and stared in surprise. " Why so ?" she asked.

" Because I am told that you have a crippled brother, whom you have to keep out of your small earnings. You cannot have enough to clothe and feed both him and yourself. I have also heard that you are a well-conducted, honest girl, and therefore it gives me pleasure to reward you by giving you double pay."

" I cannot take it."

" Why not ?"

" Because I know what the others would say. They would joke and tease me about your being my lover, and I should get so tormented that I could not stay in the place."

Ivan was so confounded by this naive explanation, given without the slightest confusion, that he could make no answer. He counted out the usual week's wages, which she stowed away in the bosom of her bodice, wished him good morning, and went her way.

He remained, his thoughts in a maze. In all his experience—and he had a good deal, for his time had not been always spent in Bondavara, and out in the world he had known many women—he had known no woman like this.

She is afraid they will say I am her lover; she is afraid they will tease her so much on that account that she may have to leave the place ! Has she, then, no idea that once I, the master, loved a girl here, she would not push the wheelbarrow any more ? Does she even know what a lover is ? She knows well that she must guard herself against one. Poor child! How earnest she was, and yet she laughed, and she did not know why she laughed, nor yet why she was grave. A savage in the guise of an angel!

He got up, locked his desk, and turned to leave his office; then again remained, thinking.

She is unlike every other woman. I doubt if she knows how beautiful she is, or what is the worth of beauty. She is Eve, a perfect copy of Eve—the Eve of Scripture, and the Eve of Milton. She is Eve, in not knowing wherefore she should blush over her own nakedness—the type of the beautiful in its primitive state, unwashed, savage, with hair unconfined, who wanders through the garden, fearing nothing, and even playing with a serpent. With men she is a woman, by herself she is a child, and yet she displays a motherly care for her little brother. Her figure is a model for a sculptor, her countenance is full of mind, her eyes bewitching, her voice melodious; and yet her hands are hard with the barrow-poles, her mind is troubled with sordid cares for her daily bread, her face is covered with coal-smut, and she has learned her songs in the street.

"The worse for her!" and, after a pause, Ivan added with a sigh, "and the worse for another besides her."

In his mind a total revolution had taken place. The intellectual spirits had for the nonce deserted him, and in their place others had come of a very different order —those demons which the blessed Antony had fought with such good effect in the desert.

When poor Ivan tried to banish these tempters by burying himself in his books and his scientific instruments the form of Evila came between him and the experiment he was busy on, just as Marguerite appeared to Doctor Faust in his laboratory; her voice sounded in his ear, her eyes glowed in the coals, and when he tried to write he found himself drawing a maiden in a blue bodice and short red skirt. It was the same with everything he undertook. Some mocking demon seemed bent on tormenting him.

Abandoning his experiments, this unfortunate man took to reading a volume of light literature. What did he open on? The loves of great and nobly-born men for lowly-born and inferior women. Thus Lord Douglas fell in love with a shepherdess, and became a shepherd for her sake; Count Pelletier took for his wife a gypsy girl, and went about the streets turning an organ; Bernadotte, the King of Sweden, sought the hand of a young girl who watched a flock of geese for a farmer; Archduke John married the daughter of a postmaster; and another Austrian duke raised an actress to the position of grand duchess; the consort of Peter the Great was the daughter of a villager; a Bonaparte married a washerwoman who had been his mistress.

And why not? Are not beauty, sweetness, fidelity, and true worth to be found under a woollen as well as under a silken frock? And, on the other hand, do we not find sinners enough in the upper circles?

Did not Zoraida kill her own children, and was she not a born princess? Faustina took money from her lovers, although she was the daughter of an emperor; the Marquise Astorgas ran a hairpin through her husband's heart; Semiramis strewed a whole churchyard with the corpses of her spouses; King Otto was poisoned in a grove by his queen; Joanna of Naples treasured the ribbon with which the king, her husband, was strangled; Jeanne Lafolle tormented her husband to death; the Empress Catharine betrayed her sovereign and consort, and connived at his murder; and the

Borgias, Tudors, Cillis, all had wives who became notorious in that they wore entwined in their crowns the girdle of Aphrodite.

And do we not find the most exalted virtue in what is called low life? The actress Gaussin, to whom her wealthy lover gave a check with *carte blanche* to write a million thereupon, only wrote that she would always love him ; Quintilla, another actress, bit off her tongue, lest she should betray her lover, who was implicated in a conspiracy; Alice, who undertook to fight a duel for her husband, and was killed; and many others who have suffered silently and died for very love.

Philosophy and history both conspired against Ivan. And then came sleep.

A dream is a magic mirror in which we see ourselves as we would be if our own wishes and inclinations were all-powerful. In his dream the bald man has hair and the blind sees.

Towards the end of the following week Ivan made the discovery that he had lost the use of his understanding. The more he endeavored to force his mind back to its original groove of abstract theories, the more the demons ranged themselves against him. One evening, in a fit of absence of mind, he overheated one of the retorts, so that it burst in his face, and the small glass particles cut his nose and cheek, and he was forced to bind up his wounds with bits of sticking-plaster. It did not occur to him that these strips of black diachylon placed obliquely across his nose did not improve his appearance. He was, however, very angry at his own folly—a folly which went still further, for he began to argue with himself in this way:

"It would be better to marry this girl than to become mad for her sake. Marry her? Who ever heard the like? A pit-girl! What a *mésalliance!* And who cares? Am I not alone in the world? Do I not form the whole family? And does not this constant thought of her come between me and my business? If this goes on I shall be ruined; and as for the *mésalliance*, is there a soul for six miles round who understands the meaning of the word? Not one; and if there should be one, he would have to seek me in the coal-pit, and he would find my face blackened with coal-dust, so that no one could see me blush for shame."

All the same, he never sought the girl. He waited for the Saturday, when he knew she would come for her weekly wages, and on that day she appeared, as usual, the last, because she was the youngest, and stood before him as he sat at his desk. But this time, when Ivan had put the money into Evila's hand, he kept the little fingers in his firm clasp. The girl laughed—perhaps at the plasters, which still ornamented her lover's face.

"Listen to me, Evila. I have something to say to you."

Evila looked uneasy; she ceased to laugh.

"Will you have me for your lover? Nay, my child, I mean you no harm; only one must play the lover before one talks of marriage."

The girl nodded, and then shook her head. "It is not possible," she said.

"Not possible! Why not?"

"Because I am already engaged."

Ivan let go his clasp of her hand. "To whom?"

"That I am not going to tell you," said Evila, "for if I did, I know very well what you would do. You would discharge him, or you would keep him back, and we cannot be married until he is taken on as a regular pitman."

"You mean as a day laborer?"

"Yes."

"And you think more of this low fellow than you do of me, your employer?"

The girl shrugged her shoulders, held her head a little to one side, and threw a look at Ivan which sent the blood coursing to his head. Then she went on, quietly—

"I gave him my promise before mother died, and I must keep my word."

"To the devil with your father and your mother!" cried Ivan, out of himself with baffled hope and rage. "Do you imagine I care what you have promised to a fellow like that? I ask you again, will you give him up and come to me?"

Again Evila shook her head. "I dare not. My bridegroom is a wild, desperate fellow; he would think nothing of doing for you, and setting the pit on fire into the bargain when bad weather was on. Good-evening!" And so saying, she ran away quickly, and mingled with her companions.

Ivan threw the day-book from him so violently that the leaves flew from one corner to another. A common creature, a wheelbarrow-girl, a half-savage, had dared to cross his wishes and refuse his offer! And for a dirty, miserable, underground miner—a common mole!

Ivan had a hard battle to fight with himself when he was once more alone in the solitude of the night. The suppressed passion of the ascetic had suddenly broken through the dams, which moderation had set up to restrain its course.

Beware of the man who professes to be above human passion, who glories in his iron will and his heart of ice; avoid him and the quiet, holy, studious man of soft tongue, who turns away his eyes from women, and shuns what others enjoy. It is upon such as these that outraged human nature revenges itself; and once the demon within gets loose, he plays a fine game to indemnify himself for all the restraint he has undergone. The love of the worldling is a small dog; that of the hermit is a lion.

With this wild beast, which he had suddenly unchained, did Ivan, the man of science, spend the long night, now walking up and down the narrow room, now throwing himself on his bed, a prey to the most horrible temptations, his heart beating with a thousand passionate desires, his thoughts running in as many evil directions. The opposition that had been made to its wishes by Evila had stimulated his passion, and also roused the pride of his nature. The master of the Bondavara mine was a man of fiery temper, kept in check by his strong command over himself; but this command seemed now at fault. He had no longer any power to lay this demon, which had got possession of him, tempting him from every side. With his powerful fist he struck himself a blow upon his chest, near to his throbbing heart.

"Wilt thou be silent? Who is master, thou or I? Do thy duty, slave. I am thy lord, thy king. Thy duty consists in nothing but keeping my arteries in motion, in pumping the air into my lungs, in forcing the blood in the right direction. When you cease your work, your illness is atrophy; but you cannot be my master, for the sovereign ruler is my will."

And as Ivan beat his breast, it seemed to him as if in a magic mirror there were reflected two forms—himself and another Ivan, with whom he waged a deadly combat. It appeared to him as if this other self had robbed him of his form and features, to perpetrate in his name the most odious sins, and as he hit out against this horrid image of himself, it slowly vanished; and then Ivan, falling back upon his pillow, cried out in a loud voice, "Never return, O fiend; never defile my sight again!"

In another hour, pale and exhausted, Ivan was seated quietly before his desk. It required an heroic effort on his part to go into prosaic calculations, to add up long columns of figures; but he forced his weary brain, his tired fingers to the task, and the slave obeyed its master, the body submitted to the mind.

CHAPTER III

THE MAN-EATER

THE morning light found Ivan still seated at his table. As daybreak and lamplight did not agree, he extinguished his lamp, threw aside his papers, and gave himself a momentary rest.

He had conquered; he was himself again. All the fire of passion had died out, the sinful images had vanished, and in his breast reigned profound peace. He had resolved upon his course; an angel had been at his side and inspired him.

It was Sunday morning. The engines which work the distillery were at rest. On Sundays the enormous water-basin, or trough, which fed the steam-pump was utilized to remove the dirt of the week from the miners. From six to seven the basin was free to the women, from half-past seven to nine to the men. The keys of the great pump-house were given over by the machine superintendent on every Saturday night to Ivan, so that no curious or peeping Tom of Coventry could hide himself there, and see these Venuses bathing through a little window, which gave upon the basin, and which was placed there to allow the stoker to see that the water-course was not disturbed when the pumps were at work.

It had never once entered Ivan's brain that he could play Tom if he were so minded. But on this Sunday morning he took the key from its nail and put it in his pocket. Don't start; he did this, not between six and seven, but shortly after eight o'clock. He wanted to see the men bathing, unseen himself. And wherefore? Because he knew the customs which prevail in coal-mines, and that when a pair are engaged, it is customary to inscribe the name of the girl upon the man's naked body. Where the miners have got this Indian and savage method is hard to say. There is a certain tenderness in it, and tenderness is more often found with the savage than the civilized man. The lovers tattoo themselves with a needle, upon the arm or shoulder, and then rub in a corrosive acid, either red or blue. Such a testimony is ineffaceable. Sometimes some poetic temperament adds two hearts transfixed by an arrow, or a couple of doves, or it may be the signs of the miner—the mallet and the pick. It occasionally happens that the relations alter, and the lover would gladly remove the name of the fickle one from his album. This can be done by placing a blister over the name, and then the writing vanishes, together with the skin; a new skin grows, and upon this a new name can be written. It is a real palimpsest. Many are not so discreet. They punctuate a fresh name under the old one, and let the register increase, until sometimes there is not a vacant place.

It did not give Ivan much trouble to find the man he sought. As soon as the water removed the black soot from the bodies of the bathers, he saw on the shoulder of one of them the name of Evila, the letters in blue, two hearts in red. His rival was an intelligent, most industrious laborer; he was called Peter Saffran, and his comrades had added the nickname—the man-eater. To this misnomer Peter had never taken any umbrage. He was a particularly quiet man, and when they teased him he took no notice. He never complained of anything, and never entered either the church or the tavern. Towards children he had a particular antipathy. If one came near him he drove it away, ground his teeth together, and threw anything he had in his hand at it. This peculiarity was so well known that the mothers always cautioned the little ones against the man-eater. For the rest, he was on good terms with every one.

Ivan, having found what he wanted, left the pump-house and returned home, placing himself before the door, so that he could see the people as they went by presently in groups towards the neighboring village to the church. He noticed that Evila was among them. He examined her critically and in cold blood, and he came to quite a scientific conclusion as to the peculiar character of her beauty, which showed a mixture of races. The small hands and feet, the slender form, the narrow forehead, the finely cut nose, the silky black hair — all spoke the Indian or Hindoo type; but the short upper lip and the long, serpent-like eyebrows were derivable from some Slav ancestor. The starry, seductive eyes were decidedly Eastern, the chin and the coloring recalled the Malay race, and the quick, sudden rising of the red blood to the velvet cheek the Caucasian — for this people blush constantly, owing to the cellular texture being fine almost to transparency.

Ivan pondered on all this as Evila passed him; he wondered also why her lover was not with her, for this was an established custom in Bondavara. Peter, however, evidently did not mind these rules of courtship; he was lounging on one of the benches outside the gates of the ventilation-oven, close to the pitmouth, his head in the air, his chin in his hand.

Ivan went to him. "Good-morning, Peter. What are you doing there, my man?"

"I am listening to the wind that is coming from below."

"Why don't you go to church?"

"Because I never pray at all."

"And why not?"

"I do nobody any harm. I neither rob nor murder, and if there is a God, He knows better than I do what is good for me."

"You are quite wrong there, Peter. In these matters there is an immense difference between educated people and what are called the children of Nature. I have my science and thought to fall back on—my intellect is my guide, and preserves me from temptation; but with you, and men like you, it is otherwise. Those who have no other knowledge but what concerns their daily labor have need of faith, of hope, of consolation, and of forgiveness." As he spoke, Ivan seated himself beside the other and laid his hand upon his shoulder. "Something is on your mind, Peter?"

Peter nodded. "There is something."

"Does it weigh on your soul?"

"On my soul, on my body—everywhere!"

"Is it a secret, Peter?"

"No, it is not. If you care to hear it, I will tell it you."

"A murder?"

"Worse than that."

"Don't you think you had better not tell it to me? It may place you in danger."

"There is no danger for me. If it were published on the Market Cross, the law could not touch me; besides, most people know it. You would hear it from some one else if not from me."

"Then tell me."

"It is a short story. When I was only a lad, not quite twenty, I went to sea to seek my fortune. I bound myself as stoker on board a Trieste steamboat. We sailed with a cargo of meal to the Brazils. Our voyage there was prosperous. On our return we took black coffee and wool. On this side of the equator we met a tornado, which broke our engine, smashed our mainmast, and drove the vessel upon a sandbank, where she foundered. Some of the passengers took to the boat; they went only a short way when she upset, and they were all drowned. The rest made a raft from the planks of the sunken ship, and trusted to this frail thing on the open sea. I was one of them. We were in all thirty-nine, including the captain, the steersman, and a merchant from Rio de Janeiro, with his wife and a three-year-old child. We had no other woman or child, for the rest had perished in the open boat. We thought them unfortunate, but now I think they were happy. Better, far better, to have died then. Out of our thirty-nine, soon only nine remained. Oh, how I wish I had been among the dead! For eight days we floated upon the water, the sport of the waves; now buffeted here and there, again in a calm, immovable, nailed as it were to the ocean, without one drop of water to quench our thirst or one morsel of food. Ten of us had died of hunger. For two days we had never eaten, and the ninth day came, and no hope of succor. The sun was burning us up, and the water reflected the heat, so that we lay between two fires. Oh, the horror of that awful time! That evening we took the resolve that one of us should be a victim for the others—that is, that we should draw lots which should be eaten by the others. We threw our names into a hat, and we made the innocent child draw for us. That child drew its own name.

"I cannot tell you, sir, the rest of the ghastly business. Often I dream the whole thing over again, and I always awake at the moment when the miserable mother cursed all those who partook of that horrible meal, invoking heaven that we might never again have peace. At the recollection of her words I spring out of my bed, I run into the woods and wait, to see if I shall be changed into a wolf. It would serve me right.

"Of the partakers of the cursed meal I am the only survivor. The thought haunts me; it burns into my very soul. Besides my own blood, the blood of another human being circulates in my veins. Fearful thoughts pursue me. The piece of human flesh that I have eaten is in me still; it has taken away all wish for any other food. I understand the delight of the cannibals. I never see a rosy-faced child without thinking what a delicious morsel his little rounded arm would be. When I behold a sickly, pale baby, the idea at once occurs to me—Why let it live? Would it not be better—"

He shuddered, and stood up. He hid his hands in his blouse, and after a pause, went on—

"Tell me now, sir, is there any relief for what I suffer? Is there a physician who can cure me, or a priest who will absolve me? I have told my story to both priest and doctor, and one has enjoined me to fast and to chastise myself, the other to drink no brandy and to have myself bled. Neither of them is worth a straw, and such counsel only makes the matter worse."

"I will advise you," said Ivan. "Marry."

Saffran looked with some surprise at his employer, and after a minute a feeble smile stole over his face.

"I have thought of that. Perhaps if I had children of my own this horror of them would disappear."

"Then why don't you marry?"

"Because I am such a poor devil. If two beggars come together, then you have a couple of paupers instead of one. One must first have something to live on."

"That is true; but you are an industrious fellow. I have long wanted to have you as a first-class pitman, but I waited to advance you until you got married. It is my rule to give all the best places to married men. I have found by experience that the unmarried ones, when they get higher pay, go straight to the bad. There is more dependence to be placed in a married man; he won't leave his place for a mere nothing. Therefore, consider the matter. After the first Saturday on which you can tell me that you have been called in church with your intended, you will receive the pay of a pitman, and I shall give you a dwelling-house for yourself."

Peter's face was a study. He could not believe that what he heard was real earnest. When this was made clear to him, he was ready to fall at the feet of his benefactor; he almost sobbed as he stammered forth some words of thanks.

"Now," cried Ivan, with friendly encouragement, "today is a Sunday. Does nothing occur to you, my friend?"

The man sprang to his feet.

"Service has not yet begun," went on Ivan; "the congregation have not all arrived at the church yet. I think there would be time for you to catch up your bride and go with her to the clergyman."

Peter said no word to this proposal, but he began to run; his legs were long, and he was soon out of sight.

He was bareheaded; he had forgotten his hat upon the seat. Ivan saw it, and took it into his house to keep, but he stood looking after the fleet lover until he had disappeared behind the stone wall at the turning. Then he went in, with Saffran's hat in his hand.

"How happy he is!" he thought, and sighed.

When he was in his room he wrote in his day-book that from the following day, Monday, he had engaged Peter Saffran as a first-class pitman with the usual wages, and that in his place another day-laborer should be taken on. When he had closed the book, his heart whispered—

"My cruel master, art thou content?"

But Ivan had his misgivings, and answered his heart thus—

"I don't believe in you, since I have seen how easy it was for you to slip on the ice. I must for the future watch closely. I am not sure of the purity of my own motives even now. God knows what lies under this apparent abnegation. Perhaps you think as a young wife— But I shall watch you closely, traitorous heart of mine; you shall lead me into no more pitfalls."

Again he consulted his account-book, and found that the increase in this year's income allowed him to take on an overseer at a very fair salary. He wrote out the proper advertisement, and despatched it that very evening to different papers for insertion. In this way he would not be thrown into daily contact with his workpeople.

CHAPTER IV

A MODERN ALCHEMIST

A FORTNIGHT had passed since Ivan sent his advertisement for insertion, when, one morning, and again it was Saturday morning, Peter Saffran came and told him that two gentlemen had just arrived, who wished to see the mine.

"They must be foreigners," he added, "since they spoke French together." Peter's life as a sailor had given him some knowledge of the French tongue.

"I shall be with them immediately," returned Ivan, who was busy pouring a green liquid through a pointed felt hat. "Let them meanwhile get into the usual miner's dress."

"That is already done; they are all ready for you."

"Very good. I am going. And how are you getting on, Peter?"

"With the wedding? Everything is in order; to-morrow we shall be called in church for the third time."

"And when shall you be betrothed?"

"It is just now Advent, and our priest will not marry us; but on the first Sunday after the Three Kings we shall have the wedding. I am not at all annoyed at the delay, for I have to get together a little money. When a man marries he must have all sorts of things—furniture and the like; and something for the cold winter into the bargain."

"And have you put by nothing out of your wages?"

"Yes, sir; I had over a hundred and fifty gulden laid by. I had spared everything on myself—food and drink, and even the pipe—and I had got together this sum. Then what should the devil do but bring the recruiting commission down here, and I had to give all my money into the greasy palm of the examining doctor, so that he might report me as being unfit for service because I squinted. It's a trick I have. I can squint for a quarter of an hour together, although my eyes are straight; on this account I shall be let off by the doctor, but my hundred and fifty gulden are gone. I shall have to squint at the marriage ceremony, for the priest only marries me because I am unfit for service."

"Well, Peter, you may count upon some help from me."

"Thank you, sir, but I don't like loans; that is like eating one's supper at dinner."

By this time they had reached the place where the strangers were waiting.

"Ah," cried Ivan, "so it is you, Felix!" and he held out his hand cordially to the visitor.

The old acquaintance whom Ivan called Felix looked as if he belonged to another generation. His soft complexion, carefully waxed mustache, short imperial, his fine, dark-blue eyes, and particularly the shape of his head, and the way it was placed on his shoulders, taken together with his elegant dress, which the rough miner's blouse could not quite conceal, betrayed the man of the world. When he spoke, his voice was almost womanly; the tone was clear and high, like one of the Pope's choir.

Felix hastened at once to put his friend's mind at ease upon a necessary part of his visit.

"I hope you will forgive our putting up at the inn. I was sure you would have made us welcome, but you are a busy man, and you would not care to be at the bother of entertaining us; besides, like all men of business, you are, I dare say, a little in the rough, and the inn is really very comfortable. May I introduce you to my travelling companion, Gustav Rauné? He is a mine-surveyor and engineer."

Ivan was well pleased at his friend's forethought in the matter of hospitality; not that he would not have made him welcome so far as lay in his power—and there were unoccupied rooms in the house which would have accommodated the two men—but his manner of life would have been disturbed. He had never for one moment thought of entertaining a guest.

"My house," he said, frankly, "is not fitted to receive my friends, and, indeed, none come; but the inn is also mine. I trust you will consider yourselves my guests while you remain here."

"We accept your offer," returned the other; "the more readily, since we have really come here on your business. Yesterday I read your advertisement. You require an overseer?"

"I do." Ivan looked doubtfully at the two gentlemen.

"No, no; it is not for me," laughed Felix. "I understand nothing of the business; but Rauné is inclined to join you, should he find that there are capabilities here for real work. Rauné is an old friend of mine. He has learned his business under Erenzoter. You know the firm of Erenzoter? He is thoroughly up in the whole thing."

Rauné all this time said not a word, perhaps for the best of reasons, that, being a Frenchman, he did not understand the language in which the others spoke. He was a small man, slight, and well-made, with penetrating eyes, a sharp-cut face, and very long mustache.

To this gentleman Ivan explained in fluent French that he would be glad to show him all the properties of the Bondavara mine before going closer into the matter of engaging him permanently.

After these courtesies they went down into the pit. Here the two men were soon convinced that each was thoroughly conversant with the whole machinery and working of a mine. Sometimes they held different opinions upon certain systems, and in the dispute or argument which would arise each disputant saw that the other had nothing to learn from him.

Rauné displayed extraordinary quickness and knowledge in valuing the coal stratum. Even without looking at the geometrical maps he was able to decide upon the probable profit, as also upon the probable extent of the layer or stratum beyond the actual ground covered by Ivan's pit. His valuation agreed in almost every particular with that already made by Ivan. By mid-day the inspection was over, and they went to the inn for dinner, having first given some time to washing and general purification. A visit to a pit is by no means a cleanly undertaking.

The afternoon was devoted to the inspection of the distilling-ovens, and in the evening they went over the foundry. When they returned from the foundry, Felix went in with Ivan to his house, while Rauné returned to the inn.

Ivan led his old acquaintance into his workroom, where, in truth, a wonderful disorder prevailed, cleared a chair, full of maps and books, for him to sit upon, and told him to light his cigar at a chemical lamp of a new construction. After a pause Felix began:

"You were always of an inquiring mind, Ivan. I remember well how at college you distanced every one. As for me, I was a pygmy near a giant. Now, tell me truly, have all your science, your industry, and your physical exertions made you a rich man?"

Ivan laughed. "This mine gives me an annual income of ten thousand gulden."

"In other words, it produces nothing, or, at least, next to nothing. You are director, overseer, cashier, engineer, secretary, bookkeeper, and conveyer of goods, and you receive, roughly calculated, just what you would have to pay these employés if you had not united all their different offices in yourself. In other words, your work, your talent, your studies, your zeal, your expenditure of thought and strength upon this mine of yours only bring you in the miserable return which any proprietor would give to a man who filled only one of these offices. As a fact, you don't get a farthing by it."

"The mine is not to blame, neither am I; it is the result of a small consumption, and, in consequence of this, the production cannot be increased."

"I will tell you in two words where the fault lies. In the present day strength is alone to be found in co-operation. In the political world the smaller states go to the wall; they are forced to tack themselves on to larger ones, and so form a union. It is the same in the commercial world; small tradesmen must give way to the larger co-operative centres, and it is better for them to understand this, and make part of a company."

"There is no danger of our foundry closing; our iron and our coal take a first place, and could not be crushed out."

"An additional reason for developing my idea — an

idea which, I may as well tell you, was the factor that brought me here. You have already guessed, I imagine, that I am not such a good fellow as to undertake the journey solely on Raune's account. He is not a chicken, and could have introduced himself. I have a great plan in my head. I intend to make you a wealthy man, and, naturally, I shall feather my own nest at the same time."

"How so?"

"I do not know where I once read this short synopsis of how different nations acquire money: 'The Hungarian seeks it, the German earns it, the Frenchman wins it, and the American makes it.' It is a most characteristic description. You have only to watch the Hungarian, how he seeks in every hole and puddle for a piece of gold; the German will work in the sweat of his brow till he gets his reward, a piece of gold; the light-hearted Frenchman will win the last piece of gold his victim has; but the Yankee sits in a corner, gnaws his finger-nails, and makes his pile. Yes, gold lies in undiscovered millions, only waiting to be 'made.'"

"Where does it lie?"

"In the capabilities of life, in bold undertakings, in the concealed treasures of the earth, which require development, and in the outlay of capital; in new discoveries, in the extension of the means of communication, in the increase of luxury, in the follies of mankind, in the exertions made by scientists; and especially in the money-box where small capitalists keep their gold, which should circulate through large channels to be of use. The number of small capitals should be thrown into one large, commercial mart, and by means of this credit every gulden would bring in three times its value. This is the art of the American; this is how to make a pile of gold. It is a splendid art, an honest art, and it seems to thrive with those who adopt it."

When he had concluded this rather long-winded exordium, Felix threw himself back in his chair with an air as who should say, "Are you not dazzled with the brilliancy of my conception? Is not Felix Kaulmann one of the greatest financiers of the day? Surely you are convinced that he is."

So far as that went, the name had a fair reputation. The Kaulmanns had always been in finance, and were well-known bankers. Of late, since Felix had inherited the business from his father, the firm were more before the public. Ivan knew his old schoolfellow well; he looked at him now quietly.

"How do you propose to make a pile out of my pit?"

"I have a big scheme in my head."

"But the whole pit is anything but big."

"So it appears to you, because you don't view it from my standpoint. You have sought for diamonds in the mine, but it has never occurred to you that there may be iron ore. This pit produces, you tell me, a profit of ten thousand gulden; that is the interest of two hundred thousand florins. I can get you a company who will buy the whole place out and out for two hundred thousand florins."

"But I would not part with my pit at any price. I am here in my element, like the mud-worm in the mud."

"You need not leave it—certainly not; on the contrary, if you wished to go, I would keep you chained, if necessary. The company will start with a recognized capital of four millions; we will form a large business, which on one side will ruin Prussian coal, on the other side will drive the English iron out of market. You shall be the principal director of the business, with a yearly salary of ten thousand florins, and two shares in the business; besides which you will be allowed to take, if you wish it, a portion of the purchase-money in bonds at par, and these will bear interest at twenty per cent. You will enjoy an income of thirty thousand florins, instead of your beggarly ten thousand florins, which you now have, and, into the bargain, hardly any work."

Ivan listened to this proposal without interrupting the speaker. When Felix had finished, he said, in a calm voice—

"My dear Felix, if I were to propose to a company ready provided with four millions the purchase of a business which up to the present had only produced ten thousand guldens profit, and which profit could never in the future realize more than eight hundred thousand gulden, do you not think I would be a despicable villain? If, on the other hand, I placed my own money in such a company, I should be equally a perfect fool."

At this clear definition of his recent proposal Felix burst into a peal of laughter. Then, passing his pliant little walking-stick behind his back, he placed both his hands on the ends, and said with an air of profound wisdom—

"You have not heard all my plan. It has not altogether to do with your colony. You know well that your pit is only a small portion of the monster coal stratum of the Bonda Valley, which stretches far away—as far, indeed, as Muld Valley. I intend to buy this entire region; it can be had now for a mere song, and when properly worked it will be worth millions—millions earned by honest means. No stealing or taking unfair advantage of any one. We only raise a treasure which lies at our feet, so to speak, which is there ready for us,

or for any one. It needs only sufficient strength on the part of those who lift it."

"That is quite another thing. Now I can understand your scheme. I will also not contradict your assertion that it is lawful and generous; but it is just because it is so that it is full of holes. It is quite true that the treasure which lies concealed in the Bonda Valley is immense—it is possible that it represents millions; but this treasure cannot be discovered, for the Bondavara property is not for sale."

"Really!"

"I will tell you why; because at this moment it belongs to Prince Bondavary, who is one of the richest men in this country."

"I should imagine that no one knows better than I do how rich he is."

"In the next place, this man is one of the proudest of our aristocrats, to whom I, for one, would not venture to make the proposal to turn his old family property—the cradle, we might say, of his race—into a mine to be worked by a company."

"Oh, so far as that goes, we have seen many an ancient race glad to do a bit of commercial dirt. The King of Italy is a crowned king; and, nevertheless, he has sold Savoy, the place from which his family took their name and the right to have a cross on their shield."

"Well, suppose the old prince were inclined to sell this property, he could not do so as long as his sister, the Countess Bondavary, is alive. Her father left the castle and the property round about to his daughter, who is now nearly fifty-eight, and may live yet another thirty years. She has grown up in that castle; she has, to my knowledge, never left it, not even for one day; she hates the world, and no human power would induce her to part with her beloved Bondavara to a coal company, not if the last remaining stratum were to be found under the castle, and without this the world should perish from want of fuel."

Felix laughed, then answered with an air of ineffable conceit—

"I have conquered greater difficulties than an old maid's fad, and for the matter of that, women's hearts are not locked with a Bramah key."

"Well, let us suppose," said Ivan, good-humoredly, "that you have overcome the prejudices of the prince and his sister, and that you have actually started your monster company. Then begin all the technical difficulties; for what is the first necessary to an undertaking of the kind?"

"A sufficient supply of money."

"By no means. A sufficient supply of workmen."

"Wherever money is plentiful, human beings are pretty sure to flock."

"Between men and men there is a wonderful difference. This is an article in which one is likely to be easily deceived. With us there is a want of first-class workmen."

"We would get men from France and Belgium."

"But the men who would come from France and Belgium would not work for the wages we give our men. They would ask double. In such a commercial undertaking, the first false step would be to raise the wages to more than the old system, for my conviction is that every industrial enterprise to be safe must work upon its own internal capabilities. We should measure our strength according to the circumstances in which we find ourselves, and we should educate our own workmen: draw them to us by learning together. The trade should extend slowly, but surely, by small experiments."

"You are too cautious. I can convince you to the contrary. For instance, a steam-engine of a hundred-horse power needs just the same labor to work it as one of four-horse power; and a small business requires as many account-books as a large one, and small undertakings in like manner, even if they are in themselves lucrative, will eventually be swamped by the larger ones on account of the want of the proper activity, without which all trade dies of itself."

"Nevertheless, there is less danger of sudden collapse in a small business," returned Ivan, reflectively. "I like a certainty."

"And what certainty have you? Suppose, just for the sake of argument, that one bright morning the Austrian minister of trade listens to the petition of the English iron masters, and that the free importation of raw iron is allowed. Your neighbor over there will at once shut his foundry, and you may go and sell your coal to the smithy, eh, Ivan?"

"I have gone into all that. Our raw iron can compete with the English, and there would be—"

"Your ideas are *rococo;* they belong to the last century. If America had worked on these lines she would not have overshadowed Europe."

"That may be. What I maintain is that foreign workmen are a bad investment. Those who come to us are, for the most part, men who cannot get on in their own country; restless fellows, ever wanting change; members of secret societies, socialists, and atheists; and so soon as they get among our men they begin disseminating their vicious doctrines, and the next thing is a strike for higher wages."

"Have you ever had a strike here?"

"Never!"

"How do you prevent it?"

"That is my secret, which cannot be told in a few words. I am, however, convinced of one thing: the first obstacle a company would have to contend against would be the price of labor, and the second difficulty would be to secure the services of a really capable overseer; one who would understand the *technique* of the business."

"We could easily get one from abroad."

"That might be; but I, as a private individual, could get one easily if I had sufficient money to pay him, for I could choose the best for my purpose, and could give him what I chose, as far as his merits deserved."

Felix laughed at Ivan's description. "That is it exactly, as if you read it out of a book; and just on this account I intend to give the complete direction of the business to a man who understands it to a T, and this man is you."

"That is a complete mistake. I do understand the working of my own small business, but I am quite ignorant of the ways of a great concern. Like many another small man, I should be a child in the hands of big speculators, and I should probably wreck the whole concern."

"You are too modest. On the contrary, I think you would outwit the big speculators."

"Well, suppose all went according to your wishes, or, rather, as it presents itself to your imagination. The great business is in full swing, delivers goods at moderate prices, and in sufficient quantity. Now comes the real objection — the topographical impediment. The Bonda coal-mine is twenty miles from the nearest railway, and twenty-five miles from the nearest river. On your way here you must have noticed the state of the roads. During four months of the year we can send no freight to a distance, and at any time the cost of transporting our coal and iron adds so much to the price that it is impossible for us to compete with either Prussia or England."

"I know all that," said Felix, stroking his beard with the coral head of his stick; "but a light railway would soon settle all this. We could run it from Bonda Valley to the principal emporium." He spoke as if running light railways were a mere trifle.

"A railway through the Bonda Valley!" returned Ivan, in a tone of surprise. "And do you really believe that with a capital of four millions you could construct a railway twenty miles long?"

"Certainly not. That would be quite a separate affair."

"And do you think you would find people ready to advance money for such an uncertain return as mere luggage traffic would insure to the shareholders in such a railway?"

Felix moved his stick from his beard to his mouth, and began to suck the top.

"And why not," he said, at last, "when the state would guarantee a certain rate of interest on the advance?"

Ivan opened his eyes still wider, and placed upon each word an emphasis.

"The state will give to this railway a guarantee of interest! You will excuse me, Kaulmann—that is not possible."

Felix answered, after some consideration, "There are certain keys by which the bureaus of even ministers of state can be opened." After this oracular speech he was silent, pressing the top of his stick upon his lips, as if to restrain his words.

Ivan drew out the drawer of his writing-desk and took therefrom a piece of black bread.

"Do you see this? People who eat such coarse stuff don't dance attendance upon ministers."

Felix threw his head back with a scornful laugh and twisted his stick impatiently between his fingers.

"*Allons, n'en parlons plus*," he said. "You have plenty of time to make up your mind, for what I have once resolved to do, that I do. I am quite ready to bet with you that I shall secure the Bonda Valley property from under the nose of the old prince and the faddy countess, and that the largest factory in the kingdom shall be established *here*, and the trade carried on with the outside world. This will all come to pass, as sure as my name is Felix Kaulmann."

"Well, I wish you every luck in your undertaking, but for my part I will have none of it."

The arrival of Rauné interrupted the conversation. The Frenchman explained that he had considered Ivan's offer, and was ready to agree to his conditions and to enter on its office at once. Thereupon Ivan gave him his hand as a sign that the agreement was concluded. Then he handed him the books and the strong-box, the former with the complete list of the pitmen, the laborers, the girls, and boys engaged in the mine; the latter with the money which was paid to them for the week's work, and he asked the new overseer to appoint a room in the inn, where he was going to live, as the place where the miners should come to be paid.

As it happened, this was a Saturday, and therefore

on this evening the overseer should enter on his new duties.

The inn was exactly opposite to Ivan's house. Groups of pitmen collected on the vacant space between the two houses. Ivan went to the window to see in what order the payments would be made by the new director. Felix also amused himself by means of his pocket-glass, staring at all the women.

"Ah!" he exclaimed, suddenly, "that little Cinderella over there in the red skirt wouldn't be bad for the model of a bronze statuette. I should like her to teach me how to say 'I love you' in the Slav language."

"Take care," laughed Ivan; "she is betrothed, and her lover is called a man-eater."

Just then Peter Saffran came out of the tavern. He had received Evila's money with his own, and offered it to her. She, however, refused to take it, and the pair went off together in good-humor with one another. The young girl's hand was upon Peter's arm, and as she passed the window they heard her singing.

"*Saperlot!* What a voice!" exclaimed the banker. "Why, she beats Thérèse. If she were in Paris—"

He didn't finish his sentence. Ivan lit a cigar, and sat smoking silently.

CHAPTER V

THE DOCTOR

The next day was Sunday. Ivan took Felix and Rauné through the workmen's colony to show them the dwelling-houses, which were clustered together like a village. This village had been made by Ivan's father. The district had been formerly occupied by the very poorest, who eat nothing but potatoes; but now the miners who lived here were well-fed and well-lodged. Each pitman had his own cottage and fruit-garden.

When the three men came to the house in which Evila lived they stood still and looked into the little yard beyond. They felt obliged to do so, first, because the door stood open, and secondly, because in the yard a scene was going on of which they were unseen spectators.

Peter Saffran was beating Evila. The lover held his betrothed by her long black hair, which fell over her shoulders nearly to the ground. He had the rich masses gathered up in his left hand and wound round his wrist, while in his right hand he had a thick plaited cord with which he struck the poor girl over the shoulders, neck, and back. As he did so, his eyes expanded until nearly all the white was visible, his eyebrows almost touched one another, his countenance grew white with rage, and through his open lips his white teeth looked like those of an infuriated tiger. At each blow of the rope he growled out—

"So you will have your own way, will you? You will defy me, will you?"

The girl made no protest against her lover's violence. She did not cry, neither did she beg him to spare her. She pressed her apron to her lips, and looked at her cruel persecutor with eyes full of the most divine compassion.

"What a beast!" cried Felix. "And he is her lover!"

"Just so," replied Ivan, indifferently.

"But you should interfere; you should not allow that pretty child to be ill-used by the savage."

Ivan shrugged his shoulders. "He has the right; she is his betrothed, and if I were to interfere he would beat her more. Besides, don't you see he has been at the brandy flask? There would be no use in reasoning with him."

"Well, I shall reason with him to some purpose," returned Felix. "I am not going to stand by and see that pretty creature beaten."

"You will do no good, I warn you. The underground laborer has no respect for men in black coats."

"We shall soon see as to that. Do me the favor to call out 'doctor' as soon as you see me take the fellow by his arm."

As he spoke, the elegantly attired Felix rushed across the narrow passage which led to the yard, and confronted the infuriated savage.

"You brute!" he cried. "Let go that girl. Why do you beat her?"

Saffran answered phlegmatically, "What is that to you? She is my betrothed." He smelled fearfully of brandy.

"Ah, so you are thinking of marrying, are you?" returned Felix, looking at the Hercules, to whose shoulder he hardly reached. "And how is it that you are not on military service, my friend?"

The cord slipped from Peter's hand. "I could not pass," he said, in a low voice. "I have it in black and white. I am not fit."

"Could not pass—not fit—when you can use your arms so well? Who was the upright doctor that gave you that certificate in black and white? Such muscles—" He touched with the tips of his gray gloves the starting muscles on the brawny arm.

"Doctor!" called out Ivan.

When Peter heard this exclamation, and felt the pressure of Felix's fingers, he let go his hold of Evila's hair. She was free.

"You just wait till to-morrow, young man," continued Felix, shaking his cane before Peter's nose—"till to-morrow, and you shall have a second examination. I shall be curious to find out what is the secret impediment which makes *you* unfit to serve your country. That is my business here."

Peter began suddenly to squint.

Felix burst out laughing. "Two can play that game, young man," and he, too, fell to squinting. "I shall pay you a visit to-morrow."

At this Peter took to his heels, and making one rush of it, was soon over the wall of the yard, and never ceased running until he reached the wood.

Ivan was astonished at the result of Felix's interference. He, who was twice as strong mentally and physically as this effeminate town-bred man, would have been routed signally, and behold, the weak one in gray gloves had chased the savage from the field, and was master of the situation! He felt vexed, yet he wished to conceal his vexation. He saw Felix calmly conversing with Evila, whose deliverer he had been. Ivan was not going to stand open-mouthed looking at the hero.

"Let us go on," he said to Rauné. "Herr Kaulmann can follow us if he wishes."

Herr Kaulmann was not inclined to continue his walk. A full hour afterwards, when they were returning, he met them. He said he had been looking everywhere for them without effect. He had done a good morning's work in their absence. Finding himself alone in the yard with the girl, he had spoken to her in a sympathizing tone.

"My poor child, what did you do to that brute, that he should ill-use you so cruelly?"

The girl dried her eyes with the corner of her apron and made an effort to smile. It was a piteous attempt, tragic in its effort to hide her sufferings.

"Oh, sir, the whole thing was only a joke. He only pretended to strike me."

"A nice joke! Look at the welts his blows have made."

He took from his pocket a little case, which held his pocket-comb, a dandified affair with a small looking-glass, which he held before her eyes.

Evila reddened over face and neck when she saw the disfiguring marks of her lover's affection. She spoke with some anger in her voice—

"Sir, you have been very kind, and I will tell you all about it. I have a little brother who is a cripple. As soon as father died mother married again. Her husband was a drunkard, and when he was tipsy he would beat us and tear my hair. Once he threw my brother, who was only three years old, down a height, and since then he has been crippled. His bones are bent and weak, and he has to go on crutches; his breath, too, is affected; he can hardly breathe from asthma, and this was stepfather's doing. But that did not soften him; on the contrary, he persecuted the poor baby, and it was ten times worse after mother died. How many blows I have had to bear, and glad I was to get them if I could only spare the child! At last stepfather fell from the shaft; he was drunk, and he broke his neck. A good thing it was, too; and since then we have lived alone, and what I earn does for us both. But now I am going to marry Peter, and Peter hates my poor crippled brother. He says he must go out and beg; that an object like him on crutches could stand at the church-door on Sundays, and in the market on week-days, and get pence enough to support himself. Oh, it is shameful of him! And to-day we had a quarrel about it. He came to take me to church, where we were to be called for the third time. I was nearly ready, but I said I should first give my little brother some warm milk, and I went to fetch it. The boy was sitting on the doorstep waiting for it.

"'Warm milk!' cried Peter, in a rage. 'I will give him what will make him fat!' and then he struck the child and tore at his ear as if he would tear it from his head. The child has a peculiarity—strange for a child —he never cries, although you might beat him to death. He opens his eyes and his mouth, but says nothing, and gives out no sound. I implored Peter to let the poor thing alone, for I loved him. This set him in a horrible rage.

"'Then let the dwarf go packing!' he screamed. 'Give him a beggar's wallet, and let him beg from door to door; there never was a more unsightly cripple than he is, so let him bring home something for his keep, the scarecrow!'"

The tears ran down the girl's face as she told this.

"How can he help being so ugly and deformed?" she went on. "It was not God who made him so, it was stepfather; and so I told Peter, and that I would rather he would beat me than that he should touch the child.

"'And I will beat you,' he said, 'if you say another word'; and then he seized hold of the child and kicked him. 'Get out of my sight, you little monster of ugliness!' he said. 'Go to the church-door and beg, or I will eat you.' And he made such a horrible face that my poor little brother shrieked with fright. I could not stand seeing him tortured in this way. I took him from him, and would have covered him up in my arms, but he ran and hid himself in the chimney. I *was* very angry.

"'If you torment him like this,' I said, 'I shall break with you.'

"Then he seized me by my hair and fell to beating me, as you saw. Now he will do it every day."

"No, no," returned Felix. "The fellow will have to serve his term; a muscular giant like him cannot shirk military duty. If every one did that, who the deuce would defend the country and the emperor? It cannot be winked at—"

"Then are you really a doctor?" said Evila, doubting.

"Of course I am, when I say I am."

A faint reflection of pleasure crossed the girl's face.

"Then perhaps you can tell me if my little brother can ever be cured?" she said, eagerly.

"I can tell you. Bring me the child."

Evila went into the kitchen, and after some trouble persuaded the cripple to come out of his shelter in the chimney. This poor victim of man's cruelty was a miserable object. He looked as if nature had exhausted the stuff of which he was made; not one of his limbs fitted the other, and his will seemed to have no power over his body.

Evila took the sick boy upon her knee, and kissing his cheek, withered like a bit of dried parchment, told him not to be afraid, for that the stranger was a kind gentleman.

Felix examined the limbs of the cripple with all the attention of an experienced surgeon, and then with a professional air said—

"The injury can still be cured; it requires only time and care. There is in Vienna an orthopedic institution expressly for such cases; cripples are there treated, and grow up strong, healthy boys."

"Ah!" cried the girl, taking hold of Felix's hand. "Would they take Janoska there? But it would cost money, which I haven't got. I might get employment in this institution where cripples are made straight again. I would serve them well if they would cure my little brother."

"I don't see any reason why he shouldn't be admitted," returned Felix, gravely, "especially on my recommendation. I have great influence, and a word from me—"

"You will say it, won't you, and God will forever bless you?" cried the girl, throwing herself on her knees and covering the hands and feet of the pretended doctor with kisses. "I will serve them; I will work for them day and night. They need not keep a dog; I will be their dog, and guard the house for them, if they will make Janoska straight, so that he need not beg at the church-door. Is it far to Vienna?"

Felix laughed. "You don't think you could carry the boy to Vienna, do you? I will manage the journey for you. When I have once promised, I keep my word. I have my carriage here; I will, if you like, take you both to Vienna."

"Oh, I will sit by the coachman, with Janoska on my lap!"

"Very well, my child," returned Felix, with the air of a patron. "I am glad to help you; therefore, if you have resolved to take your brother to Vienna to have him cured, I shall give you the opportunity. Be ready to-morrow morning when you hear the post-horn sound. That rough fellow who beat you just now will be taken by the pioneers corps, who recruit next week, and he will have to serve his four years. Now, here is some money for you, that you may buy some warm clothing for the boy, for the nights are cold, and I travel day and night."

The sum of money he placed in the girl's hand took away her breath, and left her no voice to thank him. Two bank-notes, ten pounds each—a fortune to a poor girl. The gentleman was a great nobleman; he was a prince. He was, however, already on his way before she could speak a word, and it would not do to run through the street after him.

Evila then gave way to her joy like a child, as she was. She laughed, ran about the room carrying the boy, set him on a seat, knelt before him, kissed and hugged in her arms his emaciated body.

"We are going away, Janoska, my heart's darling, in a coach to Vienna. Ho, ho, little horse, ho! In a coach with four gee-gees all hung with little bells! And Janoska will sit in my lap. Janoska will have good medicine and good food, and his feet and his hands, his back and his chest will get straight. He will be a big fellow, like other boys. Then we will come home, not in a coach, but on our feet. We go in a coach, and we come back on two feet without a crutch!"

Then the poor little cripple began to laugh like her. Evila ran off to the store, and bought for the child a warm winter jacket, a cap, and boots; still, she could not, even with these stupendous purchases, spend half of the money. What she had left she determined to return to the gentleman.

Now it was full time to go to church. Her friends wondered to see her come in alone. They asked her where was Peter? Evila answered she had not seen him that day. It went against her conscience to tell a lie before mass, but then, when one is placed in a situation that one must lie, what can be done? A woman or a girl who has been beaten by her betrothed or her husband must deny it. God pardons the lie, and society demands it.

Peter Saffran was nowhere to be seen in the church. Evila felt terribly ashamed when the clergyman from the pulpit gave out for the third time the banns of her marriage. And there would be no marriage! Tears came into her eyes and sorrow filled her heart at the thought that she was leaving her home, her bridegroom, her friends, all the places she knew, the things she was accustomed to, and was going out into the world alone. These thoughts preyed upon her all day, until she was obliged to go out and look for Peter Saffran. She suspected where she would find him.

In the depths of the woods at the bottom of a mountain ravine lay a cottage, or hut, where, at the time of the recruiting, the men and boys who wanted to avoid the conscription would hide themselves for weeks, until the officers would have gone on to another place. Not one betrayed their hiding-place; and here, no doubt, Peter lay concealed. Evila went blindly through the thicket. The night was dark, the wood still darker.

From the mountain came the growling of the hungry wolves. The girl trembled with fear, but went her way, nevertheless, resolved to find her betrothed, although she was sure he would again beat her. On the path she picked up a stick, and as she went along she beat the bushes, crying, "Go away, wolf!" But her heart beat wildly when, with a rustling sound, some beast flew away through the brushwood. She was getting deeper into the wood, and every moment it was growing darker; still she kept on her way.

At last through the darkness she saw the glimmer of a light in a window. This was the hut. Her breath came shorter as she drew near to the house, from whence came the sound of bagpipes mixed with shouts. They were very merry inside. She stole softly to the lighted window, and peeped in. They were dancing. Evila knew the girls who were there; they were none of her companions; she and her friends crossed the street when they met these. The piper sat upon the pig-trough, and when he blew his instrument grunted like so many pigs.

Among the men Evila saw Peter Saffran. He was in high spirits, leaping so high as he danced that his fist struck the ceiling. He danced with a girl whose cheeks had two spots of red paint. Peter had both his arms round her waist; he threw her up and caught her again, kissing her painted face.

Evila turned away in disgust and hastened back through the woods, unmindful of the cries of the wolves and the howling of the wind. She had not even her stick; that she had dropped, and she had no means of beating the bushes.

*   *   *   *   *   *   *

That evening Felix Kaulmann came again to Ivan.

"I want to have your last word," he said. "Will you join my speculation?"

"I don't change my mind so quickly," returned Ivan, coldly. "My answer is the same as it was this morning—I will not."

"Very well. I have acted in a friendly manner in this matter, and now I tell you frankly that, as you do not choose to join me, I shall start the company alone, always leaving it open to you to rescind your determination and to join me if you wish. I cannot say fairer than this, and I trust we shall always be good friends. You will forgive me if I try to pick up some of the diamonds which are scattered about."

"I leave you perfectly free to do what you can."

"I shall avail myself of your permission, and the day will come when I shall remind you of your words."

Ivan's forehead contracted as he thought, "What does he mean? What can he take from me? Not my coal-mine; that is mine by right of possession, and the law protects me. The cut on the neighboring mountain? So he may! What I have suffices for me."

"Good-luck to your company!" he said, aloud; "and many thanks to the director."

So they parted. Early next morning Ivan was roused from his sleep. It was the post-horn which sounded the note of Felix Kaulmann's departure. Ivan wished him a happy journey, then fell asleep again. Later, as he was leaving his house, he met Peter Saffran at the door. The miner presented a sorry figure. His features bore the impression of his night's dissipation; his eyes were bloodshot, his hair ragged, his dress in disorder.

"Now, what is it?" asked Ivan, angrily.

"Sir," said the man, in a hoarse voice, "that doctor who was with you yesterday—his name?"

"What do you want with him?"

"He has carried off Evila!" burst out Peter. In wild agitation he snatched the hat off his head, tore his hair, and raised both his hands to heaven.

In the first moment Ivan was conscious of feeling a cruel satisfaction.

"It serves you right, you beast!" he said. "Serves you right! What business had you to ill-use the girl—your promised wife—on the very day that you were called for the third time?"

"Oh, sir," cried the miserable man, his teeth chattering, and beating his head with his hands, "I was drunk! I did not know what I did; and, after all, it was only a few blows with a light strap. What was that? With us common people it is nothing. A woman likes a man the better when he cudgels her. It is true; but to leave me for a gentleman—"

Ivan shrugged his shoulders and went on his way. The miner caught him by the tail of his coat.

"Ah, sir, what shall I do? Tell me, what shall I do?"

Ivan, however, was in no mood for giving advice; he was angry. He pushed Peter away, saying, sternly:

"Go to hell! Run to the tavern, drink brandy, then choose among the girls whose company you frequent another bride, who will be only too glad if you are drunk every day in the year."

Peter took up his hat, put it on his head, looked Ivan in the face, and, in an altered voice, said:

"No, sir, I shall never drink brandy again; only once in my life shall I taste the accursed thing—once. You will remember what I say, and when I smell of it, when I am seen coming out of the public-house, or when you hear that I have been there, then stay at home, for on that day no one will know how or when he will die."

Ivan left the man standing, and going back into his house, shut the door behind him. His first satisfaction at the news was passing away. This miserable peasant, who had dared to be his successful rival, had lost the treasure which he coveted. The fool had the pearl in his keeping, but he didn't know how to value it, and he had let it fall. That was good; but where had it fallen, this pearl so white and lovely in its purity and innocence? His soul was full of sorrow as he thought how in his eyes it had lost all its value. The girl who had seemed to him so virtuous, who kept her troth so faithfully, whose simplicity had been what he really loved—she had fallen at the first word from a villain. She refused her master, who had honorably offered her his name, his house, his all. But he had not the gifts of the other; he was not a dressed-up fellow, with town manners and seductive ways; he had not the tongue of a seducer, and had not promised her jewels and fine clothes, balls and operas. It was the same story with all women, and Mahomet was right when he gave them no souls, and no place either on earth or in heaven.

CHAPTER VI

COUNTESS THEUDELINDE

THE mistress of Bondavara was at this time fifty-eight years old. Ivan had not overstated her age when he gave Felix the information. Countess Theudelinde had long since given up the world. The renunciation cost her very little; she had never been in touch with it. Up to her fourteenth year she had grown up in the house of her father, the prince; at that period her mother, the princess, died. The governess of Theudelinde was beautiful, the prince was old. The countess—only the firstborn can have the princely title; the younger children are all counts and countesses—could not, for various reasons, remain under the paternal roof; she was sent out of the way and to finish her education at a convent. Before she went, however, she was betrothed to the Marquis Don Antonio de Padua, only son of the Marquis de Colomorano, then eighteen years of age. It was settled between the two fathers that when Antonio was twenty-four and Theudelinde twenty, she should be fetched out of her convent, and both should be united in wedlock by Holy Church. This arrangement was carried out so far as Theudelinde spending six blameless years in a most highly respectable convent. She was then brought home, and the marriage bells were set ringing. But, horror of horrors, when the girl saw her betrothed husband, she shrieked and ran away! This was not the man she had promised to marry; this one had a mustache! (Naturally, for he was an officer in the hussars.)

Theudelinde had never seen a man with a mustache. Six years before, when she was at home, all the distinguished guests who came to her father's house, the magnates, the ambassadors, were all smooth-shaved, so were the man-servants, even the coachman. In the convent there was only one man, the father confessor; his face was like a glass. And now they proposed to marry her to a man all hair! Impossible! The saints and the prophets of old wore beards, that was true; some of them had a good deal of hair, but none had it only on the upper-lip. The only one she could remember with this adornment was the servant of the high-priest in the Stations of the Cross, which, to a pious mind like Theudelinde's, was conclusive. She would hear no more of the marriage; the betrothal rings were returned on both sides, and the alliance was at an end.

After this the countess avoided all worldly amusements. Nothing would induce her go to a ball, or to the theatre. Nevertheless, she did not seem inclined to take the veil; she had strong leanings towards this wicked world, only she wanted one of a different sort, without the wickedness. She desired out of the general chaos to create an ideal, and this ideal should be her husband. He should be tender, faithful, no winedrinker, no smoker; a man with a smooth face, a pure soul, a sweet-sounding voice; a gifted, sympathetic, patient, amiable, soft, romantic, domestic, pious man; prudent, scientific, literary, distinguished, well-born, much respected, covered with orders, rich, loyal, brave, and titled. Such a *rara avis* was impossible to find. Countess Theudelinde spent the best days of her life seeking a portrait to fit the frame she had made, but she sought in vain; there was no husband for her.

When the countess had reached thirty there was a halt. The ideal was as far off as ever. She was anxious to come to terms with the world, but the world would have none of her. Her day was past; she had no right to any pretensions. She found herself in the position of having to choose between utter renunciation or acceptance of the world, with all its wickedness. At this critical juncture the old prince, her father, died, leaving the countess the property of Bondavara, together with the castle. Here Theudelinde retired to nurse her ideal, and mourn over her shattered idols. Here she was absolute mistress, her brother, to whom the property reverted, leaving her to her own devices.

The countess carried out, therefore, her theories unmolested, and her dislike to beards and mustaches had free play. The growers of these enormities were banished from her presence, and, as was only a natural consequence, as time went on her hatred of the male sex increased. No man was allowed in the neighborhood of the countess. She only suffered women about her—not alone in the house, but outside. The garden, the conservatories, were attended to by women — unmarried women, all. Matrimony was as a red rag to Theudelinde, and no one durst mention the word in her presence. Any girl who showed any inclination to wear the "matron's cap" was at once dismissed with contumely. Even the "coachman" was a woman; and for the reason that it would not have been fitting to sit upon a coach-box in woman's clothes, this female Jehu was allowed to wear a long coachman's cloak, a man's coat, as also a certain garment, at the bare mention of which an Englishwoman calls out, "Oh, how shocking!" and straightway faints. Truly, at the time this history was written, in our good land of Hungary, this very garment played a serious part, since it was the shibboleth and visible sign of fidelity to the governing powers, and of submission to the mediators; in truth, ever since those days the "leg of the boot" has been worn. So it came to pass that Mrs. Liese wore this thing, the only one of the kind to be seen in the castle. Liese, also, was allowed to drink wine, and to smoke tobacco, and, needless to say, she did both.

Fraulein Emerenzia, the countess's companion, was, so to speak, the exact counterpart of her noble mistress. The countess was tall and slender; she had a white skin, her features were sharp, her nose almost transparent, her lips, scarlet in color, were shaped like a bow; her cadaverous form bent forward; her eyelids fell over her lack-lustre eyes, her face appeared to have two sides which didn't belong to one another, each half having a totally different expression; even the wrinkles didn't correspond. She wore her hair as it was worn in the days of her youth, as it was worn when Caroline Pia was married, and as it is possible it will be worn again. Her hands were fine, transparent; they were not strong enough to cut the leaves of a book with a paper-knife. Her whole being was nerveless and sensitive. At the slightest noise she would shriek, be seized with a cramp, or go off in hysterics. She had certain antipathies to beasts, flowers, air, food, motion, and emotion. At the sight of a cat she was ready to faint; if she saw a flesh-colored flower her blood grew excited. Silver gave everything an unpleasant taste, so her spoons were all of gold. If any women crossed their legs she sent them out of the room. If the spoons, knives, or forks were by accident laid crosswise on the table, she would not sit down; and if she were to see velvet on any of her attendants she was thrown into a nervous attack, from the bare idea that perhaps her hand might come in contact with this electric and antipathetic substance.

Fortunately for her household her nervous fears kept her quiet at night. She locked and double-locked the door of her room, and never opened it until the morning came—no, not if the house were burning over her head.

Fraulein Emerenzia was, as we have before said, the counterpart of her mistress, in so far that she affected a close imitation of her ways, for in her appearance she was a direct contrast, Emerenzia being a round, short, fat woman, with a full face, the skin of which was so tightly stretched that it was almost as white as the countess's; she had a snub nose, which in secret was addicted to the vice of snuff-taking. Her dress and her manner of doing her hair were identical with the countess's fashion in each, only that the stiff-set clothes had on her small body a humorous expression. She affected to be as nerveless as the countess; her hands were as weak—they could not break a chicken bone. Her eyes were as sensitive to light, her antipathies were as numerous, and she was as prone to faints and hysterics as her patroness. In this direction, indeed, she went further. So soon as she observed that there was any cause for emotional display, she set up trembling and screaming, and so got the start of the countess, and generally managed to sob for a minute longer; and when Theudelinde fell fainting upon one sofa Emerenzia dropped lifeless upon another; likewise, she took longer coming to than did her mistress. At night Emerenzia slept profoundly. Her room was only separated from that of the countess by an ante-chamber, but Theudelinde might tear down all the bells in the castle without waking her companion, who maintained that her sleep was a species of nervous trance.

One man only was ever allowed entrance into the Castle of Bondavara. What do we say?—no man, no *masculinum*. The language of dogma has defined that the priest is *neutrius generis*, is more and less than a being of the male sex; bodily he can be no man's father, spiritually he is father of thousands. No one need think he will here read any calumnies against the priesthood. The pastor Mahok was a brave, honest man; he said mass devoutly, baptized, married, buried when called upon, would get up in the middle of the night to attend the death-bed of a parishioner, and would never grumble at the sacristan for waking him out of his first sleep. The pastor wrote no articles in the *Church News*, neither did he ever read one. If he wanted a newspaper he borrowed from the steward the daily paper. When his clerk collected Peter's pence, Pastor Mahok sent it with an additional gulden or two to the office of the chief priest; but this did not prevent him sitting down in the evening to play "tarok" with the Lutheran pastor and the infidel steward. He held to having a good cellar; he had a whole family of bees in his garden, and was a successful cultivator of fruit. In politics he was a loyalist, and confessed he belonged to the middle party, which in the country means just this, and no more, "We vote for the tobacco monopoly, but we smoke virgin tobacco because it is good and we have it."

From this account every one will understand that during the course of this narrative this excellent gentleman will offend no one. We would, in fact, have nothing to say to him were it not that he came every day, punctually at eleven o'clock, to Bondavara Castle to hear the countess's confession, and that done, he remained to dinner, and in both directions he honestly earned his small honorarium. There was a general air of satisfaction in his whole appearance, in his double chin, in his fresh color, in his round, shining face.

To-day the excellent man was punctual. The countess, however, was not. Just as eleven o'clock struck, the spiritual man knocked at the door of the sitting-room. Only the voice of Emerenzia answered, "Come in!"

The smile of greeting on the countenance of the visitor was reflected on that of the companion. It was the meeting of two full moons.

"The countess is still locked in her room," Emerenzia said in a whisper, as if afraid that her voice could penetrate into the third room.

The pastor expressed by a movement of his hand and an elevation of his eyebrows that the sleep of the just was not to be disturbed. The good man was not aware that it was the toilette of the just that was then in progress. These mysteries were conducted by the countess in private. No one, not even a faithful maid, was admitted until Theudelinde was clothed, and for this reason her garments were made to close in front.

The priest made use of this unexpected delay to search in the pocket of his coat, and to draw from thence a mysterious something, which, after first casting a look round the room, to make sure no one was spying on him, he pressed into the fat hand of the countess's companion, who hastily concealed this surreptitious something in the depths of the pocket of her dress, expressing her gratitude by a friendly nod, which the pastor returned by a courteous movement which expressed, "No thanks are necessary for so small a service." Whereupon Emerenzia, turning away, half-shyly drew the something carefully out of her pocket, peered into the contents of the same, held it close to her nose, drinking in the scent of the something, turning her eyes up to heaven, and again to the pastor, who, on his part, expressed by the motion of the thumb and forefinger of his left hand, "Excellent — special brand!" Then, no longer able to restrain her feelings, the companion took from the mysterious packet between the thumb and forefinger of *her* right hand something which she placed in both nostrils, and sniffed up in silent ecstasy. It was the pastor's pleasure to fill Emerenzia's snuff-box with the very best mixture. This was the platonic bond which existed between them—the mutual desire of two noses for one ideal.

Yellow snuff is not an unattainable ideal. In the ordinary way of business a quarter of a pound can be procured for a few pence; but common snuff was as different from the priest's mixture as cherry brandy is from Chartreuse, or Veuve Cliquot from the vintage of Presburg. This is easily understood by those who take snuff. How is it that a clergyman always has the best tobacco? How does he prepare it? Does he get it prepared? These are broad questions that a man of liberal mind dare not ventilate. Even if he knew, it would not be advisable to make use of his knowledge. One thing is certain, the best tobacco is used by the Church. A bishop, who died not long since, left behind him a hundredweight of the most heavenly stuff, two ounces of which fetched a ducat.

The quiet *tête-à-tête* between the two snuff-takers was disturbed by the sound of a bell; then a metal slide in the door of the countess's room opened, and a tray with an empty teacup was put through. This was a sign that the countess had breakfasted.

Every door in the castle had sliding panels, some large, others small. The slides were made of copper, the doors of strong wood, with brass locks and fasteners. The door of the countess's bedroom was all of iron, covered on the inside with a tapestry curtain. Since no man was allowed in the house, it was necessary to have a defence system against any possible attack. This system included some cleverly-constructed machinery, by means of which the countess, by pressing her foot, could raise up the flooring, and precipitate any bold invader of the sacred precincts of her bedroom into a cellar without light or exit. From the alcove of her bed an electric telegraph connected with the fire-tower, so that by raising her finger the alarm-bell could be set ringing, and in case of danger the masculine inhabitants of the adjacent farm-houses and hunting-lodges could be summoned without a moment's delay. In Emerenzia's room there was likewise a communication with this electric apparatus, and to the door were affixed the different signs by which the countess expressed her wishes. The cup signified that the waiting-maid was required, a book would have meant that the companion was needed.

Emerenzia, therefore, sent the girl to her mistress. When her work was finished the bell rang again, the book appeared, and the companion went to the countess. After a short time she returned, and opened the door for the pastor, while she whispered to him softly—

"She has seen the spirits again; she has much to tell you."

We will follow the pastor into his penitent's room; but no one need be afraid that he or she is about to listen to the lady's confession. When the pastor had closed the door behind him, he came to the countess, who sat in a large armchair, looking pale and exhausted.

She signed to the priest to take his place in another armchair opposite to her.

"Have you seen them again?" he asked.

"I have," said the countess, in an awed whisper. "All happened in the same way as usual. So soon as the clock-tower had sounded midnight, there rose from below, as if out of the vault, a fearful chorus of voices intoning the *De Profundis*. It was a ghostly, terrible sound. I could distinguish the solo of the celebrant, the antiphon, the chorus; and between them loud laughter, diabolical words, the shrieks of women, and the clatter of glasses. I heard comic songs accompanied by wild howls; then, again, the soft, pious hymn succeeded by the wild disorder. I pinched my arm to see did I dream. Here you can see the mark. 'Twas not dreaming. I got up; I wished to convince myself that I was awake. I took my pencil and note-paper, and when a distinct tune reached my ear I wrote it down. Here is the paper. You understand music."

The priest threw a hasty glance over the ghostly melody, and recognized a well-known Hungarian volkslied — "Maiden with the black eyes, let me taste thy lips." Undoubtedly an unclean song to issue from the family vault at midnight!

"And, gracious countess, have you never heard the peasants singing this in the fields?"

The countess drew herself up with dignity. "Do I frequent the places where peasants sing?" she made answer; and then continued her story. "These notes are sufficient proof that I was awake; my nerves were too excited to allow me to sleep again. Moreover, I was drawn by an invincible desire to go to the spot from whence the sound came. I dressed myself. I am certain that I took out my grass-green skirt of Gros de

Naples, with a flounce of cashmere. I called none of my servants; every one in the house was asleep. An extraordinary courage awoke in me. Quite alone I descended the steps which lead to the family vault. When I reached the door both sides opened of themselves; I entered, and found myself in the presence of my departed ancestors. The monuments were all removed, the niches empty; the occupiers of both sat round the long table which stands in the vault, in the identical dress in which they are painted in the portraits which hang in the hall, and by which their calling in life is distinguishable. My great-uncle, the archbishop, in full canonicals, celebrated mass before the requiem altar; my grandfather, the chancellor, had large parchment documents before him, upon which he affixed the state seal. My great-uncle, the field-marshal, in armor, and with the marshal's baton in his hand, gave orders. My ancestress Katherine, who was a lady of the court, and of remarkable beauty, rolled her eyes about, and in her whole face no feature moved but those glittering eyes; and my aunt Clementina, the abbess of the Ursuline Convent, sang psalms with my uncle, in which the others from time to time joined."

"But the laughter, the tumult, the comic songs?" asked the pastor.

"I am coming to that. At the other end of the table sat some of my more distant relatives—my young cousin Clarissa, who danced herself to death; and a cousin, who was a celebrated flute player; and my great-uncle Otto, who was devoted to hazard, and now rattled dice into a copper goblet, and cursed his bad-luck when he made a bad throw; also another cousin, who died on the very night of her marriage, and still wore a faded wedding wreath; finally, my uncle Ladislaus, who was banished from the family circle early in the century, and whose frame hangs in the picture-gallery empty, his portrait being removed."

"How did you know him, then?" By this question the pastor hoped to check the flow of the countess's visions.

Theudelinde, however, answered that her uncle Ladislaus, being a rebel and a heretic, had not alone been declared a traitor, but had incurred the ban of excommunication. He was taken prisoner and beheaded. "And therefore," she added, with an air of conviction, "it was easy to recognize him by his death's-head. Likewise, during his lifetime he ignored the king's express command, and was the first to introduce tobacco-smoke into the country, and on this account, at his execution, he received the punishment awarded to the smoker, of having a pipe-handle run through his nose. Last night, as he sat at the table, he held between the teeth of his monstrous death's-head a large meerschaum pipe, and the whole vault smelled in the most fearful manner of tobacco-smoke."

This remark convinced the priest that the countess had been dreaming.

"Between both my cousins," she went on, "the nun and the bride, there was an empty chair. There I felt obliged to seat myself. The bride wished to hear of the fashions; she praised the stuff of my Gros de Naples dress, taking it between her fingers, which, when they touched mine, were cold as death itself. The upper end of the table was covered with green cloth, the lower end with a yellow silk table-cloth, embroidered with many-colored flowers. At this end every one laughed, talked, sang noisy songs; while at the top the psalms were intoned and the antiphon was sung. Both sounded horrible in my ears. The dishes contained cooked hazel-hens and roast pheasants, with the feathers sticking in their heads; sparkling wine filled the cups. I was pressed to eat and drink, but neither the food nor the liquor had any taste. Once the bride, my cousin, as is the custom with very young girls, offered me the spur of the pheasant's breast, saying, jokingly, 'Break this spur with me, and we shall see which of us two gets a husband first.' I seized hold of my end of the spur; I tugged and tugged, and at last broke it. The largest half remained in my hand. The bride laughed. 'Theudelinde shall be the first married!' she cried. I blushed; it seemed to me something terrible that the spirits of my dead ancestors should be so frivolous."

The worthy pastor said nothing. Nevertheless, he was minded to agree with his penitent. He could not imagine why blessed souls, or even condemned ones, should occupy themselves breaking pheasant bones with an old maid, of all people in the world.

"What gave me most offence," continued Theudelinde, "was the outrageous behavior of my uncle Ladislaus. One minute he shrieked, then laughed loudly, sang horrid songs. Again he broke out into fearful curses, scorned the saints, the pope, the sacraments, made witticisms that brought a blush to the faces of the ladies, and blew all his tobacco-smoke over me. I shook the skirt of my green silk to prevent the horrid smell sticking to it, but I felt this precaution was of little use. My uncle Ladislaus began then to tease me, and said I had concealed the prophetic bone in the pocket of my green dress. My face glowed with shame, for it was true. I denied it, however, whereupon he began to swear in his heathenish way, and to thump with his fists on the table until the vault resounded with his blows. My cousins put their hands over his mouth. Then he spoke through his empty eye-sockets. It was terrible! He cursed all the saints in the calendar and the emperor. My great-uncle, the archbishop, stretched out his hands and damned him; my grandfather, the chancellor, sealed the sentence; and my great-uncle, the field-marshal, drew his sword and cut off my uncle's death's-head. The head rolled over, and fell at my feet, still holding the pipe between its teeth, and blew its filthy breath over me. Then I arose and fled."

The pastor had now made up his mind that the whole story was nothing but the dream of an hysterical woman. It was strange, however, that the countess should have the same vision so often, and that it should always begin in the same manner.

As she now concluded her recital with the words, "As I took off my silk dress it smelled horribly of tobacco-smoke," a brilliant idea came to Father Mahok.

"Will you excuse my asking you where your green dress is?" he asked, gravely.

The countess betrayed some embarrassment.

"I do not know. My wardrobe is in the care of Fraulein Emerenzia—"

"Allow me to ask you the question, did you not take the dress off in this apartment?"

"I no longer remember. Emerenzia has been here since; she may know."

"Will you grant me the favor, countess, to send for Fraulein Emerenzia?"

"Certainly. She will be here in a minute."

The countess pressed her finger twice on the electric apparatus, and the companion entered.

"Fraulein," said the countess, "you remember my

green Gros de Naples silk, bordered with a trimming of fur?"

"Yes; it is a pelisse of peculiar cut, with hanging sleeves, and fastened by a silk band and buckle."

"That is the dress," returned the countess. "Where is it?"

"In the wardrobe. I hung it there myself, first putting camphor in the sleeves, that the moths might not get at the fur."

"When did you do this?"

"Last summer."

The pastor laughed slyly to himself. "Now," thought he, "the countess must be convinced that she dreamed the whole scene she has so accurately described."

"Have I not worn it since last summer?" questioned Theudelinde.

"Not once. The open-hanging sleeves are only for the hottest weather."

"Impossible!"

"But, countess," put in the priest, "it is easy to convince yourself of what ma'm'selle says. You have only to look into the wardrobe. Who keeps the key?"

"Ma'm'selle Emerenzia."

"Do you command me to open the press?" asked the companion, with a discomfited look.

"I do," answered the countess, nodding to the pastor to follow her into the next room.

Emerenzia, her face puckered into an expression of annoyance, drew her bunch of keys from her pocket, and placed one in the lock of an antique and highly ornamented press, of which she threw the doors open. At least fifty silk dresses hung there, side by side. The countess never allowed any of her clothes to get into strange hands; no man's eye should ever rest upon what she had worn. Through this museum of old clothes Emerenzia's fingers went with unerring certainty, and drew forth the oft-mentioned green silk dress with the fur trimming.

"Here it is," she said, shortly.

The pastor was triumphant, but the countess, whose nerves were more impressionable than those of ordinary mortals, grew suddenly pale and began to shake all over.

"Take that dress down," she said, in a whisper. And Emerenzia, with a jerk, tore it from its peg. What, in Heaven's name, had come to the pastor and her mistress?

The countess took it from her hand, and held it, while she turned her head the other way, across his nose.

"Do you smell it?" she said. "Is it tobacco-smoke?"

Father Mahok was astonished. This fine silk dress, straight from out of a lady's wardrobe, smelled as strongly of the commonest tobacco as the coat of a peasant who had passed his night in an ale-house. Before he could answer Theudelinde's question she was ready with another. From the pocket of the green Gros de Naples she now drew forth a broken pheasant bone.

"And this?" she asked. But here her strength was exhausted. Without waiting for a reply, she fell fainting on the sofa.

Emerenzia, sobbing loudly, fell helplessly into an arm-chair. The clergyman was so upset by the whole thing that, in his embarrassment, he opened the doors of three more wardrobes before finding the one which communicated with the sitting-room. Then he summoned the servants to attend to their mistress. *The evidence of witchcraft was proved.*

CHAPTER VII

THE COUNTESS'S ALBUM

The worthy Pastor Mahok was of opinion that the mystery of the countess's dress smelling so strongly of tobacco-smoke could not be accounted for by any law of Nature, and judged, therefore, by the light of his priestly office, as well as from his worldly experience, that these diabolical visions were matters worthy of deep consideration on his part. They occupied his mind during dinner, which he partook of in company with the countess's companion, but of the subject of his thoughts he spoke no word to her. They were alone at table. The countess remained in her room, as was her habit when she suffered from what was called "cramps," and her only refreshment was some light soup. After dinner she again sent for the pastor.

He found her lying on the sofa, pale and exhausted; her first words had reference to the subject which filled both their minds.

"Are you now convinced," she said, "that what I told you was, indeed, no dream?"

"Doubtless there has been some strange work going on."

"Is it the work, think you, of good or bad spirits?" asked the countess, raising her eyes.

"That can only be ascertained by a trial."

"What sort of a trial, holy father?"

"An attempt to exorcise them. If these spirits who every night leave their graves are good, they must, by the strength of the exorcism, return to their resting-places, and remain there till summoned by the angel's trumpet to arise on the last day."

"And in case they don't return?" inquired the countess, anxiously.

"Then they are bad spirits."

"That is to say, damned. How do you know that?"

For a minute there was a struggle in the pastor's mind; then he answered, boldly:

"This night I shall keep watch in the castle."

"And if you hear the unearthly noises?"

"Then I shall descend into the vault, and scatter the ghosts with holy water."

The countess's face glowed with fervor as she exclaimed:

"Holy father, I shall accompany you."

"No, countess; no one shall accompany me but my sacristan."

"The sacristan! A man! He shall not put his foot in this house!" cried the countess, excitedly.

The pastor, in a soothing voice, explained to her that his sacristan was almost as much a part of the Church as himself; moreover, that he was absolutely necessary on this occasion for the performance of the exorcism; in fact, without him the ceremony could not take place, seeing that the sacred vessel containing the holy water, the crucibulum and lanterns, should be carried before him to give all due effect to the religious rite.

Under these circumstances Countess Theudelinde gave her consent, on the condition that the obnoxious male intruder should not enter the castle itself. Still more, the pastor promised to watch in the greenhouse after the castle gates were locked.

According to these arrangements, when it began to get dark, Father Mahok arrived, bringing with him his sacristan, a man of about forty, with a closely shaved mustache and a very copper-colored face. The pastor left him in the greenhouse, and proceeded himself to the dining-room, where the countess was awaiting him for supper. No one ate a morsel. The pastor had no appetite, neither had the countess, nor her companion. The air was too full of the coming event to allow of such a gross thing as eating.

After supper the countess withdrew to her room, and Herr Mahok went to the greenhouse, where the sacristan had made himself comfortable with wine and meat, and had kept up the fires in the oven. The servants had been kept in ignorance of what was going on; they had never heard the midnight mass, nor the wild shrieks and infamous songs of the inhabitants of the vault, and the countess would not allow the ears of her innocent handmaidens to be polluted with such horrors. Therefore, every one in the castle slept. The pastor watched alone. At first Herr Mahok tried to pass the long hours of the night in reading his prayers, but as his habitual hour for sleep drew near he had to fight a hard battle with his closing eyelids. He was afraid that if he slumbered his imagination would reproduce the countess's dream, to which, be it said, he did not give credence; at the same time, he did not wholly doubt. Generally, he found that his breviary provoked sleep, and now he thought it better to close the book, and try what conversation with the sacristan would do as a means to keep awake.

The clerk's discourse naturally turned upon ghostly

appearances; he told stories of a monk without a head, of spirits that appeared on certain nights in the year, of hobgoblins and witches, all of which he had either seen with his own eyes or had heard of from persons whose veracity was unimpeachable.

"Folly! lies!" said the excellent pastor; but he could not help a creeping sensation coming over him. If he could even have smoked, it would have strengthened his nerves; but smoking was forbidden in the castle. The countess would have smelled it, as the giant in the old fairy tale smelled human flesh.

When the sacristan found that all his wonderful tales of ghosts and hobgoblins were considered lies, he thought it was no use tiring himself talking, and as soon as he ceased sleep began to fall upon his eyelids. Seated upon a stool, his head leaning against the wall, his mouth open, he slept profoundly, to the envy, if not the admiration, of the good pastor, who would willingly have followed his example. Soon some very unmusical sounds made themselves heard. The sacristan snored in all manner of keys, in all variations of nasal discord, which so jarred on the pastor's nerves that he several times shook the sleeper to awake him, with the result that he slept again in no time.

At last the clock on the castle tower chimed twelve. Herr Mahok struck the sacristan a good blow on his shoulder.

"Get up!" he said. "I did not bring you here to sleep."

The clerk rubbed his eyes, already drunk with sleep. The pastor took his snuff-box to brighten himself up with a pinch of snuff, when suddenly both men were roused out of all the torpor of sleep by other means. Just as the last beat of the clock had finished striking the unearthly mass began to be intoned in the vault below. Through the profound silence of the night was heard the voice of the priest singing the Latin mass, with the responses of the choir, accompanied by some instrument that sounded like an organ, but which had a shriller tone, and seemed to be a parody of the same.

Over the whole body of Herr Mahok crept a ghostly shiver.

"Do you hear it?" he asked the sacristan, in a whisper.

"Hear it? Who could help hearing it? Mass is saying somewhere."

"Here, under us, in the vault."

"Who can it be?"

"The devil! All good spirits praise the Lord," stammered the worthy pastor, making the sign of the cross three times.

"But it seems that the evil spirits praise the Lord as well as the good ones," returned the clerk.

This assertion of his was, however, quickly contradicted, for in the middle of the next psalm a diabolical chorus struck in wildly, and the air resounded with—

> "Come, dearest, come to me,
> Come, I am at home;
> Two gypsies play for me,
> And here I dance alone."

Then followed shrieks of laughter, in which women's shrill cackle mingled with the hoarse roar of men and the wildest discord, as if hell itself were let loose.

The poor priest, who had trembled at the pious psalms, nearly fell to the ground on hearing this pandemonium. A cold sweat broke out all over him; he knew now that the countess was right, and that this was, in truth, the work of the evil one.

"Michael," he said, his teeth chattering with fear, "have you heard—"

"I must be stone deaf if I didn't—such an infernal din!" replied the other. "All the spirits of hell are holding a Sabbath—"

Just then there was the tinkle of a bell. The tumult subsided, and the voice of the celebrant was once more heard intoning mass.

"What shall we do?" asked Herr Mahok.

"What shall we do? Descend into the vault and exorcise the evil spirits."

"What!" cried the priest. "Alone?"

"Alone!" repeated Michael, with religious fervor. "Are we alone when we come in the name of the Lord of armies? Besides, we are two. If I were a priest, and if I were invested with the stole, had I the right to wear the three-cornered hat, I should go into the vault, carrying the holy water, and with the words, 'Apage Satanas,' I would drive before me all the legions of hell itself."

The excellent pastor felt ashamed that his ignorant sacristan should possess greater faith, and show more courage in this combat with the powers of darkness, than himself; still, fear predominated over his shame.

"I would willingly face these demons," he said, in a somewhat hesitating manner, "were it not that the gout has suddenly seized my right foot. I am not able to walk."

"But consider what a scandal it will be if we, who have heard the spirits, have not pluck enough to send them packing."

"But my foot, Michael; I cannot move my foot."

"Well, then, I will carry you on my back. You can hold the holy water and I will take the lantern."

There was no way out of this friendly offer. The pastor commended his soul to God, and, taking heart, resolved to fight the demons below, armed only with the holy insignia of his office. The good man, however, did not mount, like Anchises on the back of Æneas, without much inward misgiving.

"You will be careful, Michael; you will not let me fall?" he said, in a somewhat quavering voice.

"Don't be afraid, pastor," returned the sacristan, as he stooped and raised the pastor on his shoulders. "Now, forward!" he cried, taking the lantern in his hands, while Herr Mahok carried the vessels necessary for the exorcism.

A cold blast of air saluted them as they issued from the greenhouse and crossed the large hall of the castle, which the glimmering light from the small lantern only faintly illumined. Half of it remained in darkness; but on the side of the wall where hung the portraits of the armed knights an occasional gleam showed Herr Mahok the faces of the countess's warlike ancestors, who had done in their day good service against the Turks. They looked at him, he thought, somewhat contemptuously, and seemed to say, "What sort of man is this, who goes to fight pickaback?"

Michael stopped before a strong iron door in the centre of the hall. This was the entrance to the subterranean vaults and cellars underneath the castle. And now the pastor suddenly remembered he had left the key of this gate in the greenhouse. There was nothing for it but to retrace their steps. Just as they reached the threshold, however, Michael suggested that something very hard was pressing against his side.

Could it be the key which was, after all, in his reverence's pocket? This suggestion proved correct, and once more he had to run the gantlet of the old crusaders and their contemptuous superiority.

The key creaked as it turned in the lock, and a heavy, damp smell struck upon them as they passed through the iron gate.

"Leave the door open," said the pastor, with an eye to securing a safe retreat.

And now they began to descend the steps, Herr Mahok remarking that his horse was not too sure-footed. He tottered in going down the steps so much that the pastor, in his fright, caught him with his left hand tightly by the collar, while he pressed the other more closely round his throat, a proceeding which Michael resented by calling out, in a strangled voice:

"Reverend sir, don't squeeze me so; I am suffocating!"

"What was that?"

A black object whizzed past them, circling round their heads. A bat, the well-known attendant upon ghosts!

"We shall be there in a few minutes," said the clerk, to encourage his rider, whose teeth chattered audibly.

While they were descending the steps the noise in the vault had been less audible, but now, as they came into the passages which ran underneath the hall, it broke out again in the most horrible discord. The passage was long, and there were two wings; one led to the cellars proper, the other to the vaults. Opposite to the steps there was a cross passage, at the end of which, by ascending some seven or eight steps and passing through a lattice door, you could get into the open air. This lattice served likewise as a means of ventilating the passages, and on this particular night there was such a strong current of air that the light in the lantern was in danger every minute of being blown out. It would have been well if that were all. The sacristan hadn't taken three steps in the direction of the vault before a terrible sight revealed itself to both men.

At the other end of the passage a blue flame burned; before the flame there stood, or sat, or jumped, a dwarfish figure all in white. It was not three feet in height, and, nevertheless, its head was of monstrous size. As the sacristan, with the pastor, drew near this horrid appearance, the blue flame suddenly flared up, throwing a bright, whitish light all over the passage, and by this light the terrified spectators beheld the dwarfish figure stretch itself out, and grow taller and taller—six, eight, twelve feet—and still it grew and grew. Its shadow danced in the light of the blue flame upon the marble floor of the passage like a black serpent. Then the fearful appearance raised its head, and the vaulted roof echoed with its howls and shrieks.

Michael's courage flew out of the window. He turned, and, burdened as he was with the weight of the pastor on his back, he ran back as fast as he could. In the middle of the passage, however, he made a false step and fell, with Herr Mahok, flat upon his face. In the fall he broke the lantern, the light went out, and left them in the dark. Groping along with outstretched hands, they missed the steps which led up to the iron gate, but after some time found themselves in the cross passage, and saw the soft light of the moon shining through the lattice window. They made at once for the door. At first there was some difficulty in opening it, but Michael managed to force it, and, to their great joy, they were once more in the open air. Over the stubble, through the thorn-bushes they flew, never pausing to look back. Singularly enough, the gout in the pastor's foot in no way affected his speed. He ran quite as fast as Michael, and in less than a quarter of an hour was in his bed. So, too, the sacristan, whose fright produced an attack of fever, which kept him a prisoner there for three days.

The next morning Herr Mahok, with many inward qualms, went up to the castle. His was an honest, simple mind; he preferred rather to believe in the wiles of the devil than in the wickedness of human nature; he credited what he had seen with his own eyes, and never sought to penetrate the dark veil which shrouds many supernatural mysteries. He believed firmly that he had now to do with damned spirits, who at their midnight orgies cracked pheasant bones to see who should first be married.

He found the countess in good humor; she was friendly, lively, and received her visitor with a smiling countenance. This change did not surprise Herr Mahok. He was by this time accustomed to the caprices of Countess Theudelinde. One day she was out of humor, the next all serenity.

The pastor went straight to the kernel he had to crack.

"I watched last night," he said.

"Oh, father, thanks, ten thousand thanks! Your mere presence has been sufficient to banish the evil spirits which have haunted the castle for so long. Last night all was peace; not a sound did I hear."

"Not a sound!" cried the pastor, rising from his chair in his astonishment at such a statement. "Countess, is it possible that you did not hear the noise?"

"Profound repose, Arcadian peace, reigned in the house, both up-stairs and below."

"But I was there, and awake. I did not dream it. And, moreover, I can show you the bruises and abrasions on my elbow; they witness to the fall we had, to say nothing of Michael, the sacristan, who is this moment in a high fever in consequence. No, never did any one hear so demoniacal, so terrible a noise as echoed through the vault last night. I was there myself, countess, in my own person. I was ready to encounter the wicked spirits; I would have met them armed with all the terrors of Mother Church, but the courage of my weak-kneed sacristan failed. I have now come to tell you that my knowledge is at an end. This castle is bewitched, and, countess, my advice to you is to leave it without delay, and to take up your residence in a city, where your family ghost cannot follow you."

The countess placed the middle finger of her left hand upon her breast, and spoke with haughty dignity:

"I leave this castle because the spirits of my ancestors dwell here! Your advice, reverend father, shows how little you know me. To my mind, it is a powerful reason for remaining. Here the spirits of my forefathers, the ghosts of ancestors, surround me. They know me, they claim me as theirs; they honor me with their visits, with their invitations, and you counsel me to abandon them. Never! Bondavara is dearer to me than ever; the presence of my ancestors has doubled its value a hundredfold."

It was on the tip of Herr Mahok's tongue to answer, "Well, then, remain here by all means, but for my part I give my resignation; provide yourself with another confessor." He restrained himself, however, and said, quietly:

"Will you tell me, countess, how it happens that, if you have these close relations with your ancestors' spirits, you heard nothing of the witch's Sabbath they kept last night?"

At this bold question the countess's pale cheeks were suddenly decorated by two carnation spots; her eyes fell before the sharp look of her father confessor, and, striking her breast with her hand, she sank slowly on her knees, whispering, in great agitation:

"Pater, peccavi. There is something which I have never confessed to you, and which lies heavy on my conscience."

"What is it?"

"Oh, I fear to tell you!"

"Daughter, fear nothing," said the priest, soothingly. "God is merciful to human weakness."

"I believe that; but I am more afraid that you will laugh at me."

"Ah!" And the pastor, at this strange speech, fell back in his chair, smiling to himself.

The countess rose from her kneeling position and went to her writing-table; she opened a secret drawer, and took from thence an album. It was a splendid book with an ivory cover, chasings of gilt enamel, and clasp of the same.

"Will you look through this album, father?"

The priest opened the clasp, took off the cover, and saw a collection of cabinet photographs, such as are generally to be found on drawing-room tables. There were portraits of eminent statesmen, poets, actors, with whose likenesses all the world is familiar. Two points were remarkable in this gallery—one, that no one was included who had any scandal connected with his name; secondly, it was only clean-shaved men who had a place in the volume. Herr Mahok recognized many whom he knew either by sight or personally—Liszt, Reményi, the actors Lendvay, Szerdahelyi, and others, together with many foreign celebrities, who wore neither beard nor mustache. Another peculiarity struck the pastor. Several of the leaves, instead of portraits, had pieces of black crape inserted into the frames. This circumstance made him reflective.

"It is a very interesting volume," he said, closing the book; "but what has it to do with the present circumstances?"

"I confess to you," said the countess, in a low voice, "that this book is a memorial of my folly and weakness. A picture-dealer in Vienna has for many years had an order from me; he sends me every photograph that comes out of clean-shaved men, and I seek among them for my ideal. I have been seeking many years. Sometimes I imagine I have found it; some one of the portraits takes my fancy. I call the man whom it represents my betrothed. I place the photograph before me; I dream for hours looking at it; I almost fancy that it speaks to me. We say to one another all manner of things—sweet nothings, but they fill my mind with a sort of ecstasy. It is silly, I know, and something tells me that it is worse than silly, that it is sinful. I have been for a long time wondering whether I should confess this as a sin, or keep silence about such foolish nonsense. What is your opinion, father?"

Herr Mahok, in truth, did not know what to say. It was true that in the Scripture some words were said about sinning with the eyes, but photographs were not named. He answered, vaguely—

"Anything further, my daughter?"

"After I had for some time been silly over one of the portraits, I saw in a dream the man it represented. He appeared to me as a beautiful apparition, we walked together through fields and meadows, arm-in-arm; a sort of heavenly halo surrounded us, flowers sprang up under our feet. We were young, and we loved one another." The poor lady wept bitterly as she related her dream, and she sobbed as she said, " Is not this a sin, father?"

Herr Mahok had no hesitation in answering. He had found the name of the sin—it was witchcraft; but the form the penance should take puzzled him. The countess, however, helped him to a decision.

"Ah," she said, sadly, "I thought it was some demoniac possession; and for these visions, sweet as they were, I must now do penance. Is it not so, father? Will it satisfy for my fault if I burn in the fire the portrait of the man who appeared to me in my dream, and fill the empty space in my book with black crape?"

This remark explained the many frames filled with crape. The pastor thought that the penance was well chosen. Nothing could be better than a burnt-offering.

Theudelinde continued, "During these visions I lie in a profound slumber. My soul is no longer on the earth; I am in the paradise of lovers. No earthly feeling chains me here below; I am a clear spirit, consequently no sound reaches me. I am as deaf to this world as if I were already dead."

"Therefore the ghostly tumult never reached you last night; you were wandering in your dream world."

"I confess it was so," whispered the countess, covering her face with her hands.

"Now, here is a nice state of things!" thought the pastor. "The dead ancestors play all manner of pranks in the family vault, while their descendant projects herself out of her human body to make love in some other region. They are, indeed, an extraordinary race. A poor man daren't even think of such extravagances, and how can I, a poor parish priest, deal with such queer goings-on? I only know how to settle with the every-day penitent, who commits the usual sins."

This complication, in truth, of the ghosts below and the bewitched countess above, was too much for a man of his calibre to deal with. It required a superior genius to exorcise the spirits and to calm the hysterical mind of Theudelinde. In the difficulty it appeared to him better to temporize.

"My daughter, the penance you have imposed upon yourself is well thought of. Have you already committed to the flames the portrait of the last demoniacal appearance?"

"No," answered the countess, with all the hesitation a young girl would have in speaking of her lover's picture.

"And why not?" questioned the priest, almost sternly. He was glad to find some tangible fault.

"It would be wrong, I think, to throw this particular portrait into the fire."

"And wherefore should it be wrong?"

Before she replied the countess opened a concealed pocket of the album and drew forth what it contained.

"Ah!" cried the pastor as he took the photograph, which he at once recognized as the Abbé Samuel, the head of an influential order which possessed many different branches.

"The photographer in Vienna had my directions to send me the photograph of every clean-shaven celebrity. He, therefore, has committed the sin of sending me the portrait of an eminent priest. The fault is mine, not his."

"And in your dreams have you wandered arm-in-arm with the original of this?" asked Herr Mahok, still holding in his hand the photograph.

"I am guilty!" stammered the countess, laying her hands upon her breast.

"Then," said the pastor, "Heaven inspired you not to throw this portrait, like that of the others, into the fire, for in this man you will find a physician able to cure your sick soul. It is really providential that this portrait should be in your hands, for the others were idle, foolish dreams. Here you have found your ideal, under whose guidance you may hope to find health and salvation. He will lead you, not in a dream, but in reality, to the blessed regions of peace and true piety, where alone, my daughter, real happiness is to be found. This man possesses strength of mind and elevation of character sufficient to exorcise all the spirits which haunt your castle, and to banish from your mind those temptations which spring from the same source as the more visible demons which we call ghosts."

CHAPTER VIII

THE EXORCIST

Acting upon the advice of Herr Mahok, the countess resolved to lay all her troubles before a new physician for her soul. That very day the pastor wrote to Abbé Samuel, who was then in Pesth, inviting him to come to Bondavara Castle.

The abbé was a man of high calling; one of those priests who are more or less independent in their ideas. He had friendly relations with certain personages, and the initiated knew that certain articles with the signature "S," which appeared in the opposition paper, were from his pen. In society he was agreeable and polished, and his presence never hindered rational enjoyment. In intellectual circles he shone; his lectures, which were prepared with great care, were attended by the *élite* of society, and, as a natural consequence, the ultramontane papers were much against him. Once, even, the police had paid him a domiciliary visit, although they themselves did not know wherein he had given cause for suspicion. All these circumstances had raised his reputation, which had lately been increased by the appearance of his picture in a first-rate illustrated journal. This won for him the general public. So stately was his air, his high, broad forehead, manly, expressive features, well-marked eyebrows, and frank, fearless look, with nothing sinister or cunning in it. For the rest, there was little of the priest about him; his well-knit, robust, muscular form was rather that of a gladiator. Through the whole country he was well-known as the independent priest, who ventured to tell the government what he thought.

For this reason the excellent Herr Mahok had for him the greatest respect. He, as an insignificant parish priest, could do nothing for his fatherland. It was true that, many years ago, he had fought more than twenty battles with the Honvéd Battalion; he had preached to his men how they should love their country, and for this he had been sentenced to death, which sentence had been commuted to ten years' imprisonment; he had passed five of those years in chains, and his feet still bore the marks of the wounds made by the heavy irons. But what were these trifles, of which Herr Mahok thought little, in comparison to the bold deeds of the Abbé Samuel, who dared to write independent articles in the papers, and to sign them with the initial of his name. To have fought with Haynau against the Russians under fire of heavy cannon, to have been in the galleys, that was a mere joke. To have the fearful police upon your track, that was serious. Herr Mahok thought most highly of the abbé's capabilities, measuring them by the loss of his own physical and mental energy—for after fifteen years, five of which had been spent in heavy iron chains, a man is not what he was.

After some days the invited guest arrived at the parsonage of Herr Mahok. The pastor related to him, circumstantially, all that had reference to the countess, with the exception, of course, of such matters as were under the sacred seal of confession. He told him about the ghosts, and his own experience under that head.

Herr Samuel received the narration with fits of laughter.

"You may laugh here as much as you like, but I beg of you not to do so before the countess; she holds to her ghosts," remarked the pastor, with an air of one who knew what he was saying.

The abbé then asked for information concerning the disposition of the rooms in the castle, how they were situated in regard to one another. He made the pastor describe minutely every particular of what he had himself been witnsss to, also how he and his sacristan had made good their escape through the lattice door.

The equipage of the countess came at the usual hour to fetch both the guests to the castle, which lay at some little distance from the village.

It was only natural, all things taken into account, that the countess on her first introduction to the abbé should lose all control of her nerves, and that she should give way to several hysterical symptoms, which could only be calmed by the abbé laying his hand in paternal benediction upon her forehead. Fraulein Emerenzia's nerves, in accordance with the sympathy which existed between her and her mistress, became at once similarly affected, and required a similar imposition of hands; but neither of the priests troubled themselves about her, and when the countess recovered from her attack, the companion did likewise.

During dinner, which was served with great elegance, the abbé discoursed upon every possible subject, and made inquiries as to the prospects of the country, the occupations of the people, the age of the servants, and so forth. He addressed a great deal of his conversation to Fraulein Emerenzia, attended to her wants; when he offered her wine she covered her glass with her hand,

and declared she never tasted anything but water, which seemed infinitely to surprise him; also, when he wished to know whether the ring on her finger was one of betrothal, Emerenzia tried to blush, and gave him to understand that, from her own choice, she meant to live and die a maid.

After dinner was over, Herr Mahok remained in the dining-room to entertain the Fraulein—that is to say, he seated himself in an armchair, folded his hands upon his rotund stomach, closed his eyes, and during a sweet doze heard the clatter of Emerenzia's sharp voice.

The abbé went with the countess into her private sitting-room. She sat upon the sofa, her eyes on the ground, waiting with much inward trepidation to hear what sentence so exalted a personage would pronounce upon the demoniacal possession. As he did not speak, she in a timid voice began—

"Has my confessor told you the terrible secret of the castle?"

"He has told me all that he knows."

"And what view would the authorities of the Church take, do you think?"

"My individual opinion, countess, is that the whole thing is a conspiracy of the living."

"Of the living!" repeated the countess. "And my visions?"

"Those can be explained by psychological means. You are of a susceptible, nervous temperament; your senses are made acquainted with the first portion of the history, your imagination works out the remainder. Your dreams, countess, are hallucinations, nothing else. Visible ghosts do not exist; those who are dead cannot live and move, for the reason that their organic powers are at an end."

The countess shook her head incredulously. To say the truth, she was ill-pleased. She had expected from so high and intellectual an ecclesiastic a very different explanation. If he could only tell us this, it was, indeed, lost trouble to send so far for him.

Herr Samuel was quick enough to read in her face what was passing in her mind, and hastened to apply a radical cure.

"Countess, I know you doubt what I say, because you have firm faith in what your eyes have seen, your ears have heard. You are quite convinced that you yourself have been many times in the haunted vault, and have there seen the spirits of your departed ancestors."

"Only last night," whispered the countess, in an awed voice, "the tumult was fearful. They told me they would come again to-night, that they would expect me."

"And have you promised to go to them?"

"When day comes I shudder from the idea, but at night some strange, mysterious power draws me to the vault; I know all fear will vanish, and I shall not be able to stay away."

"Very good. Then to-night I shall go with you to the vault of your ancestors."

At these words a sudden flush covered the pale face of the countess. The living portrait! She should go with him—where? Perhaps into hell. She trembled at the thought; then with a violent effort recovered her composure, and said, in a hesitating manner—

"I do not know. I do not think it would be possible. I should have to let my household into the secret."

The abbé understood the nature of the question, and all the consequences it involved.

"That would not be necessary. On the contrary, your household must know nothing of my visit."

The countess looked at him. She was puzzled, agitated. What could he mean? He could not imagine for a moment that he was to spend the night with her—alone?

The abbé read her thought and answered quietly—

"I shall go away now with Pastor Mahok. I shall return about midnight, and will knock at your door to announce my arrival."

Theudelinde shook her head. "That is impossible. In winter every door in my house is locked by seven o'clock. To reach my suite of rooms, you should pass through no less than seven doors. First the castle door. This is watched by my portress, an old woman who never sleeps; besides, two monstrous bloodhounds keep guard there. They are chained to the door with long chains; they would eat you if you tried to pass. Then comes the door of the corridor, to which there are two locks; my companion keeps the key of one, my housekeeper the key of the other, and to open it you must awake both. The third is the door to the staircase; the cook has the key under her pillow, and she sleeps so soundly, and the whole house is astir before she moves. The fourth is the entrance to the secret lattice passage; this is in the keeping of the housemaid, a nervous girl, who, when it grows dark, would not go into the next room. The fifth door leads to the chamber of my own maid, a very modest young person, who would not open the door to a man were he prophet or saint. The sixth door is that of Fraulein Emerenzia, my companion; she falls into violent hysterics if at night any one turns the handle of her door. The seventh and last door is that of my dressing-room, which is fitted with a peculiar self-acting lock, a new invention. I ask your reverence if, under such conditions, you could make your way here at midnight?"

"Permit me, in my turn, to put a question to you. You have given me to understand that you descend constantly to the vault of your ancestors. How does it happen that you pass through all these well-guarded doors?"

Over the countenance of the countess a triumphant smile passed. The superstitious woman could repel the attack of the scientist.

"Oh, I do not pass through any of them! From my bedroom a secret staircase leads to the chapel vault. I go down this staircase."

It would have been only natural that the abbé on hearing this should have proposed to conceal himself in the library, and there await the countess. But he read the character of his hostess and knew that such a proposal would have shocked her prudish mind and have offended her so deeply that, in all probability, she would have refused to listen any further. She required the most delicate management; this the quick-seeing abbé recognized perfectly.

"I am still of the same mind," he said, calmly. "I shall knock at your door this night at twelve o'clock."

At these words the countess was seized with a nervous shudder, but the abbé went on without taking any notice—

"If you believe that there are unearthly beings who are possessed of mysterious powers by which they pass through locked doors and make themselves visible to some human beings, invisible to others, then why should I not have this power also? But you imagine that because I am only a man born of dust I cannot infringe the laws of nature. Let me remind you that there is a natural explanation for all that may seem to you incomprehensible. Witchcraft is now no longer a mystery.

We do not now burn Boscos and Galuches upon funeral piles. Do not for a moment think that I am a Bosco or a Paracelsus. I repeat that what I promise I will perform; at the same hour at which the ghosts begin their orgies will I knock at your door with the words, *In nomine Domini aperientur portæ fidelium*—'In the name of the Lord may the doors of the faithful be opened.' Remember, no one but us two is to know anything of my coming to-night. Till then may the blessing of God be with you."

Theudelinde was much impressed by her strange visitor. His confidence infused courage into her weak mind, while his masterful ways influenced her like a spell. He addressed her from such a superior height that she felt it would be almost desecration not to place the utmost faith in his promises, and, nevertheless, he had promised to perform an impossible thing. How could she reconcile the two, unless, indeed, she had to do with a being of another world? She saw from the window the carriage drive away with the two clergymen. She watched them get in; she remained at her post until the carriage returned empty.

The female Jehu showed to the other servants the *pourboire* she had received; it was a new silver piece. It passed from hand to hand. What a miracle! Of the fifteen million inhabitants of Hungary, fourteen million five hundred thousand had never seen such a thing as a silver piece of money. There was a clergyman for you, of a very different pattern from that other, who gave, every Sunday, a fourpenny piece wrapped carefully in a piece of paper, to be *divided* among the waitresses!

The time passed slowly to the countess; the clock seemed to go with leaden weights. She wandered through all the rooms, her mind revolving in what possible manner, by what possible entrance a man could find his way into the castle. When it had struck seven o'clock she saw herself that every door which communicated with her wing was carefully locked; then she sat herself down in her own room. She took out the plan of the castle, which had been prepared by the Florentine artist who had built it. It was not the first time she had studied it; when she had received the castle as a present from her father, she had made herself mistress of every particular concerning it. The building was three times larger than her income could afford to maintain. She had, therefore, to choose which wing she would occupy. In the centre there were fine reception-rooms, a banqueting-hall, an armory, and a museum for pictures and curiosities. This portion was out of the question. Also, from this portion of the castle a concealed staircase led to a subterranean passage. This could be used as a means of escape, and had no doubt served such a purpose when the old castle had been besieged by the Turks. The grandfather of the countess had walled up these steps, and no one could now get into the secret passage. The left wing, which was similarly constructed to the one which the countess inhabited, had served as a sort of pleasure residence to her pleasure-loving ancestors. There were all manner of secret holes and corners in it, communications of all kinds connecting the rooms, doors behind pictures, concealed alcoves, and the like. The architect's plan showed these without any reticence. Theudelinde naturally turned away in horror from the idea of inhabiting this tainted wing, so full of sinful associations; she set up her Lares and Penates in the less handsome, but more homely, right wing, where were a few good rooms fitted for domestic life, an excellent library, and the family vault below. It contained no other secret staircase than the one which led to the tombs of the departed members of the family. For the rest, Countess Theudelinde had taken care to wall up all the passages which led to either the centre or left wing of the castle, and there was no means of communication between them and her apartments. All the chimneys had iron gates to shut off any possible entrance that way; every window was provided with strong iron bars. It would have been impossible for even a cat to effect an entrance into this enchanted castle.

The countess, meditating on all these precautions, came to the conclusion that there was only one way by which the Abbé Samuel could introduce himself into the house, and that was by a secret understanding with some one of her household. But again, setting altogether aside the high character borne by the priest, which would render such an act upon his part improbable, the very nature of the circumstances attending his visit made it impossible. He had never been absent from the countess for a minute, except during his short walk to the carriage, and then Herr Mahok had been his companion. Theudelinde, therefore, dismissed the idea from her mind. She sent her household early to bed; she complained to Fraulein Emerenzia of suffering from pains on one side of her head. Immediately that sympathetic companion complained of pains on the other side of her head. When the countess thought she would try to sleep, Emerenzia felt the like desire; she wrapped her whole head up in warm cotton wool, and snored without mercy.

Theudelinde shut herself up in her bedroom and counted the minutes. She tried to play Patience, but the cards would not come right; her mind was too much disturbed. She took out her Bible, splendidly illustrated by Doré. She looked at all the pictures; she counted the figures of the different men and women upon those two hundred and thirty large plates; then the horses and the camels, till she came to the scenes of murders. Then she tried to pass the time by reading the text. She counted which letter of the alphabet was repeated the most frequently upon one side of the page. For the greater part the letter *a* was the favorite. *e* came next, then *o*, also *u*; *i* was the worst represented. This was in the French print. In the Hungarian text *e* had the majority, then *a*, *o*, and *i*, and, last of all, *b* and *u*. But of this she also wearied. Then she sat down to the piano, and tried to calm her agitation by playing dreamy fantasias; neither did this succeed. Her hands trembled, and she could not sustain herself at the instrument, she was so wearied; and as the fatal hour of midnight drew nearer she gave up making efforts to distract her mind, and abandoned herself to thoughts of the impending ghostly tumult. She found herself altogether under the influence of her ancestral spectres, for she was always consumed with *ennui* until the noise began. Then a sort of fever would come to her; she would undress herself, crawl into bed, draw the coverings over her head until she broke into a perspiration, and then fall into a deep sleep. The next morning, when she awoke, she really believed that she had witnessed the scenes of which she had only dreamed.

This night she drew forth her talisman, the photograph of the abbé, and tried to find some strength by considering it. She placed it before her on the reading-desk and sat gazing at it. Was he really a superior being, at whose command the doors of the castle would fly open, spectres would vanish, and the gates of hell would close upon them? It could not be that such things would happen. The more the night advanced the greater grew her nervous fears. Her heart beat loudly. It was not so much the nightly ghosts that she dreaded, but this new and equally unearthly visitor. What was he? A wizard, an enchanter like Merlin of old, or a saint come to exorcise and banish her tormentors?

The weary lagging hours went by, until at last the pendulum of the old clock began to vibrate, and its iron tongue gave out midnight. The countess counted every stroke. Its vibration had hardly ceased when, punctual to its usual time, the infernal noise began; from the vault below the tones of the mass reached Theudelinde's ears. She was, however, listening for another sound, listening with feverish anxiety to catch a stealthy footfall in the adjoining room, to hear the rattle of a key surreptitiously moving in the lock. Nothing! She came to the door, and, putting her head to the keyhole, strained her ears in vain. All was still. It was now a quarter past midnight; the tumult in the vault below was in full swing—the witches' Sabbath, as it might be called, with its yells, shouts, songs, prayers; it was as if all the devils of hell had given one another rendezvous in the company of the countess's ancestors.

"He will not come," she thought, and trembled in every limb of her fever-stricken body. It was folly to expect it. How could a man accomplish what is only permitted to spirits?

She retired to the alcove and prepared to lie down. At this moment she heard a tap at the door of her sitting-room, and, after a moment, a low voice spoke in firm tones—

"In nomine Domini aperientur portæ fidelium."

It was the signal given by the abbé. Theudelinde gave a shriek; she nearly lost her senses from fright, but gathered herself together with a supreme effort. It was real; no hallucination, no dream! He was at the door, her deliverer. Forward!

The countess ran to the door and opened it. The crisis gave her unusual strength. This might be a trap, and instead of a deliverer she might find herself opposite to a robber or murderer. Under the carpet lay concealed the trap-door; the midnight visitor stood on the very spot. One pressure of the secret spring and down he went into the abyss below. Theudelinde had her foot on the spring as she undid the door.

There stood the abbé before her. No appearance of his clerical calling was to be seen. He wore a long coat, which reached to his feet, and carried neither bell, book, nor candle, wherewith to exorcise the spirits. In his right hand he held a thick stick made of rhinoceros' skin, and in the left a dark lantern.

"Remain where you are," said the countess, in a commanding voice. "Before you set foot in this room you shall tell me how you got here. Was it with the help of God, of man, or of the devil?"

"Countess," returned the abbé, "look about you. Do you not see that every door in your castle stands open? Through these open doors I have passed easily. How I passed through the court is another thing. I will tell you that later."

"And my household, who sleep in those rooms?" said the countess, in an incredulous voice.

"The curtains hang round every bed; I have not raised them. If your household be asleep, they will no doubt sleep as the just do, without waking."

The countess listened, only half believing what she heard; she was growing nerveless again. She led the abbé into the sitting-room, and sank exhausted upon the sofa.

The tumult in the vault was indescribable.

"Do you hear *it?*" she said, in a whisper.

"I do hear, and I know whence it comes. I am here to face those who cause this unseemly riot."

"Have you the weapons that Holy Church has provided for such a task?" asked Theudelinde, anxiously.

The priest for all answer held towards her the strong staff he carried.

"I have this good stick, countess."

"Do you hear above all the tumult that strident voice? It is my uncle Ladislaus," cried the countess, grasping the abbé's arm with both her hands. "Do you hear that horrible laugh? It is my uncle's laugh."

"We will soon learn the author of that unpleasant cachinnation," remarked the priest, quietly.

"Why, what do you propose to do?"

"I shall go down and join the worshipful society below."

"You will descend into the vault? What to do?"

"To pass judgment upon that unruly gang, countess. You promised to accompany me."

"I promised!" and Theudelinde retreated from him, her eyes staring wildly, her hands pressed to her breast.

"It was your own wish."

"True, true! I am so confused; my thoughts are all astray. I cannot recollect them. You here, and that fearful noise below! I am terribly afraid."

"How? You who had the courage to go among the ghosts by yourself, are you afraid now that *I* am with you? Give me your hand."

The countess placed her trembling fingers in the abbé's hand, and as she felt the firm, manly clasp, an unusual sense of strength and protection possessed her; she ceased to shake and shiver, her eyes no longer saw shapes and fantasies moving before them; her heart began to beat steadily. The bare touch of this man's hand gave her new life.

"Come with me," he said, in a decided voice, while he stuck his whip under his left arm, and with the right drew the countess after him. "Where are the keys of the secret staircase, and of the room through which we must pass?"

Theudelinde felt that she could not let go his hand for one minute. She was for the moment, so to speak, mesmerized by his superior mind. She crawled after him submissively; she should follow him, were it to the very gates of hell itself. Without a word she pointed to the key cabinet, an antique piece of furniture which would have made the joy of a bric-à-brac collector, and in which there was a drawer full of keys.

Without a moment's hesitation the priest put his hand on the ones that were wanted. It was no miracle that he should do so, although to the weakened mind of his companion it appeared to be miraculous; on one of the keys there was the well-known sign of a vault key, the crucifix.

The abbé now drew aside the curtain which concealed the secret passage to the library, and here, at the first step, he was met by a certain proof, if such were wanting, to show him the credit to be given to the countess's statements that she was in the habit of descending to the vault: as he opened the door a mass of cobwebs blew into his face. The countess, however, was firm in her hallucination. It is a phase of such nervous disorders as hers to believe that what they have dreamed is actual fact; they can even supply small details.

As the countess went up the steps she whispered to her companion—

"A window is broken here, and the wind whistles through it." And as they turned the angle of the steps there was a narrow slip-window which in the daytime gave light to the staircase, the panes of which were actually broken. She had never seen this. When they came to the door of the library she confided to the abbé that she was always frightened to pass the threshold.

"It is such a ghostly place!" she said. "When the moon shines through the shutter of the upper window it throws white specks upon the mosaic pattern of the marble floor, which makes it look like some mysterious writing. In one of the corners between two presses there is a glass case with a skeleton in it; in another case the wax impression, taken after death, of Ignatius Loyola."

Everything was precisely as the countess related. The moon shone through the upper panes of glass, the skeleton stood in his glass case, the waxen head of the dead saint lay in the other, but the countess had never crossed the threshold. In her childhood her nurse had told her these tales of the Bondavara Castle, and when she had become its mistress her first care had been to lock these rooms. Ten years' dust lay on the carpets, on the chairs and tables; cobwebs hung from the ceilings, mice played games in the deep wainscots, for no one ever came here.

At the moment in which the countess and her companion entered the library a certain peace reigned in the vault below. The tumult seemed lulled; there were neither shrieks nor demoniacal songs to be heard. From the mortuary chapel, however, the notes of the organ reached the ears of the two listeners. It sounded like the prelude which is played in church before mass begins, only the chords of the prelude were all discords; it was as if the organ were played by a condemned spirit.

The countess stood before the chapel door, her breast heaving with emotion. She caught hold of the abbé's hand with a strong grasp, and kept him from turning the key in the lock. She trembled in every limb.

"What are those fearful tones?"

Then came a confused sound, as of many voices intoning the vespers. One voice, which imitated the monotonous delivery of the celebrant, began to sing in Latin the words of a hymn—

> "Bacchus, prepare the libation."

Another voice answered in the same tone—

> "And hasten, brethren, to drink!"

Then a third took up the text in a parody of the *Gloria*—

"Gloria Baccho, et filiæ ejus Cerevisiæ et Spiritui vini, sicut erat in Baccho natus, et nunc, et semper, et per omnia pocula poculorum. Stramen."

The countess felt her whole body turning into ice; fear mingled with horror. She understood the impious parody.

Now the organ accompanied the antiphon.

"Date nobis de cerevisia vestra; quia sitiunt guttura nostra"—"Give us of your beer; our throats are dry."

Then followed the psalm—

"Brother to brother spoke these words: shall two goblets of beer quench man's thirst?"

"Two, three, five, six are not enough for man's satiety."

"Blessed be Bacchus, who gave us beer."

Then followed the Capitulum.

"Brethren, attend, and do as I command ye. Before ye leave the ale-house for your own homes empty all the pots, leave not a drop therein, but tilt them and drain every drop of wine. This do from goblet to goblet. Stramen."

The countess felt, as she listened to this profanity, what a damned soul must experience when for the first time it consorts with devils. But now a hellish chorus broke forth of men's and women's voices, yelling out a parody of a hymn—

> "Bacchus, who gave us drink,
> Art thou not called the god of liquor?
> Grant us all the holy grace,
> Strength to drink in every place,
> So that, drinking everywhere,
> We for glory may prepare
> In thy everlasting wine-cellar."

This was followed by the ringing of the bell, and the priest's voice intoned the blessing.

"Bacchus be with you."

The chorus answered, "And with thy pint-pots."

Then came the Oratio—

"Let us eat. O all-powerful Bacchus, since thou hast created this society of ours for thine own honor, grant to us its continuance, and give to us a constant supply of brave topers, who never may cease drinking from goblet to goblet."

And the chorus answered, "Stramen."

The countess was not able any longer to hold herself up. She sank upon her knees, and looked up at the priest in mute horror. Hardly knowing what she did, she gazed in utter despair at the tall figure lit up as it was by the rays of the moon, which played round his head like a halo.

The abbé put the key into the lock of the chapel door. The countess caught his hand; her fright amounted to agony.

"Do not—do not open it!" she cried. "Inside is hell let loose."

With an elevation of his head, the abbé answered proudly—

"Nec portæ inferi—the gates of hell shall not prevail"; and then he turned the key, and the heavy iron door swung open, and disclosed the actors in the strange drama.

On the altar all the candles were lighted, and their light showed with distinctness every incident of the performance, every feature in the faces of the performers.

What a scene!

On one side of the vault ran a long table, round which was seated, eating and drinking, not the countess's ancestors and ancestresses, but all the servants of her household. The maids, who were so strictly guarded, were here in the company of the men who were so rigorously excluded. The countess could, therefore, see that these were flesh-and-blood ghosts which had so long haunted her ancient castle. Each of her handmaidens had a lover in either the steward, bailiff, gamekeeper, or clerk in the neighborhood. The nervous housemaid, who at night was afraid of her own shadow, was now drinking out of the glass of the innkeeper; the virtuous maid was embraced by the mayor's footman; the portress, an elderly virgin, held a jug in her hand, while she executed a clog-dance upon the table. All the rest clapped hands, shrieked, sang at the top of their voices, and beat the table as if it were a big drum. The shepherd, who represented the countess's grandfather, sat upon the monument of the chancellor, his legs round the cross, and played the bagpipes. It was this instrument which at the burlesque of vespers imitated the harmonium. Upon the gravestone of the first archbishop the beer-barrel was set up. The maids were all dressed in the countess's silk dresses, with the exception of the female coachman, who, as usual, wore man's clothes, but by way of symmetry her lover, the coachman of the neighboring brewery, was dressed in woman's clothes. The countess recognized on the head of this bearded fellow her nightcap, and round his body her cloak, trimmed with her best lace. Worst of all, at the top of the table sat Fraulein Emerenzia, on very intimate terms with her neighbor, a young lawyer. She wore the skirt of a favorite dress of Theudelinde's, a flame-colored brocade; the body could not fit her corpulent form, so she had her mistress's best lace shawl wrapped round her. Her face was red; she had a large tumbler of wine before her, and she smoked a pipe. The modest Emerenzia!

The men were all drunk and noisy, the women screamed in an unearthly manner; the bagpipes squealed; the table resounded with thumps and the clatter of the portress's clogs. From the altar came the voice of the mock priest, his arms outstretched in blessing. Through the din the words "Bacchus vobiscum" were heard, and the tinkle of the bell. This mock priest was no other than Michael the sacristan, who brought all the church ornaments confided to his care. He wore the pastor's vestments, and on his head an improvised skull-cap. The acolyte was the parish bell-ringer.

The countess was cut to the heart. The terrible ingratitude, especially of these girls, to whom she had been as a mother—more anxious indeed than their own mothers to keep them pure and innocent—wounded the poor lady who had taught them to sing hymns on Sunday, had fed them from her own table, and had never allowed them to read a novel or hear a bad word. And this was the outcome of her efforts. They insulted the graves of her ancestors, played upon her nervous fears, destroyed her rest, nearly drove her mad with their ghostly noises, wore her clothes at their orgies, and, worse insult of all, she, a high-born lady and a pure woman, had the degradation of wearing these same garments, defiled as they were with the smell of wine and stale tobacco.

Bitter as such ingratitude was, it counted as nothing in comparison with the profanation of using the holiest things of religion, the sacred ornaments of the Church, to carry out these impious rites. "Woe to them from whom scandal cometh," says the Scripture, and this woe means pain and suffering that no soothing balsam can alleviate.

A mortal terror still filled the countess's heart. She was in the presence of those who had no control over their already besotted senses. If these drunken savages, these unsexed women, found their revels were discovered, what was to hinder them tearing her to pieces? There was only one man between her and them. Theudelinde looked at her solitary protector. His eyes gleamed with such apostolic anger that her timid soul grew fearful of the consequences, both to him and to herself, of his just wrath. She seized both his hands, to hold him from venturing among such demons. The abbé easily freed himself from the clasp of her weak fingers. In one bound he sprang down the steps, fell upon the false priest as he was in the act of pronouncing his final stramen; with the butt-end of his rhinoceros whip he gave him two blows.

What the countess now witnessed was truly no vision. She saw how one man, armed with no more formidable weapon than a horsewhip, ventured into the midst of the hellish assembly, with one hand seized the table and overturned it and all that was on it of dishes, glasses, and wine-cups, with the other cracked his whip in the faces of the guests, who sprang to their feet in all the terror of detection, like to the profaners of the Temple. They were driven towards the door of the vault, the abbé's whip descending on their shoulders with impartial justice. They went tumbling over one another, howling and screaming, pressing onwards and pursued by the flagellation of the abbé. The bagpipe player in his haste missed his footing, those behind stumbled over him, and so lay all in a heap together. Not one went without carrying a remembrance of the abbé's strong arm, for he spared no one. No effort was made at reprisals; the criminal who is caught seldom shows fight. These last were, moreover, taken by surprise, and the clergyman was possessed of extraordinary strength; one man who tried to drag the horsewhip from his hand was dealt such a blow in his face that he was glad to relinquish his hold and take to his heels without loss of time.

"Give it to them! give it to them!" cried the countess, who had no pity for her former servants, who had to pass her as they made their way pell-mell to the door. Emerenzia covered her head, not from shame, but fearing her face might get a blow. Almost the last was the sacristan, whose clerical dress hindered his speed, and whose back was so battered by the abbé that the vestment he wore hung in ribbons.

After the last guest had departed, the abbé closed

the heavy door of the vault and returned to where the countess was standing. His face wore an almost glorified expression; it was the consciousness of having asserted his strength. As he approached the countess fell on her knees, and made as if she would kiss his feet, but the abbé raised her.

"Compose yourself, countess. Your present situation needs all your strength. Do you know that at this moment there are only two persons in this castle, for I have locked the door which leads to the court-yard. This folly is played out. You see now that no wicked spirit had any part in it. It was no ghost, only human beings who have had to do with this miserable business."

"What shall I do?" asked the countess, constraining herself to speak calmly.

"Take my lantern. I am going to lock the lattice door, so as to stop any entrance from this side. But you can return by the way we came, back to your own apartment, where I advise you to make yourself some tea; you are freezing with cold."

"Must I go back all that way alone?"

"Remember the words, 'If God is with me, who is against me,' and you can never be alone. To see ghosts is an illness; the method of curing it must be heroic."

And as he saw that the countess, in spite of her efforts, could not subdue her nervous tremor, he took her by the hand, and, returning with her to the library, led her to the glass case which enclosed the skeleton, and opened the door.

"Were you afraid of this? Why, it is nothing to fear. It is a standing proof of the wisdom of God. Every limb of this wonderful collection of bones tells us the Almighty created man to be ruler of the earth. Look at the skull; upon this arched forehead is written the birthright of humanity, in every corner and line of the face the superiority of the white race over all others. This skull teaches us how deep should be our gratitude to an all-seeing Providence who has created us the superior over all other beings on the earth. The sight of a skull should cause no shudder in the breast of man; it should give rise to feelings of thankfulness and reverence, for it is the symbol of the great love which our Heavenly Maker has for the creature He has made and chosen from all eternity."

As he spoke the priest laid Theudelinde's cold hand upon the skull of the skeleton. The countess trembled no more. New life and strength born of the words of this singular man seemed to infuse themselves into her veins. She looked another being.

"Now go to your room," said the abbé. "I shall soon follow, but I must first put out the torches on the altar. We must not have a conflagration on our hands."

"I am quite ready to go alone," returned the countess. "My foolish fears are cured, but I am now concerned for you. Perhaps those wretched servants of mine are still about, and if you venture into the vault in the dark they may fall upon you and take their revenge for being discovered."

"Oh, I am provided with what would soon scatter such cowards as they are," said the abbé, drawing a revolver from a secret pocket. "I had resolved to use stringent measures with them if necessary. Now, in God's name, retire to your room, countess."

Theudelinde, without another word, took the lantern and went through the long library. The priest watched her until she had crossed the passage, and had opened the door of her own apartment. He then hastened back to the vault. In the passage he saw a blue flame burning on a tin dish.

"Alcohol and ammonia mixed together," murmured the priest. "This is what frightened Herr Mahok." Close to it lay the winding-sheet and mask. The abbé pushed the vessel with the flame into the corner, for he knew that in an encounter with an adversary it would be little profit to have an illumination, and then he went down the dark passage carefully. No one was there; they had all run away, and were probably running still. The lattice door stood open; he drew it to, and barred it carefully; then he returned into the vault and locked it also, having first extinguished the lights, with the exception of one, which he took to light him back to the countess's room.

He found her sitting composedly before the tea equipage. She had obeyed him. As he entered the room she rose, and, folding her hands upon her breast, cried:

"Most holy saint and apostle!"

"You must not give me such exalted titles," said the abbé, smiling. "What I have done does not merit such high-sounding terms. I have accomplished no miracle, for I had to do with mortals only. One circumstance which appears to you in a miraculous light is easily explained. I allude to my entering a house wherein all the doors were locked. But first, will you pour out the tea?—and if you will give me a cup I shall be grateful, for the occurrences of the last hour have somewhat excited me. Then we will talk the whole affair over."

The countess gave her guest his tea, then sank back in her arm-chair, and wrapped herself in her cloak; she was still shivering.

"That the supposed ghostly appearances and noises were in no sense supernatural was borne in on me," continued the abbé, as he sipped his tea, "from the first moment Herr Mahok took me into his confidence. I was convinced that the nocturnal disturbance was the work of your own household, and it served their purpose to make it as ghost-like as possible. The situation had been created by your over-caution, countess. Your women servants were not allowed to hold communication with the opposite sex; they, therefore, found other means to meet, and to give a cover to these illicit meetings they set up an atmosphere of ghostly mystery, by which their goings-on were well concealed. The conspiracy was perfectly carried out. If they had conducted their sinful intercourse on any other lines you would have long since discovered them. When the pastor told me that he and his sacristan had escaped through the lattice door, I suspected that it was through this door the men found their way into the vault, and that the sacristan must be a participator in the plot, whatever it was. Moreover, I calculated that the women must, of necessity, find their way through the cellar passage, and that, therefore, they would naturally leave every door in the house *open*, so that their return might be conducted without any danger of awaking you by noise, such as unlocking doors. The countenance, the coloring, the eyes of your companion betray her; it is easy to see what she has been, and that, moreover, she drinks. I knew to-day at dinner that she was a hypocrite. She held forth against all alcoholic drinks; that settled her with me. I had no doubt that I should find all the doors open; and I did. In order to make no noise I came on foot to the garden door. Countless footsteps in the fresh snow showed me that the company had already assembled. From the open garden door the footprints led to the lattice door, and thence to the vault.

This door was put to. I pushed it open and was in the passage. I went to the left, up the steps to the cellar passage; the door was open. I could not count upon finding every door open; it was exactly as I imagined. The only difficulty lay in passing through your wardrobe-room, which has no key, but a peculiarly constructed spring-lock. I felt certain that your maids would borrow some of their mistress's silk dresses, and therefore the spring-lock would be arranged so as not to betray by its loud snap the return of the stolen garments to their proper place. On looking closely I found this to be the case; the lock was kept in its place by the insertion of a penknife, which could be easily withdrawn. Therefore, countess, you have, night after night, slept in this castle with every door open—in real danger—at the mercy of robbers, or even murderers; all the time frightened to death with ghostly noises, which kept you a prisoner to your room, not venturing to call your treacherous servants. Countess, you have been terribly punished."

"Punished!" stammered the countess, her face growing even paler.

"Yes, punished; for you have richly deserved to suffer."

Theudelinde fixed a horrified look on the abbé.

"Countess, at your door," said the priest, sternly, "lies the heaviest portion of the sins into which your servants have fallen. You have, in fact, driven them into vice. Your eccentric rules, bizarre and ridiculous ideas, made your women servants liars and induced their irregularities. Nature punishes those who revolt against her, and the long years during which you have isolated yourself from the world and from society have been flat rebellion, which has brought its own punishment. You now stand before two judges, Heaven and the World; Heaven is ready to punish you, the world to laugh at you; and the wrath of Heaven and the ridicule of the world is equally hard to bear. How do you mean to protect yourself against both?"

The countess sank back annihilated. Only just recovered from the anxieties, horrors, and dangers of this dreadful night, she was not able to face the denunciations of the priest, which were, in fact, only the echo of her own conscience. The torture was greater than all she had undergone. There was silence in the room, during which the words rang in Theudelinde's ears like the tolling of a bell.

"How shall you face the anger of Heaven and the ridicule of the world?"

At last she thought of a way out of the difficulty, and, raising her head, she said, in a low voice:

"I will hide my miserable head in a convent. *There* the ridicule of the world will not reach me; there, kneeling before the altar, I will day and night pray to God to pardon my fault. You, oh most reverend father, will perhaps use your influence with the abbess of some convent—I should prefer the very strictest order—and get me admitted. There I shall find a living grave, and no one will ever hear my name. I shall leave this castle, and all my fortune, together with my savings of the last few years, to your order, with only one condition, that every night at twelve o'clock vespers shall be sung in the family vault, which has been desecrated by such abominations as have been practised there."

The countess's voice, which was low and broken in the beginning, gathered strength as she made this renunciation of her worldly goods.

The abbé rose up as she finished, and took her trembling hand in his, while, with a haughty elevation of his head, he answered :

"That everything may be quite clear, I beg you will understand, countess, that neither I nor my order need, nor would accept, the donation of your castle, your property, or your money. It is not our custom to take advantage of weak-minded persons in a moment of contrition, and to extort from them compensation for their sins in the shape of their worldly goods. We have no desire to acquire property in so sneaking and contemptible a manner, and therefore, countess, in the name of my order, I decline to spend the night singing vespers in your family vault, or the day in living on your fortune. This idea you may dismiss altogether from your mind."

These words filled the countess with admiration. She had already felt herself singularly attracted by this man. This proof of his disinterestedness and indifference to worldly considerations completed his dominion over her mind, and subjugated her to his authority. She listened submissively while he continued his admonitions.

"For the rest," he said, "I should recommend you to abandon all ideas of conventual life, which is quite unsuited to a person of your nervous, excitable nature. You would find neither peace nor happiness; on the contrary, you would be a prey to all manner of scruples and disquieting thoughts. There are those who find a refuge and salvation in a cloister; for you it would be a foretaste of damnation, and in all probability you would end like the hermit who fled from the world to pray to God, and instead of praying, cursed Him."

The eyes of the countess glared at this awful prospect, but she murmured to herself, "True, quite true!"

"The recollection of your faults has banished you from

the Church and has robbed you of all power to pray," continued the priest, in a harsh voice.

"True, quite true!" sobbed the countess, and beat her breast. "I can never again enter a church, and I dare not pray." Then with a cry of despair she threw herself at the feet of the abbé, and with feverish strength clasped both his hands, while she screamed out, "Where shall I go, if not to the Church of God? Who shall help me, if I cannot pray to Him?"

The clergyman saw it was necessary to soothe her terrible excitement.

"Your proper refuge is in your own heart," he said, gently, "and your good deeds shall plead for you."

Theudelinde pressed the priest's hand to her burning forehead. Then she rose from her kneeling position and stretched out her arms.

"Command me. Advise me. What shall I do?"

"Return to society, and take the place your rank and wealth entitle you to hold."

The countess fell back a step, and stared at the abbé, her face all astonishment.

"Return to the world! *I* who left it five-and-twenty years ago! I should be the laughing-stock of every one were I to seek, at my age, pleasures which I long ago renounced."

"Countess, you have voluntarily thrown away that portion of your life to which the world offers its best gifts; but there still remains to you that other half, wherein you can acquire the esteem of the world—that is, if you avail yourself of the means necessary for success."

"My father, remember that in that circle which you wish me to enter I shall meet nothing but contempt and humiliations. The present generation don't know my name, my contemporaries despise me."

"But there is a magic circle in which every one is recognized and no one is despised. Would you wish to enter this circle?"

"Place me in this circle, father. Where is it to be found?"

"I will tell you, countess. Your nation is passing through a crisis; it may be called the battle for intellectual freedom. All are striving to place themselves on a footing with the intellectuality of other nations—philosophers, poets, industrials; men, women, boys, graybeards, magnates, and peasants. If they all knew how to strive together they might attain their purpose, but all are divided; each works for himself and by himself. Individual effort is doomed to failure, but united, certain of success."

The countess listened in breathless astonishment. She did not understand where the abbé was leading her.

"What is wanting in this tremendous struggle is a centre. The country has no centre. Debreczyn is thoroughly Hungarian, but its religious exclusiveness has narrowed its sphere of influence. Szegedin is well suited, but it is far too democratic. Klausenburg is indeed a Hungarian town. The aristocracy are to be found there, and a certain amount of culture, but it lies beyond the Kiralyhago, and the days of the Bethlens and the Bocskais are over. Pesth would be the proper centre; it has every qualification. I have been through the five quarters of the globe, and nowhere have I found such a place. In Pesth no man troubles himself about his neighbor, and each man believes that the world is made for him alone. The first look of the city takes one by surprise; the fine embankment along the broad Danube River, the beautiful squares and streets, with the six-story tin houses, each in a different style of architecture. Side by side are palaces built in the Roman, Moorish, Spanish, or Renaissance style, with, perhaps, the occasional introduction of a quaint Dutch mansion or Gothic structure. Opposite to the great edifice of the chain bridge rises a large stone bandbox with four towers; this is called the Basilica, but it looks more like a giant scaffold than anything else. On all sides rage monster factory chimneys, which vomit forth volumes of poisonous smoke upon the town. Factories, docks, academical palaces, redoubts, tin card-houses, art conservatories, are crowded one over the other. The academy interferes with the business of the docks, and the noise of the shipping-trade disturbs the academicians. The smoke of the steam-engines suffocates every one; while the town-hall, with all its ornamented peaks and minarets, says to the stranger, 'Come nearer, friend; this is Constantinople.'"

The countess could not help smiling over this graphic description.

"The inner town," continued the abbé, "is a labyrinth of narrow, irregular streets, which were built when the site of the present town-hall was only a marsh for the pigs to wallow in. In spite of the narrow proportions, these streets contain some of the finest shops in Europe. The contrasts are something wonderful; the finest equipages jammed against the overladen wagons conveying merchandise; the most elegantly dressed women jostling against beggars in rags. The prettiest women are to be seen in this quarter, and this in face of a wind that drives all the dust into the eyes. In the suburbs houses are rising on all sides with marvellous rapidity, little and big, in every style and variety, giving more dust for the wind to play tricks with. The whole place is a stony wilderness, with here and there a small green oasis not bigger than a private garden. Round about the city lies a Sahara, the earth of which is constantly dug up, so that the sirocco is never in want of dust. This is the exterior appearance of Pesth, which in itself presents the different features of a manufacturing town, an emporium for trade, and a city of arts and science, as well as those of the capital of an empire and of an American colony, where men of all classes assemble to make their pile of gold, but when this is secured hurry away to spend their winnings in other places.

"So far as social conditions are concerned, and these, after all, concern us most," said the abbé, with a quick look at his listener, "they are as complicated as the commercial interests of Pesth. Each class is surrounded, so to speak, with a Chinese wall. Trade and the stock-exchange are altogether in the hands of Jews and Germans. This would not be so much an evil were it not that a great amount of fraudulent speculation goes on, and at every turn of the money market in Vienna the funds go down. The Hungarian element is made up of tobacco-merchants and hand-workers; there are, besides these, about twenty thousand Slavonians from the hills, who are day-laborers. Pesth is, or should be, the headquarters of national education. It is, however, not the fashion to support it. It should be also the centre of science and literature; it is not, however, considered good 'ton' to cultivate anything but foreign literature. Pesth can boast of very distinguished *savants*, and of a very haughty aristocracy; but no one is allowed to enter this magic circle but those who belong to the upper ten. The whole society is on a wrong footing; each one fights his own battle, bears his own burden; the finest ideas are lost because no one understands the other. A common standpoint is wanting. All healthy life is dying out, full freedom of thought and action being strangled by the iron laws of the short-sighted government, which forbids discussion of any kind.

"The Reichstag and the Comitatshaus are both closed. The only free ground left is that of general society; but here class prejudices step in. A certain portion of our aristocracy are too indifferent to trouble themselves to do anything for the general good; the rest are too fond of their own ease and amusement; they acknowledge no other aim in life but their own pleasure. There are some, however, who do know what their duty is, and who would willingly make sacrifices to fulfil it, but during the last ten years they have suffered such a loss of income that they are no longer in a position to bear the expense which would be entailed by opening their houses. There are others, those most fitted by intellect as well as by position to be leaders. Alas! they will never return to Pesth; it is to them full of tragic memories, which haunt the houses where they once lived, and which have banished forever the laugh and jest from those walls. Therefore it is that we have arrived at this position, that there is not a single centre where the clever, the good, the nobleman, and the gentleman can meet on equal terms; and without this no real good can be done."

"Then let me create this centre!" cried the countess, rising to her feet and addressing the abbé with an inspired look. Her whole being seemed changed by this new thought, which had been skilfully suggested by the words of the clergyman, who seemed well pleased at the effect he had produced.

"Then you understood," he said; "and for you the advantages will be incalculable. Here is the shelter you require. If you come to Pesth, if you live there as befits your rank and your fortune, you can assemble round you the very cream of society. To your *salon* will come every one, distinguished not alone by birth, but by talent—politicians, artists, poets, magnates, priests, prelates, and laymen; the aristocracy of the land and the aristocracy of intellect shall be alike represented. Your mission will be to further by this means the apostolate of truth, of culture; and, by so doing, to assist the progress and development of your own nation, and for the rest your own position will be most honorable. As hostess and mistress of such you will be respected and admired."

The countess seized the clergyman's hand in both hers, and covered it with kisses, while in her excitement she sobbed:

"I thank you, I thank you, I thank you!"

"Do you not see, countess, that there is a vocation for you besides that of conventual life?"

"You are a prophet."

"In the meantime, may I ask you a practical question? For the task which you have undertaken with such praiseworthy zeal there are certain material qualifications absolutely necessary, the first being a sufficient income. May I ask you to give me your confidence on this delicate subject?"

"I am rich," answered Theudelinde. "I have my capital at good interest. Likewise, out of my savings I have bought a fine mansion situated in the best part of Pesth; it is at present let."

"You will now take it into your own hands," said the abbé, "and have it properly appointed, suitable to your rank. So far as your securities go, it may be better to invest your capital differently. We shall see. How much does your yearly income from the Bondavara estate amount to?"

"About twenty thousand florins."

"How large is the estate?"

"From about nine to ten thousand acres."

"Then the return is far too small. The agent is to blame for this; this income would be too little to support the position you now intend to hold. Twenty thousand florins would not be nearly enough to keep up an establishment on a proper footing in Pesth."

The countess was surprised. She said, humbly, "I imagined it was a great deal of money."

"So it is for living in the country; but Pesth is as dear, if not dearer, than Paris. To keep a proper establishment going, and take the position of a leader of society, such as it is your ambition to be, you must at least command a yearly income of forty thousand florins."

"But I cannot do that. What shall I do?" Theudelinde said, in great distress.

The abbé's lips parted in a smile. "Oh, we will manage it for you! For the rest it will not be difficult. The rental of the estate must be overhauled; you must get a better agent, a more enterprising steward. I myself do not understand finance, but I have friends in the inner circle of the stock-exchange, and one or other of these will undertake to advise you as to your affairs when you are settled in Pesth. In any case, I am quite certain that your land is let too low, it should bring in double the interest you get from it. I know so much of political economy."

The countess was delighted at these words. What a friend to have! Her income to be doubled! Truly this abbé was sent to her from heaven.

"Do as you think best," she said. "I give you full power to act for me."

"Then, if you will allow me, I shall have your property revalued, and fresh leases made. This will double your income, and it will only cost you a trifle—a factor's fee, in fact."

Theudelinde was like a child in her joy—like a child in her submission to her spiritual adviser, to whom she looked up as a father, a counsellor, a true friend.

All this he might be; but it was also true that from the date of this conversation the owner of Bondavara lost her hold on her own property forever.

CHAPTER IX

"AN OBSTINATE FELLOW"

COUNTESS THEUDELINDE was beside herself with joy. She ran to her bell-apparatus, touched the spring, and the machine put itself into motion.

"What are you doing, countess?" asked the abbé, in some amazement.

"I am desiring my steward to be sent for at once."

"By what messenger?"

And then for the first time the countess remembered there was not a living soul in the house.

She grew very grave.

"It is truly a problem," continued the priest, "to know how we are to get out of the castle."

"What do you mean?" asked Theudelinde, who was so weak-minded that she always required to have everything explained to her.

"We two are quite alone in this house," returned the abbé. "If I go away to get the necessary assistance for packing up your things and making the arrangements for departure I must leave you alone here."

"I would not for all the world remain alone here."

"Then you have the alternative of accompanying me on foot to the nearest post-house in the adjacent village."

As he spoke the snow-storm was heard outside beating against the window. Theudelinde shivered.

"Why cannot we drive? My horses are in the stable."

"But I can neither harness them nor drive them."

"Oh, I should never think of such a thing!"

Nevertheless, the countess had now to consider whether she should remain alone in the castle or take the alternative of accompanying the priest in a heavy fall of snow.

"Somebody is knocking at the door," said the abbé.

"It must be my steward," returned Theudelinde. "He has heard what has happened, and has come to our assistance."

"But there is no one to open the door. Your portress was one of the ghosts."

"She was the old witch who danced on the table."

"Have you by chance a second key?"

"It hangs there on that large bunch to the right."

"Then I will take it with me, in case there is none in the lock."

"But the dogs, father, they will tear you in pieces. They are fierce to strangers."

"I will call them by their names, if you will tell me what they are."

"I don't know their names," returned the countess, who never troubled herself about such a common thing as a watch-dog's name.

"Then I must shoot them."

"But, father, as gently as you can." By this Theudelinde did not mean to appeal to his compassion for the dogs, but to remind him to spare her sensitive nerves.

The abbé took his revolver and went on his mission; he carried no lantern with him, for daylight had come.

Both the watch-dogs lay one on each side of the doorway. They were chained loosely, so that they could keep well clear of one another, but it was impossible to pass between them to the door; if you escaped being bitten by one, the other was sure to tear you. The abbé, therefore, to get to the door, had to shoot one and wound the other. He then drew the bolt, and saw a man standing before him, a revolver in *his* hand.

"Who are you? What do you want?" asked the priest.

"Who are you, and what brings you here?" returned the stranger.

"I am the Abbé Samuel, the countess's confessor."

"And I am Ivan Behrend, the countess's next neighbor."

The abbé lowered his pistol, and changed his tone to one of courtesy.

"You must confess that it is rather an unusual hour for you to come," he said, smiling.

"Honi soit qui mal y pense," said Ivan, putting his weapon into his pocket. "I came at this unusual hour in consequence of a letter which I received this very night, in which I was informed that the castle was in a state of confusion, and the countess was in great need of help."

"The cause of the confusion—"

"Oh, I know, that was also in the letter. Therefore, I have come to do what I can, although I am aware the countess admits no man into her house, especially at this hour."

"She will receive *you* most certainly. Allow me first to close the door. There is absolutely no one in the house. Take care of the dog on the left-hand side; he is still alive."

"You have shot the other?"

"Yes; you heard the shot and drew your revolver?"

"Naturally. I did not know who might have fired the pistol."

Both men ascended to the apartments of the countess. The abbé entered first to prepare her.

"We have got unexpected help," he said; "a neighbor of yours, Ivan Behrend."

"A doubtful person," returned Theudelinde, scornfully. "He is an atheist."

"It does not matter in the present crisis whether he be a Thug, a Mormon, or a Manichæan, we have great need of his help. Some one told him of the plight you are in, and he wishes to see you."

"I will not see him, or speak to him. I beg you will confer with him instead of me."

"Countess, if this man is what you say, a heretic, he may say that he will not confer with one of my cloth."

"Very well. I suppose I must see him, but you will be present?"

"If it should be necessary."

The countess rolled her shawl round her, and went into the reception-room, into which the morning light was breaking. Abbé Samuel thought it necessary, however, to light the candelabras on the chimney.

Theudelinde, with a freezing air, asked Ivan to take a chair, and placed herself at a considerable distance from her visitor. She signed to him to begin the conversation.

"Countess, this night while I was busy reading, some one tapped at my window, and when I opened it thrust this note into my hand. It is written by your steward."

"By my steward!" exclaimed the countess, in a tone of surprise.

"It is written in his style, and quite unfit for you to read. I will tell you what interests you. The steward says that your entire household, without any exception of sex, have made good their escape, and that he is following their example."

"My steward also! And for what reason?"

"He gives the reason in his letter. I suspect, however, it is only a pretext on his part to conceal a very criminal design. I am of opinion that he has robbed you."

"Robbed me!" repeated the countess.

"Do not alarm yourself; there are different sorts of robbery, such as being an unfaithful steward, injuring your land, making profit to himself to your disadvantage. This man, I imagine, played this game, and has now tried to give a humorous turn to his flight, so that the laugh may be turned against you. This is my idea."

The countess was obliged to acknowledge that her neighbor was both a clever and a kind-hearted man.

"In this letter," continued Ivan, "your steward states that after what has happened he could never dare to look you in the face again, as he could not convince you that the late scandals in the castle had gone on without his knowledge. I did not believe these words. I felt certain that you had dismissed your household on finding out how grossly they had deceived you; therefore, my first care on getting this letter was to send a messenger on horseback to the nearest telegraph-station with a message to your banker in Pesth, to tell him that the agent of the Bondavara estate had absconded, and on no account to honor his checks. I thought it was probable he had liberty to draw in your name."

"This was really very practical and thoughtful on your part," said the abbé. "The countess must feel most grateful to you."

Theudelinde bowed her head graciously.

"One reason that brought me here," continued Ivan, "was to know if you approved of what I had done, and also to offer you my assistance in case you wish to leave the castle. I will help you to get away, and I will send my people to look after your property till you can make further arrangements."

"This is really most neighborly and friendly, and the countess owes you a debt of gratitude," repeated the priest, again assuming all responsibility.

"I am merely doing my duty," returned Ivan. "And I would add that if you should be in any difficulty as to the necessary funds, which is very likely, as the steward and bailiff have both made off, don't let this for a moment distress you; I can lend you ten thousand florins."

The Abbé Samuel whispered to the countess to accept this offer in the spirit in which it was meant, and on no account to say anything of interest.

Theudelinde accordingly held out her hand with gracious dignity to her chivalrous neighbor, who drew from his pocket the money in bank-notes. The countess wished to give him an acknowledgment, which he declined, saying the money was lent for such a short time that it was not necessary.

"And about leaving the castle," he said. "How soon do you start?"

"The sooner the better!" cried the countess.

"Then, if you will allow me to suggest a plan for accomplishing the first stage of the journey, which is the difficult part of the business, in the first place it will be necessary to pack up what you need. Will you be good enough, countess, to select the trunks you mean to bring? When this is done I will harness the horses; then we must lock and seal the rooms, and my servants will watch them until you send your proper people. This done, we can set out; and as we shall have to pass the steward's house, we can call there, and look for any books he may have for keeping the accounts of the estate. They would be useful."

"I shall not go there; I don't want any accounts."

"Very good. Then we shall go straight to the inn in my village."

"What to do?"

"Because the post is there. We must get post-horses."

"And why post-horses? Cannot I drive my own horses?"

"No."

"And why not?"

"Because they are screws. They would not reach the next station."

"My horses! Why do you say they are screws?" asked the countess, angrily.

"Because they are in bad condition."

"Bear!" thought Theudelinde. "He answers me so roughly."

"I shall not enter the inn," she said, determinedly. "I go nowhere where men drink. Cannot I wait at your house until the horses are changed?"

"Certainly. I am charmed to receive you, countess; only you will find nothing suitable for you. I live alone *en garçon.*"

"Oh, that does not matter," returned the countess, with an air of indifference.

"Will you have the goodness, then," said Ivan, "to begin your preparations and select the clothes you mean to pack up?"

Theudelinde gave a strange smile. "My packing will not take long; my luggage will not be heavy. Will you make a good fire while I go to my wardrobe? It is very cold in this room."

In the sitting-room there was a large marble fireplace, and in the ashes of the grate some sparks still lingered. Ivan put some wood on the smouldering fire, and soon a genial blaze glowed in the chimney. It welcomed the countess, who presently returned, carrying in her arms a heap of dresses and clothes of all description.

Ivan looked at her in dismay. "You are going to pack all those?"

"Yes, and as many more, which still remain in my wardrobe."

"But, countess, where?"

"Here," returned Theudelinde, as she flung the bundle on the fire.

It filled up the whole fireplace, and the fire, catching the light materials, there was presently a crackling sound, while the old chimney roared again with joy over such a splendid contribution.

The two men looked on in silence at this *auto-da-fé*.

Ten times did Theudelinde go backward and forward to her room, each time returning with fresh armfuls of finery, and when these were exhausted, her linen, boots, shoes, etc., followed; while at each sacrifice the flames in the chimney leaped and danced, and the wind blew the flames up the chimney, where they roared like so many demons.

"Well, this sort of packing makes short work," thought Ivan, but said nothing.

The clergyman stood with his hands behind his back. The countess's eyes danced, her cheeks were flushed, her activity was unceasing. When all was consumed she turned to Ivan with a triumphant air.

"It is finished," she said.

"And may I ask in what toilette your ladyship intends to travel?"

"In the clothes I wear, and my fur cloak."

"Then I shall go and get the carriage."

When he was gone the countess, assisted by the abbé, put on her fur pelisse lined with sable. She took with her nothing that she had ever used; in her opinion everything was defiled.

After a few minutes Ivan returned, and announced that the carriage was at the entrance. The doors were then locked, and a seal affixed to each.

When they entered the hall the sight of the dog which the abbé had spared presented a difficulty. If they left him he would die of hunger. The countess thought it would be better to shoot him also. Ivan, however, was more merciful.

"I will chain him to the carriage, and he will follow us."

Theudelinde was certain the hound would bite him; but the dog's instinct assured him that it was a friend who now approached. He allowed Ivan to put on his chain, and licked his hand to show his gratitude. All was now done. Ivan locked the gates, gave the key to the abbé, who with the countess was already seated in the carriage, jumped on the coach-box, and drove away from Bondavara Castle. They went slowly, for the two miserable nags, which were dignified with the name of carriage horses, could hardly drag them along. They were spent with age and starvation, and were only fit for the knacker's yard.

As the vehicle turned in the direction of the coal-mine Ivan remarked a cloud of smoke in the distance, and soon after they met a group of laborers carrying requisites for putting out a fire, hurrying in the direction of the smoke. On being questioned they said the granary of the noble countess was burning, but that they hoped to extinguish the fire.

"I think it will be easily done," Ivan said. "The steward set it on fire to conceal the defalcation in the crop."

The countess was indignant, but Ivan remarked dryly that property had its duties, and that those who never looked after their own interests were fair game for the thief.

A rough, ill-mannered man!

It was full daylight before the noble coach, drawn by the pair of noble nags, made its way through the heavy snow into the Bergwerk Colony. The wretched beasts were steaming as they drew up at Ivan's door. Ivan's first care was to call the postmaster to take them to his stable, and to order a good pair of fresh horses to replace them. Then he led his tired guests into his workroom. All the other rooms were cold and cheerless, so he took them where there was warmth and light.

In the room everything was in the utmost disorder; it was hard to find a place where the countess could sit down. She looked about her with astonishment at the strange objects which encumbered the tables and chairs; every available spot was taken up by some extraordinary, diabolical-looking invention. She cast a look of terror at the chemical laboratory, upon whose furnace the coals still glimmered, testifying to the experiment upon which Ivan had been at work when interrupted by the steward's tap at the window.

"Cagliostro's workshop," she whispered to the abbé. "There are mysterious things done here."

What annoyed the countess far more than the evidences of mystery and magic which surrounded her was the idea that she was the guest and the debtor of this rough, common fellow. She, rich, well-born, a faithful child of the Church, owed her rescue from a most unpleasant position to this obscure, godless tradesman. If she could only pay him the heaviest interest for his loan, and had not to say "thank you!" And yet she had to swallow the indignity.

Ivan, after an absence of a few minutes, returned, followed by a maid carrying a tray with the steaming breakfast. She laid the cloth, and set out the cups and coffee-cans. The countess would gladly have made some excuse to avoid tasting the food presented by her unholy host, but the abbé, who was a man of the world, drew his chair to the table, and invited Theudelinde to follow his example, "For," he said, "we shall not get anything to eat till the evening, as there are no inns on our road; and you want refreshment before your long journey."

When the countess saw that no demons seized upon the clergyman, and that the coffee of the Warlock seemed innocent of all evil, she, too, came to the table and sipped a few spoonfuls, but she found it was execrable stuff; the milk was not so bad, and she contented herself with that and bread.

Ivan began to talk about the weather—a very general subject of conversation; but herein there was this difference. Instead of an ignoramus, it was a meteorologist who handled the theme. Ivan assured the countess that both the barometer and his English glass pointed to fine weather, the sun was as warm as in May, their journey would be excellent. As he spoke, Ivan drew back the thick green window curtains, and let in the bright sunlight to enliven the half-darkened room. The first effect of this sudden eruption of light was to show the countess her own face reflected in a large concave mirror which hung on the wall opposite to her.

It is an undoubted fact that we all like to see our reflection in a glass; our eyes wander to it naturally, and the most earnest orator, in the midst of his finest peroration, will gesticulate to his own image with more satisfaction than to a crowded audience; but it is a totally different thing if it should be a magnifying-glass. What a horrible distortion of ourselves—head as large as a cask, features of a giant, expression that of a satyr; a sight too dreadful to contemplate.

"What an awful glass you have there," said the countess, peevishly, as she turned her back to the mirror.

"It is undoubtedly not a toilette mirror; it is a glass which we use in chemical experiments to test the highest degrees of heat."

Here the abbé, who wished to air his scientific knowledge, put in—

"As, for example, for burning a diamond."

"Just so," returned Ivan. "That is one of the uses of a concave mirror; it is necessary for burning a diamond, which requires the flame of a gas retort."

The countess was grateful for the abbé's remark, for it gave her a happy inspiration.

"Do you mean to tell me," she said, addressing Ivan, "that a diamond is combustible?"

"Undoubtedly, for the diamond is, in fact, nothing but coal in the form of a crystal. With the necessary degrees of heat you can extract from the patrician diamond ninety florins carat weight, the same amount of invisible gas or oxide of coal as from the plebeian lump of coal."

"That is proved by the focus of the magnifier," remarked the abbé.

"I don't believe it," said the countess, throwing back her head.

"I am sorry," returned Ivan, "that I cannot give you a proof that the diamond is combustible. We do not use such costly things for mere experiment, but have splints for the purpose, which are cheap in comparison. I have, however, none of these by me."

"I should like to be convinced, for I do not believe it," repeated the countess. "Will you make the experiment with this?" As she spoke she unfastened a brooch from her dress, and handed it to her host. The centre stone was a fine two-carat brilliant. Theudelinde expected that Ivan would return it to her, saying, "Oh, it would be a pity to use this beautiful stone;" and then she would reply, "Then pray keep it as a slight remembrance;" and in this manner this perverse individual would have been paid and forgotten. But, to her amazement, the countess found she had deceived herself.

With the indifference of a philosopher and the courtesy of a gentleman Ivan took the brooch from its owner.

"I conclude you do not wish to have the ornament melted," he said, quietly. "I will take the diamond out of its setting, and if it should not burn you can have it reset."

Without another word he extracted the stone with a little pincers, and placed it at the bottom of a flat clay saucepan; then he opened the window, which lay in the full blaze of the sun. He placed the saucepan upon a stand in the middle of the room and just in front of the countess; then he took the magnifying-glass and went outside, for in the room the sun's rays had not power to concentrate themselves upon the mirror.

The countess was now certain that the trick would not succeed, and that she would have an opportunity of offering the diamond to Ivan on the pretext of repeating the experiment when the sun's rays would be more powerful.

Ivan, when he had found the proper spot outside the window, directed the rays from the apex of the burning-glass straight upon the saucepan, where the diamond was waiting the moment of its annihilation. The stone emitted a thousand sparks. As the sun's rays touched it, it threw out as many colors as are in the rainbow; it seemed as if it were to be the victor in this fight. All of a sudden the fiery rays condensed themselves in a narrower circle upon the doomed diamond, the small room was filled with a blinding light that turned everything into silver; not a shadow remained. Out of the saucepan shot a ball of fire like a flash of lightning; the next minute the burning-glass ceased to work.

Ivan still stood outside the window. He spoke to the countess, who was transfixed with astonishment.

"What is in the saucepan?" he asked.

"Nothing."

Ivan returned to the room, hung the mirror in its place, and returned to the countess her brooch without its centre stone.

The abbé could not help remarking, dryly, "That little drama is fit to be played before a queen."

But now the postilion blew his horn, the countess put on her fur pelisse, and was escorted to the carriage by Ivan. She was obliged to give him her hand, and to say the words, "God be with you."

When the carriage had gone a little way she said to the abbé, "That man is a sorcerer."

But the clergyman shook his head. "He is far worse; he is an inquirer into the secrets of nature."

"H'm! he is an obstinate, disagreeable man."

CHAPTER X

THE HIGHER MATHEMATICS

THE counting-house of the firm of Kaulmann stands in the same place where it stood fifty years ago. The entrance is as it was, and the very panes of glass are identical with those through which the founder of the house, in 1811, was wont to make his observations—as from an observatory—upon the countenances of the passers-by, when a rise or fall in the funds was expected. He knew what an excellent barometer the faces of a crowd make, and how much can be gleaned by observation; so too a chance word, which is let fall as it were by accident, often contains the germ of much truth, and is, to an experienced man, in a measure prophetic.

The young head of the house did not set much store by the counting-house business. He had higher aims. He lived on the first floor in luxurious bachelor chambers; his sitting-room was a museum, and his writing-table was crowded with bronzes and antiques; his inkstand was a masterpiece of Benvenuto Cellini's—or, perhaps, a good imitation in galvanized plaster; his pen was gold, with a diamond top; he used gold sand for blotting-paper; the sand-sifter was made of porphyry, the pen-holder was a branch of real coral, the paper-weight a mosaic from Pompeii, the candle-shades of real crystal, the cover of the blotting-book Japanese. Every article had a value of its own, from the Turkish paper-knife to the paper itself, which was of all sorts and descriptions, from the thickest vellum to the most delicate straw note, perfumed with mignonette and musk. In spite of these elaborate arrangements, no one had ever been known to write at this so-called writing-table. The science cultivated by Felix Kaulmann did not require the use of pen and ink; it was purely mental work. Felix worked night and day; during his sleep, even, he worked, but no trace of his labor was to be found on paper. When he amused himself—dancing, riding, making love—he seemed altogether occupied with the subject on hand; he worked, nevertheless, all the time. He had a certain goal at which he was aiming; for this he lived, for this he strove, and this alone aroused his interest and his enthusiasm; he never forgot for one moment the aim of his life. He had something more to do than to make a pen travel over paper; he had to move men.

One day, not long after the events in the Castle of Bondavara, the Abbé Samuel was seated in Felix Kaulmann's room. Both were engaged in serious conversation. Before them an elegant equipage of fragrant Mocha, whose fumes mingled with that of the Latakia, which our friend the abbé smoked from a genuine Turkish pipe. Felix only smoked cigars.

"Well, here is your agreement with the countess. As you wished for thirty-two years, it is regularly drawn up. And now I should like to know of what use it can possibly be to either you or your company. It is not enough for the countess to sign it; it wants the signature of the prince to make the contract advantageous to you, for the countess has only a life-interest in the Bondavara property. As soon as she dies it goes to the prince, or to his grandson, and then your agreement is null."

"I know that," returned Felix, knocking the ash from his cigar; "and for this reason we must take care and keep the old girl alive. Let her have a good time, and she will live to a great age. It is very hard to kill an old maid, especially if she has lots of money. Besides, I am not so careless as you suppose. I have looked into the matter; I have seen the will of the old prince, and I know all its provisions. There is a clause that makes me pretty safe. When Countess Theudelinde goes off the reel, her brother, the present man, or his heirs, are obliged to compensate all those, either tenants, householders, or creditors, who may have erected any buildings on the estate. You see, the old prince considered that it would be more than probable that his crazy daughter might, in a fit of holy enthusiasm, build either a church or a convent, and he thought he would give the heirs the advantage of her generosity. It never entered into his head that any one would erect a factory, a refinery, or open a mine. Now you see how useful this clause is to me; the heirs will not be in a position to refund us the two millions of money we are putting on the property."

"Unless they find another company to advance them the money."

"That would not be so easy. First of all, it would have to go into the very intricate affairs of the Bondavara family; then it would require immense capital, great energy, and a certain amount of risk. For the rest, I can see as far as my neighbors. I don't sit with my hands in my lap, I can tell you, and I have not put all my money on one card."

"Right! By-the-way, what has become of the little wild kitten you brought away from the Bondavara mine?"

"I have placed her for the present in Madame Risan's school; she is being educated, for she has extraordinary capabilities, although in a general way she is a stupid creature. She has a splendid voice, but she cannot sing, as singing is nowadays; she has a wonderfully expressive face, but does not know how to make use of it; she is full of feeling, and speaks no language but her mother-tongue."

"Do you mean to educate her for the stage?"

"Certainly."

"And then?"

"I intend to marry her."

The abbé raised his eyebrows in some astonishment.

"I should hardly have thought," he said, coldly, "that a pupil of Madame Risan's would be likely to make a satisfactory wife, although she might be an excellent actress."

Felix looked haughtily at his visitor, then shrugged his shoulders, as who would say the abbé's opinion on this point was indifferent to him. For a few minutes the men smoked in silence; then, with a sudden clearing of his face, Kaulmann said, in his blandest manner:

"I want to ask you a question. You know the ins and outs of the marriage laws. Is there any means by which a marriage can be set aside without having recourse to the divorce court? That is always attended with great expense and a good deal of scandal; and if the other side should be obstinate and malicious, it can drag for an interminable time."

"I know of only one other method. We will suppose that you are already married according to the rules of the Church in this country. You wish, for some reason, for a dissolution of this marriage. Well, you have only to go to Paris, and take up your residence in the bank-ing-house your firm has there. Your father was a French subject, so are you. According to the French law, no marriage is valid that is not solemnized before the civil authorities; therefore, the remedy would be in your hands. A short time ago the process was tried by the French court. A certain count had married in Spain; the eldest son of this marriage sought to recover his birthright, which had been forfeited in consequence of his father's having neglected to be remarried before the registrar in France. The court, however, pronounced the Spanish marriage invalid, and yours would be a similar case."

Felix got up from his seat. "I thank you," he said, "more than I can say. If the recollection of our youthful friendship didn't remind me that our compact was always to *love* one another, I should certainly feel that I owed you a heavy debt."

"For what?" returned the abbé, lifting his eyes in some surprise. "It is well for you to remind me of our young days. Was I not then the debtor of your father? What did he not do for me? He found me a miserable, overworked, ill-paid student; he made me your tutor, and so opened for me the road to better things. Oh, I never forget! But let us not talk any more of the past."

"No, for the future is before us, and we shall work together. Now, I must ask you, as the countess's representative, to sign the necessary papers. There is the contract, and here is the check for the first half-year's rent, and here is another check for the sum of forty thousand gulden on my cashier."

"To whom payable?"

Felix answered by pressing the check into the abbé's hand, while he whispered in his ear:

"To the friendly representative."

The other shook his head, with a wounded look on his face. "You mean to offer *me* a present?" he said, haughtily.

"You do not understand," returned Felix. "This money does not come from me; it forms part of the expenses of the company, and in all such undertakings figures under the head of 'necessary expenses.'"

As he spoke, Felix lit another cigar, and looked slyly at his companion, as who should say, "You see what a capital fellow I am!" Round the abbé Samuel's mouth a contemptuous smile flickered as he tore the check for forty thousand gulden into four pieces; then he laid his hand upon the banker's shoulder.

"My dear boy," he said, "I had the whole Bondavara property in the hollow of my hand; it was mine to do as I chose with it. I did with it as I do with these pieces of paper." He threw the torn check into the grate. "Know me, once for all. I am no begging monk. I am a candidate for high honors; nothing will content me but to be ruler of a kingdom."

The haughty air with which the abbé said these words impressed the banker so much that he laid down his cigar and stared vacantly at his visitor.

"That is a great word," he said, slowly.

"Sit down and listen to what I shall disclose to you," returned the priest, who, with his hands behind his back, now began to walk up and down the room, pausing from time to time before his astonished listener, to whom he poured out a torrent of words.

"The whole world is in labor," he said, "and brings forth nothing but mice. And wherefore? Because the lions will not come into the world. Chaos rules everywhere—in finance, in diplomacy, in the Church. One man who would have intellect enough to see clearly could be master of the situation. But where is he to be found? Fools in embroidered coats are the leaders; therefore we see a country governed by incapables, who do not know even where to begin. They would fain force it to submit, but are afraid to use the necessary means. They oppress it, and at the same time live in dread of what it may do. And this same country does not itself know what to-morrow may bring, whether it shall submit, pay the demands of its oppressors, or appeal to arms against their tyranny; neither does it know who is its foe, who is its friend, with whom to ally itself, against whom to fight; whether it will go on submitting, whether it shall break out into curses or wild laughter at its own follies. The country still possesses one element, which stands, as it were, neutral between the two parties; this element is the clerical; the Church is a power in Hungary."

Felix's face grew darker; he could not imagine what all this would lead to. But the abbé had now paused, and was standing before him.

"What do you think, my son," he said, "would be the reward due to the man who could find a way out of this mass of confusion—who could unite the classes, and bring them into conformity with the wishes of the government? Do you not think that there is nothing which would better further your Bondavara speculation than a submissive deputation of priests and people, who would give a promise of fidelity to the minister? One hand washes the other; he who brings about such an unlooked-for condition of affairs must be recompensed. Now do you understand what use this would be to you?"

"I think I begin to see."

"And what office do you think should be offered to

the man who brings the peasant's frock into subjection and elevates the mitre?"

Felix clasped his hands together. That was his answer. The clergyman resumed his walk up and down the room; his lips were compressed, his head in the air.

"The primate is an old man," he said, suddenly.

Felix leaned back in his chair. He could see better in this position the various expressions which passed over the abbé's face. He started when the abbé murmured, almost under his breath:

"The pope is still older."

There was a moment's silence, and then the abbé continued, speaking fast and with excitement:

"Dwarfs are at the rudder, my son; dwarfs who believe that their impotent efforts will stem the storm. The Church is in danger of going to pieces, and they make use of the old worn-out means of support. Listen to my words. All the efforts of Rome are fruitless; it tries to maintain its dignity with Peter's pence, and has allowed millions to slip through its fingers. Only here in Hungary has the Church any property left. I know well that in the minister's drawer there is a paper prepared which only needs the signature of the state to become law; it only requires a slight pretext, and Vienna will declare war against the clerical power in Hungary. She will fight it upon the liberal principle, and those who oppose will be the unpopular, the losing side. It is only a question of time. The deficit grows daily, the government is in a hole, the treasury is empty, there is no loan possible. Hence a fight over the budget, or a trifling war somewhere. You know the proverb, 'When the devil is hungry he eats flies.' The clerical property in Hungary is the fly, and Austria will make one bite at it. The chair of St. Peter and the Church property in

Hungary are both in danger. How is the danger to be averted? Let us put our shoulders to the wheel; let us be more patriotic than the democrats, more loyal than the prime-minister, more liberal than revolutionists; let us save the Church property from the government, and the Church itself from the revolution. Let us throw into the market a gigantic loan of a hundred millions upon the property of the Hungarian Church for the rescue of the throne of St. Peter. What do you now think of the man who could do this thing? What should be his reward?"

"Everything," stammered Felix, his mind confused over this bewildering, yet fascinating, programme.

"To this great work I have destined you," said the abbé, with a solemn, majestic air. "Your Bondavara speculation is necessary, for with it you can make a *coup* which shall bring you a world-wide reputation, your name shall be on a par with that of the Strousbergs, the Pereiras, with that of Rothschild itself. This is the reason why I have given you my support. When you are firmly established, then I shall say to you, 'Lend me your shoulder,' upon which I shall climb where I will."

After this Felix sank into a waking dream. Before his eyes gleamed the gigantic loan, and through a mist he saw the tall form of the abbé with a crown upon his head.

CHAPTER XI

SOIRÉES AMALGAMANTES

ONE winter's morning Ivan Behrend, to his great astonishment, received a notice from the president of the Hungarian Academy of Arts and Science. This notice set forth that the members of the physical, scientific, and mathematical department had in the last general assembly chosen him as an honorary member of the before-mentioned departments; and before being elected member of the academy itself he should, in conformity to the established custom, read before the assembly his first address. Ivan was petrified with amazement. How had such an honor come to him? He who had never written a scientific paper in any periodical; who had no connections or friend in the academical assembly, who was not a magnate, or had played no part in political life. He was puzzled; he could not conceive who had brought forward his name. Could it have been, he thought, that in some way his chemical researches had reached their ears? In which case, as he told himself, every director of a mine, every manager of a factory, would be considered a philosopher and made member of the Academy, for every one of them possessed as much knowledge as he did. There was no use in thinking about it; the honor had come to him, and should be accepted. Ivan thought it best not to look the gift-horse in the mouth; he therefore wrote to the secretary, expressing his gratitude for the unlooked-for honor conferred upon him, and stating that towards the end of the year he would present himself in Pesth, and read before the illustrious assembly his inaugural address. Then he considered the subject of this address long and carefully, and spent much of his time over its elaboration. It was an account of microscopical crustations, the study of which he had followed closely during the boring of an artesian well, and which during ten years he had perfectly mastered. It took him until late in the autumn to complete his essay on the subject.

In many places, where such scientific research is valued at its proper merit, his paper would have been appreciated, and would have even caused a sensation; but we are bound in honesty to confess that it did not do so in Pesth, and that during the sixty minutes allowed by the canon law of all institutions for such lectures, the microscopical crustations produced an amount of yawning unprecedented, even among academicians.

After the reading of the lecture was over the very first person to greet the neophyte and offer his congratulations was the Abbé Samuel, and then a light burst suddenly upon Ivan. He now saw who it was who had discovered his talents, and who had been his patron. It was something of a fall to his vanity; he had thought—well, it didn't matter, the abbé was doubtless as learned as any one in the assembly, and his thanks were due to him. Small attentions, it is said, consolidate friendship.

Ivan decided to spend some days in Pesth; he had business to do. During the week several papers noticed his academical address; the most merciful was one which announced he had given an interesting lecture upon the "Volcanic Origin of the Stalactites." Ivan's only consolation was that in his own country no one read

The Referate, and that abroad no one understood it, as it was written in Hungarian. He was wrong, however; some one did read it—but of this again. One day, as Ivan was making his preparations for his homeward journey, he received from the Countess Theudelinde Bondavara a card of invitation for a *soirée,* which would take place three evenings later.

"Aha!" thought Ivan, "another thank-offering. It is well that it did not come sooner."

He sat down to his writing-table and answered the invitation in the most courteous manner, regretting his inability to avail himself of it in consequence of his immediate departure from Pesth. He was in the act of sealing the letter when the door opened and the Abbé Samuel was announced. Ivan expressed his great pleasure at receiving so distinguished a visitor.

"I could not let you leave Pesth without coming," answered the abbé, in his most friendly manner. "My visit was due, not only because I am much indebted for your kind assistance at Bondavara, but also because I felt it a necessity to tell you what an honor I count it to know such a distinguished scholar as you have proved yourself to be."

Ivan felt inclined to say that he was neither distinguished nor a scholar; he remained, however, silent.

"I trust," continued the abbé, seating himself upon the sofa, "that you intend to make a long stay in Pesth?"

"I am leaving to-morrow," returned Ivan, dryly.

"Oh, impossible! We cannot lose you so soon. I imagine you have a card for the Countess Theudelinde's next *soirée?*"

"I regret that I am prevented from accepting her agreeable invitation; I have pressing business which necessitates my return."

The abbé laughed. "Confess honestly," he said, "that if you had no other reason to return home, you would run away from an entertainment which would bore you infinitely."

"Well, then, if you will have the truth, I do confess that a *soirée* is to me something of a penance."

"These *soirées*, however, are on a different footing from those *réunions* which, I agree with you, are more pain than pleasure, and where a stranger feels himself 'out of it,' as the saying goes. Countess Theudelinde aims at having a *salon*, and succeeds admirably. She receives all the best people. I don't mean by that generic word only the upper ten, but the best in the true sense, the best that Pesth affords in art, in literature, in science; the aristocracy of birth, talent, and beauty."

Ivan shook his head incredulously. "And how does such a mixed gathering answer?"

The abbé did not reply at once; he scratched his nose thoughtfully.

"Until they get to know one another, it is perhaps somewhat stiff. But with intellectual people this stiffness must soon disappear, and each one will do something to keep the ball rolling. You have an excellent delivery; I noticed it the night of your lecture. You could easily find a subject on which to lecture which would interest your listeners by its novelty, surprise them by its profundity, and amuse them by its variety; their intellect and their imagination would be equally engaged."

It was Ivan's turn to laugh, which he did loudly. "My excellent sir, such a subject is unknown to me. I confess my ignorance; neither in print nor in manuscript have I met with it."

The clergyman joined in the laugh.

At this moment a servant brought Ivan a despatch, which claimed instant attention, so that the receipt might be given to the messenger who waited for it. Ivan begged his guest to excuse him if he opened this urgent document. The abbé, with a wave of his hand, requested him not to mind his presence.

As Ivan read the letter a remarkable change passed over his face; he grew suddenly pale, his eyebrows contracted, then a sudden rush of color came into his cheeks. He held the letter before him, read it several times, while his eyes had a wild stare, as if he had seen a ghost. Then all at once he fell to laughing. He thrust the letter into his pocket, and returned to the subject he had been discussing.

"Yes, yes," he said, "I shall go to Countess Theudelinde's *soirée*, and I shall give a lecture before her guests such as they have never heard the equal; that I promise you. Science and poetry, imagination and learning mixed together, with dates and genealogy, so that the *savants* present will not know what to think; I shall give a lecture which will make every geologist a prince, and every princess a geologist. Do you follow me?"

"Perfectly," returned the other; not, indeed, that he saw what Ivan meant, but that he wished to encourage him. "That will be the very thing—first-rate!"

"What do you say to illustrations by means of an electric-magnetic machine, eh?"

"A capital idea, and amusing. My dear friend, you will have a *succès*."

"May I ask you to convey to the countess my acceptance of her invitation? I shall require a large apparatus."

"I can assure you in advance that the countess will be charmed at your kind offer. As for the apparatus and arrangement, leave that to her, she will be overjoyed when she hears that she is to expect you."

The abbé then took his leave, fully contented with his visit. Ivan again read his letter, and again sat staring into space, as if a ghost had appeared to him.

People said the Countess Theudelinde's *Soirées Amalgamantes* would certainly make history. The mixture was excellent: grandees jostled elbows with poets; academicians with prelates; musicians, painters, sculptors, actors, critics, professors, physicians, editors, sportsmen, and politicians of all shades gathered under one roof. It was a bold experiment, a brilliant society *in thesi*. Neither was there wanting the element of female attraction; all that Pesth held of beauty, charm, and grace lent its aid to the scheme of amalgamation.

Count Stefan, a cousin of Countess Theudelinde, was a great help to her *soirées*, for he was a well-informed and cultivated young man, able to talk on all subjects, and especially on the poetry of the world. As for the Countess Angela, she was a classic beauty; her grandfather was a political celebrity—a great man, who had a surrounding of all kinds, bad and good. It was therefore quite in keeping, according to the usages of society, that when an unfortunate outsider was presented to Countess Angela, he should, after the third word or so, make mention of her illustrious grandfather, Prince Theobald of Bondavara, and inquire after his health. After this question, however, the Countess Angela never addressed the stranger another word. She allowed him to speak, if he so wished, and to retire in some confusion. Even the most dried-up specimen of university learning felt aggrieved. His heart could not resist the first glance of those heavenly eyes, so sweet and friendly, now so cold and haughty. And yet what had he done?

The poor man will probably never know; he is not in the inner circle.

Countess Angela was indeed a perfect ideal beauty; this cannot be too often repeated. A pure, noble face, with classical, well-proportioned features, nose and lips finely cut, long, straight eyebrows and lashes, which veiled the eyes of a goddess. When these eyes glowed, or when they were half-closed under their downy lids, they looked black, but when they laughed at you, you would swear they were blue. Her hair was rich, of that most lovely of all shades, chestnut brown; her whole countenance betrayed that she knew herself to be charming, that she was aware that she was the centre, at all times, of admiration, and that such knowledge pleased her well. And why not? A woman must be very silly not to be aware that beauty is a gift and a power.

But what was the reason of her cold looks at the mention of her grandfather's name? Just what one might expect from a woman with her face. All the world— that is, her world—knew that she and her grandfather, Prince Theobald of Bondavara, were at daggers drawn. The wily old politician had given his only and beautiful granddaughter to a German, Prince Sondersheim. She was to consolidate some political matter, only she didn't see it in that light, and refused to ratify the bargain, not caring for Sondersheim; and, for the matter of that, neither did he care for her. But, then, it didn't mean so much to him. Angela had her ideal of married life, however, and so she quarrelled with her grandfather because he pooh-poohed her ideals and called them romantic folly. Upon this she vowed she would never speak to him again, and he, being angry, told her to leave his house, which she did at once, and came to her Aunt Theudelinde, who had just set up at Pesth, and was glad to have so bright and beautiful a niece. Since then she had refused all communication with her grandfather. This was the reason that she would not even hear his name mentioned; and it never was, except by ignorant outsiders, or "know-nothings," as the Yankees call them.

The Abbé Samuel had wit enough to see that the *Soirées Amalgamantes* were not the success they should be. Conversation did not suffice; amalgamation was at a standstill. The young girls sat in one room, the married women in another; the men herded together, looking glum, but not so bored as the women. Then the abbé, considering what ought to be done, had a happy idea. He introduced dramatic representations, dramatic readings, concerts, which were a decided success. Soon conversation became lively, strangers got to know one another; when they rehearsed together duets and little pieces their stiffness wore off. The women seemed different in morning dress, free from the restraints of the grand toilette; they grew quite friendly, and later on they found a subject upon which they discoursed quite at their ease. It must be confessed, however, that after midnight, when the readings, the concert, or the representation was over, and the outsiders had gone home to their beds, society began to enjoy itself. The young people danced, the old played whist or tarok, and they stayed till daybreak. They would have done the same had the scientists, the poets, the artists remained; they didn't want them to leave, but, naturally, these people felt themselves out of it, and, besides, they could not sit up all night like the others, so they went home very properly; they knew their place.

The Abbé Samuel understood how to manage matters. Whenever the countess was to have a particularly good evening he took care it should get talked about, and the names of the performers, their parentage and history, together with any interesting circumstance, true or false, should be subjects of conversation for days before. In this way he sent about Ivan Behrend's name with a great many details as to his interesting life in the mines, his extraordinary cleverness, and the wonderful lecture he was going to give at the countess's next *soirée*.

The abbé knew his world, and how to whet its curiosity by exaggerated reports.

"Is it true that, for one experiment only, he burned a brilliant belonging to Countess Theudelinde which was worth eight hundred gulden?"

"The stone weighed four carats, and was worth fifteen hundred pounds."

"We must give him a good reception. See, here he comes, escorted by Abbé Samuel!"

The gentleman who had just spoken, and who was the Countess Angela's cousin, was Count Edmund, a handsome young man of about twenty-two years of age. He hastened to meet Ivan and the abbé as they entered the door, and introduced himself as nephew to the lady of the house. He took Ivan by the arm in the most friendly manner, and led him to Count Stefan, uncle to the countess. The count was a man of intelligence and reading; he assured Ivan there were those in the room who were much interested to hear his lecture. After this he was presented by his new friend to several distinguished-looking persons with decorations, who all pressed his hand, and spoke in the most friendly manner. The beginning of the evening was the most agreeable portion. The abbé and Ivan finally made their way into the next room, where the ladies were assembled, and here they found the Countess Theudelinde, who received them, and especially Ivan, most graciously. The young man, Count Edmund, again took possession of him, and, laughing and talking, led him up to the Countess Angela, to whom he was introduced with a great flourish. Before this lovely vision Ivan bowed, feeling somewhat stunned, yet not shy or awkward.

"You come very seldom to Pesth," said the young countess, with a reassuring smile.

"It is some time since I have been here; but I understand this is your first visit, countess. You have never lived in Pesth?"

Angela's face assumed its cold expression; she felt sure he was going to inquire for Prince Theobald.

"I do not see," she said, in a sarcastic voice, "what it is to any one whether I have ever been in Pesth."

"It is not an uncommon accident," returned Ivan, quietly, "that a man visits a place where he has never been before; but when many people meet in the same spot, it looks as if there was something more than accident in such a gathering; and in this instance, where so many brilliant personages are brought together, it seems as if Providence had more to do with it than mere chance."

At these words Angela's face cleared. "Then you believe in Providence? you acknowledge there is such a thing as Divine ordinance?"

"Undoubtedly, I do believe."

"Then we shall be friends." She turned away as she spoke, and Ivan took this movement as a signal to retire.

After a quarter of an hour's further waiting, Edmund came to tell him that everything was in readiness in the lecture-room, and the company had already gathered there in considerable numbers. Ivan, therefore, ascended the stage, which had been erected at the farther end of the large room, and, holding his papers in his hand, addressed his audience. He had a pleasant voice, his manner of address was perfectly unaffected, composed, and taking. From the first moment he held the attention of the audience—his subject was *Magnetism*.

CHAPTER XII

RITTER MAGNET

WHEN the lecture had concluded the lamps were carried out of the room, and only the candles in the lustre were left lighted. Ivan then exhibited to the astonished spectators the electric light. Many of them had never seen such a clear, beautiful light as this ball of virgin-like purity. It looked like one of the heavenly planets, as if Venus had descended from her place in the firmament and was shining on the company. The candles in the lustre burned blue, and threw shadows on the wall. Every face lost all trace of color from the effect of this strange illumination; people whispered to one another, almost frightened. Ivan, standing upon the platform, looked like some magician of old, his features chiselled like a statue, his eyes in deep shadow; and what added considerably to the picturesque effect, and heightened the charm of this noble assembly, was the strange coloring given by the light to the splendid national costume worn by the company, and the enamelled appearance of the jewels on the ladies' necks and arms.

The eyes of every one were directed to two persons, while an involuntary "Ah!" was whispered about at the extraordinary transformation produced in their appearance. One was Countess Angela. The light seemed to have taken from her face that pride and self-satisfaction which, although natural in one so beautiful, gave an earthly expression to her face, and somewhat marred its beauty. Now she looked a heavenly vision, with the expression of a glorified spirit who had done with earth and had soared upward to her true home in heaven; all earthly passions, joy, sorrow, love, and pride, had vanished. Such was the miraculous effect of the magic light. The other transformation was in Countess Theudelinde. She was seated in an armchair, raised upon a sort of divan. The magic light touched her face gently, and gave it a fairy-like expression; the noble features were spiritualized, her naturally pale coloring became transparent, the brilliants in her magnificent tiara sparkled over her forehead as a garland of stars; she was sublime, and for five minutes the most beautiful among the beautiful. It was, nevertheless, many a long year since her mirror had told her she was beautiful. This, too, was the miraculous effect of the magic light. Round the hall there were large pier-glasses set into the wainscot, which reflected every one of the company. Theudelinde, therefore, could see herself beautified. She sighed as she thought, "I look like Queen Mab."

Suddenly the miraculous light went out, and the room, lit only by the candles, seemed in total darkness. "Ah!" in sorrowful tones was echoed through the assembly; people rubbed their eyes and recognized the familiar faces again. Alas! it was over too soon. There were no more angels, fairies, queens, or heroes; only a group of excellent every-day people, counts and countesses. The face of Angela again wore its proud, vain expression, and Theudelinde was once more stiff and ill-tempered.

Ivan now descended from his platform, and received the congratulations and compliments due to his efforts.

There were different opinions, of course, but they were private. Every one joined in praising the lecturer to himself.

Ivan thanked every one for their approval, but with a coldly reticent manner, and soon disengaged himself from his admirers to go in search of his hostess; he wished to thank her for her kindness.

Theudelinde received him with smiles. Countess Angela was with her, leaning on the back of her aunt's chair. The young girl had just said:

"You looked, auntie, quite lovely—a perfect Queen Mab."

The smile these words had called to Theudelinde's face still lingered round her lips when Ivan presented himself. For these five minutes of beauty she was indebted to this man, and was not ungrateful. She gave him her hand, and thanked him in the most gracious manner for the enjoyment he had given her.

"I owe you something," returned Ivan. "When you honored my house with a visit, you gave me a diamond which you allowed me to burn before your eyes. I now in return for your goodness on that occasion give you this diamond, which was created before your eyes." With these words he handed her a piece of carbon, which he had taken from the voltaic pillar. "As I explained to you in my lecture, coal can be changed by electricity into a diamond, and in this condition can cut glass."

"Ah!" cried the Countess Angela, her eyes beaming with pleasure, "let us try the experiment now. Where is there a glass? Yes, one of the pier-glasses. Come."

Countess Theudelinde was also excited. She stood up, and went with the others to the pier-glass.

"Write one of the letters of the alphabet," said Angela, and watched Ivan attentively. She was curious to see the letter he would choose. If he were vain, as very likely he was, he would write his own initial "I"; if a toady and flatterer, like most of the people round her aunt, he would choose "T," as the countess's initial; and if he were a silly fool, like so many other men, he would write "A." In either of these cases he would have seen on the beauty's face a scornful smile.

Ivan took the piece of coal, and with the point wrote on the glass the letter "X." Both ladies expressed their astonishment at seeing the coal write, and Countess Theudelinde assured Ivan it should be preserved carefully with her other jewels.

Countess Angela stood so near Ivan that the folds of her dress touched him.

"I believe," she said, slowly, "every word you told us. I beg of you do not tell me that all your romantic descriptions were but the necessary clothing of a dry scientific subject, meant to make it palatable to your silly, ignorant audience, and to raise in their minds a wish to seek further, so that they might in so seeking acquire a taste for knowledge. I do not want to seek, I believe implicitly all you said; but of this world of wonder and miracles I would know more. How far does it go? What more do you see, for the magician must know everything?"

The young countess looked into Ivan's eyes as she spoke with a strange magnetic power impossible to resist. Such a look as this had often dazzled men's brains.

"You said, also," continued Angela, "how fiery and strong are those who live in this magnetic kingdom, but that they have no credit for the virtues they possess; it is due to the working of magnetism. I believe this also. Magnetism has, however, two poles, the north and the south pole. I have read that the opposite poles are drawn to one another, and the homogeneous drift asunder. If, therefore, in the magnetic kingdom hearts are drawn to one another, seek one another, love one another, which is an immutable fact, so also is it an immutable fact that there must be human beings who hate one another with an undying, a deadly hatred, and that such hatred is no sin. Am I not right?"

Ivan felt that he was driven into a corner; he understood the drift of the countess's question. Here his knowledge of natural philosophy came to his assistance.

"It is true," he said, "that so far as life upon the earth is in question, there must also exist antipathies and sympathies. You have studied magnetism, you have read of the poles, therefore you must know that there exists an equator, or line, which is neither north nor south. This is the magnetic equator, that neither draws the magnet nor repulses it, and here there is perfect peace. Just such an equator is found in every human heart, and however a man may be carried away by the passions of love or hatred, his line remains unchangeable, and those who dwell there dwell in peace."

"And who are the people who live under the magnetic equator?" asked the countess, with curiosity.

"For example, parents and their children should dwell there."

The young girl's face was covered with a vivid blush; her beautiful eyes shot a battery of lightning glances at Ivan, who remained quite unmoved under this battery.

"We must talk more of this," she said, with sudden dignity.

Ivan bowed before the haughty beauty, who turned and left him to the company of her aunt or of his own sex. He preferred the latter.

Meantime, the lecture being over, a rush had been

made to the refreshments. The army of outsiders were the first in the field. If they were of little account elsewhere, they took first place at the buffet, and here the citizen showed distinctly his origin.

Ivan mixed with the company, and conducted himself as one accustomed to such society, and quite at his ease in it, and he was well received. The men were very civil towards him; every man under forty used the friendly "thou" in addressing him; he was made one of themselves. It didn't matter much, as he was said to be leaving Pesth the next day, and would be lost in the depths of Mesopotamia. Some one said he came from Africa. They tried teasing him a bit, all in a friendly way, and were pleased to find this pedant was an excellent fellow, who took the joke in good part, laughed heartily at a well-delivered thrust, and returned it with a sly hit, which never offended any one's feelings.

"He is one of us," they said. "This man is up to everything; he is a capital fellow. We must give him a good time."

"Is it true that you don't drink wine?" asked the Marquis Salista of Ivan.

"Once a year."

"And to-day is not the anniversary?"

"No."

"Then we have drunk enough for one year; let us be moving."

Some of the men returned to the drawing-room; these were, for the most part, the young fellows, and those who wished to dance. The ladies, after their tea, had begun to play quadrilles, and even the "Csárdás" for those who wished for it.

Count Stefan, however, drew away the better portion

of the men to his quarters, which were on the second story of the countess's house. Here he entertained in his way. His rooms being on the other side of the house, no noise penetrated to the story below, which was necessary, as the count's champagne was of the very best, and given with no sort of stint; it flowed, in fact. Ivan, who was of the party, showed himself in a new light; he drank wine; his toasts were spicy, his anecdotes fresh and amusing, his wit sharp and unrestrained; and although he drank freely, he didn't turn a hair, he was quite steady.

"Brother," hiccoughed Count Geza, who towards two o'clock was half drunk, "the captain and I have agreed that when you are quite done up we shall carry you home and put you to bed; but, my dear friend, my dear Ritter Magnet, the misery is that I don't think I can get up the stairs; I am quite done. Therefore, take your wings and fly, and let the captain take his, and both of you fly home. As for me—" Here the count laid down on the sofa and fell asleep.

Every one laughed; but the name he had given Ivan —Ritter Magnet—stuck to him.

"Do you care to play cards, my learned one?" said the Marquis Salista.

"Once every three years."

"That is not often enough."

The marquis could not at this moment explain why it was not often enough, for at this moment Count Stefan acquainted his guests that it was time for them to depart, seeing that the ball below stairs had broken up, and every one had gone away. The countess's rest, therefore, might be disturbed by any noise overhead. Every one agreed that this was quite proper.

"Only," said Salista, "there is no need for us to go

home. Let us have the card-table. Let us spend our time well. Who is for a game?"

Three players soon presented themselves; Baron Oscar was one of the first. But the fourth? The captain called to Ivan.

"Now, my learned friend."

Count Stefan thought it necessary to inform the stranger, who was his guest, that at the tarok-table the stakes were very high.

"Only a kreuzer the point," said the captain.

"Yes, but kreuzer points in such a game often amount to seven or eight hundred gulden to the losing side. These gentlemen have changed a simple game into a hazardous venture."

Ivan laughed. "Every day of my life I play hazard with nature itself; every day I speculate with all I have on a mere chance, and play only one card." So saying, he rolled his chair to the green table.

The game commenced. The game of hazard, as it is generally played, is a game of chance, it needs only luck and boldness; a drunken man can almost win by accident. But as it is played in Pesth it is something quite different; what is called luck, chance, accident, is here allied to skill, prudence, consideration, and boldness. The tarok-player must not only study his cards, but also the faces of his adversaries. He must be Lavater and Tartuffe in one; he must be a general who develops at every moment a fresh plan of campaign, and a Bosco who can, from the first card that is played, divine the whole situation; he must, however, be generous, and sacrifice himself for the sake of the general good. Therefore it was that the spectators pitied Ivan when he sat down to the card-table to play with these three masters of the game.

It was seven o'clock when the players rose from the card-table. As Ivan pushed back his chair, the marquis said to him:

"Well, comrade, it is a good thing for the world at large that you only drink once a year and play cards once in three years, for if you did both every day there would be no more wine in Salista's cellar nor no gold left in Rothschild's bank."

Ivan had, in truth, stripped the three gentlemen.

"Nevertheless, we must have a parting cup," continued Salista. "Where is the absinthe?" As he spoke he filled two large glasses with the green, sparkling spirit, of which moderate people, regretting this prudence, it may be, never drink more than a liqueur glass.

Count Stefan shook his head over what he considered a bad joke, but Ivan did not shrink from the challenge; he clinked his glass with that of the captain, and emptied it without drawing breath. Then, with his most courteous bow, he took leave of his host, Count Stefan, who on his side assured him it would always be a pleasure to receive so delightful a guest.

As Ivan made his way into the anteroom his step was steady, his air composed. Not so the marquis; the dose had been too potent for him. He insisted upon claiming Ivan's astrakhan cap as his, and, as there was no use arguing the matter with an inebriate, Ivan had to go home in the military helmet of a hussar officer. On the staircase the captain maintained that he could fly, that he was one of the inhabitants of the magnetic kingdom, and had wings. The others had all the trouble in the world to get him down the stairs. When he came to the first floor he thought of paying the Countess Theudelinde a visit, to thank her for her kind reception of his lecture, for he was the lecturer, and he was ready to blow out the brains of any one who contradicted him. He was with great difficulty got into a *fiacre*, and driven to his hotel. When he got there he had to be carried to his bed, where he lay in a deep sleep until late in the following day.

Meantime Ivan, after a short rest, went about as usual, wrote his letters, and paid some visits.

"He carries his liquor like a man," said Count Stefan. And from this time all the world called him the knight of the magnet.

The knight was to be met everywhere. He had numerous visitors; he was invited to the best houses. He was elected honorary member of the club; he had been introduced by the abbé. The club had three classes of members — the day grubs and the evening and the night birds. In the daytime the library, which was an excellent collection of rare books, was visited by all the *littérateurs* of Pesth. From six to eight came the lawyers and the politicians to play whist and talk politics, and from eight until midnight the men of fashion had their innings. In this way two men might go every day to the club and never meet one another.

Ivan first ransacked the library; then he distributed his time equally. He thought no more of returning home. He enjoyed everything and went everywhere, never missing on the opera nights to pay a visit to the Countess Theudelinde's box on the grand tier.

In the second week of his stay the countess gave her ball. Ivan was invited, and went.

"Shall you dance?" asked the captain.

"I haven't done so for fifteen years."

"It suits men of our years to look on," remarked the marquis, languidly. "No man dances now after two-and-thirty."

Looking on was pleasant enough. The nameless grace and wonderful agility displayed by the aristocratic, fashionable woman was a sight for the gods to admire. Countess Angela was to-night surpassing fair. She wore a rose-colored dress, with a body, in the Hungarian fashion, all studded with pearls; the sleeves were of lace. She had taken a fancy to dress her hair like the peasant girls, in two long tresses plaited with ribbons; it suited her to perfection. But men get tired of everything, even of a sight fit for the gods. After supper one said to the other:

"Let us make use of our time; the young fellows can dance; let us play tarok."

Ivan played cards every day. He played most games well; he never disputed with his partners. He could lose with a good grace; when he won was not elated. When he held bad cards he showed no ill-temper, and seldom made a mistake. He was looked upon as an acquisition, and for a *savant* he was really a useful man. On this evening he was in exceptionally goodluck.

Suddenly Count Edmund came into the card-room in a violent hurry. He said to Ivan:

"Throw down your cards. Angela wishes to dance a turn of the Hungarian cotillon with you."

Hungarian cotillon! Strange times, that we should have a Hungarian court, a Hungarian ministry, Hungarian silver and gold coins. That is nothing wonderful; it is only natural, it is fate, and due to us. But a Hungarian cotillon belongs to the day of agitators. We dance the cotillon to the air of "Csárdás."

Ivan obeyed Angela's mandate. When he came to her he bowed low before her.

"You wouldn't have troubled yourself to come near

me only I sent for you," she said, in a tone of gentle reproach.

"Into the presence of a queen one doesn't intrude; we wait to be summoned."

"Don't try and flatter me; if you do like the others I shall treat you as I do them, and not speak one word to you. I much prefer your way, although you are always offending me."

"I do not remember to have ever offended you."

"Because you do nothing else. You know that very well."

It was now their turn; they joined the waltzers, and no one would have guessed that it was fifteen years since Ivan had danced.

Meantime, in the card-room there was some gossip over this new whim of the young countess. Count Edmund, as he shuffled the cards, declared his cousin Angela was bewitched about this Ritter Magnet.

"Ah, is that so?" cried the Marquis Salista.

"Don't you believe him," interrupted Count Stefan. "I know our pretty Angela; she is as full of mischief as a kitten. As soon as she remarks that a man has a hobby-horse, she makes him ride it, puts it through all its paces, caracoling, leaping, *haute école*. This is her trick: once she knows the subject which interests a man, she talks of it with such an earnest face, such sympathetic eyes; and when he has left her, charmed at her intelligence, her sweetness, she ridicules the unfortunate devil. This is the way she treated poor Sondersheim, a very brave young fellow, who has only one fault, that he worships Angela, and she abhors him. She laughs at everybody."

"That is true; but she praises Ivan, not to his face, but behind his back to me, and not because he is a man of science, a geologist, but because he is such a brave man."

"That is another of her tricks; the artful puss knows right well that the praise which comes at third-hand is the sweetest of all flattery."

"I take good care not to repeat one word to Ivan."

"There you show him real friendship," remarked Salista, laughing.

In the ball-room the dancers had returned to their places.

"You were ready to leave Pesth," Angela was saying, with a charming pout. "You needn't deny it; the abbé told me."

"Since then circumstances have detained me longer than I expected," returned Ivan, coolly.

"Have you got a family at home?"

"I have no one belonging to me in the world."

"And why have you not?"

This was a searching question.

"Perhaps you already know what my business is. I have a colliery; I work with the miners, and spend my day underground."

"Ah, that explains everything," said Angela, regarding him with tender sympathy. "Now I understand that you are indeed right. It would be terrible to condemn a woman to the sufferings a miner's wife must endure. What can be more terrible than to take leave of her husband each morning, not knowing whether they will ever meet again; to know he is in the depths of the earth while she breathes the fresh air of heaven; to fancy her beloved is perhaps buried alive, and she cannot hear his cries for help; that even if it is not so, that he is surrounded by a deadly atmosphere, that it only needs a spark to become a hell, in which her darling would be lost to her forever? I can understand how a woman's heart would break under such a daily agony; even to her child she would say, 'Do not run so fast, else a stone may fall on your father's head and kill him.'" Then, with a sudden change of expression, Angela turned angrily to Ivan. "But why do you stay down in the mine like a common miner?"

"Because it is my element, as the battle-field is that of the soldier, the sea of the sailor, the desert of the traveller. It is with me as it is with them—a passion. I love the mysterious darkness of the world underground."

The warmth with which Ivan spoke these words kindled an answering enthusiasm in his listener.

"Every passion is absorbing," she said, "especially the passion for creation and for destruction. I understand how a woman would follow a man she loved, not only to the field, but into the battle itself, although the art of war has now become a very prosaic and second-class affair, and has lost every trace of idealism. I confess, however, the heroism of the miner is to me incomprehensible. A man who occupies himself with dead, cold stones is to me like that Prince Badrul-Buder in the 'Arabian Nights,' who was turned into a stone, and whose wife preferred a living slave to her marble husband. I prefer those who penetrate to unknown regions of the globe, and I could envy the wife of Sir Samuel Baker, who travelled by his side all through the deserts of South Africa, holding in one hand a pistol, while the other hand was clasped in that of her husband. Together they bore the burning heat, together repulsed the savage wild beasts. Hand in hand they appeared before the King of Morocco, and what the arm of the husband failed to procure was given to the charms of the wife. I can place myself in the position of this woman, who, alone and deserted in the Mangave wood, sat through the livelong night with the head of the wounded traveller on her lap and a loaded pistol beside her. To heal his wounds she ventured into the woods and found herbs; for his food she contrived to cook in the desert. She did this for the only man she loved, whose only love she is and has ever been. Her name is known and revered in every place where Europeans have penetrated."

Again they had to join the circle of dancers, and when they returned to their place Angela resumed the conversation:

"What I said just now was sheer nonsense; the whole thing was the outcome of despicable vanity. A miserable idea to travel through countries where a woman is hardly to be distinguished from a beast, and that because she walks upright; where the ideal of beauty is to have the upper lip bored into a big hole, so that when laughing the nose is visible—ridiculous! And then to be proud because she was the most beautiful woman, and her husband perforce was faithful to her. A great thing, indeed, to be the queen of beauty amid monsters of ugliness! No, no; I know of something better, far bolder. A woman, Fraulein Christian, has accomplished a journey alone on horseback all across the steppes of Asia. What if a man and a woman had the courage to penetrate through the Polenia Canal to the warm seas discovered by Kane? or if a man and a woman had the courage to cast anchor in the regions of the north pole, and to the inhabitants of that magnetic kingdom boldly say, 'Compare yourselves with us; we are handsomer, stronger, more faithful, happier than you are'? That would be a triumph; and such a journey I would willingly undertake."

As she said these words, Angela's eyes gleamed upon Ivan with the splendor of the aurora borealis. Ivan decided within himself upon a sudden experiment.

"Countess, if you have the passion or desire to visit strange worlds, and to excite the benighted inhabitants to a proper emulation for something better, truer, more intellectual than that they have hitherto known, if this is really your laudable wish, I can recommend to your notice a country equally in need of such enlightenment, and infinitely nearer to you."

"What is it?"

"It is Hungary."

"But are we not in Hungary already?"

"Countess, you are in it, but not of it. You are merely visiting us. You do not know what and who we are. You need not go so far as the poles or Abyssinia; here is a new world open to you, a large field where your passion for creating and improving can be easily gratified."

Angela opened her fan, and with an air of indifference fanned her white bosom.

"What can *I* do? I am not my own mistress."

"You are not your own mistress, and, nevertheless, you rule."

"Over whom?"

"Countess, it would only need one word from you to bring the green palace and all it contains from Vienna to Pesth. The society here requires that leading personality which now in Vienna is lost among the crowd, whose existence is spent in aimless inaction. Pesth needs the prince, your grandfather. He adores you. One word from you would give to our life a new being; one word from you and Prince Theobald would reside here."

Angela ceased fanning herself; with an angry gesture she folded her hands, and turned an angry look upon Ivan.

"Do you know that the subject you have just mentioned is so distasteful to me that any one who has ventured to name it to me has forfeited my acquaintance?"

"I am quite aware of the fact, countess."

"And why have you dared to approach the subject?"

"I will tell you, countess. Because of an old connection between our families."

"Ah, that is something quite new. I have never heard of it."

"Possibly not. One of your ancestors was a cardinal, and one of mine was a minister in Patak—a great difference in their relative positions, no doubt; and this difference had a terrible result for my ancestor. The cardinal condemned him to the galleys for life. The minister had, however, only one word to speak, as the cardinal told him, and he would be free. That word was *abrenuncio*—'I renounce,' or 'recant.' He would not say the word, however, and so he went to the galleys. As they were putting round his neck the iron collar, from which the chains hang which fasten the slave to his bench, your ancestor, the cardinal, who was not a hard-hearted man, with tears in his eyes entreated my ancestor to say the word 'abrenuncio.' The minister, however, not only refused, but called out 'Non abrenuncio.' In the same manner I now stand opposite to you and repeat the same words—'Non abrenuncio.' This is the *rapport* between us. Would you treat me as the cardinal did my ancestor?"

Countess Angela tapped her fan upon her knee as she whispered between her small white teeth, and with a cruel smile upon her lips:

"What a pity that those days are past! If I were in the place of my ancestor I would order you to have iron goads driven under your nails."

At this formidable threat Ivan burst out laughing. After a minute Angela followed his example and laughed also.

It was rather a bold experiment to meet the young beauty's wrath with a burst of laughter, but it was a good answer to her foolish speech. The countess felt now that she had given cause for laughter; but she was offended, nevertheless, and with a haughty look at the offender she seated herself.

Ivan did not move from her side. A cotillon, even though it be the "Hungarian," has its uses. One partner cannot leave the other if they wish to separate.

In the meantime a young man, one of the stupid persons of society, came to Ivan and whispered in his ear that Edmund sent him to say he should return to his game; the luck had changed, and the heap of gold Ivan had left was lost.

"Tell him he has done well," returned Ivan; and he took his pocket-book from his breast-pocket and handed it to the messenger. "Tell him to make use of what is in this," he said, "and lose it, if necessary." And he remained where he was.

Angela never turned her head to him again. The cotillon lasted a long time; Count Geza, who led it, wished to show that the Hungarian presented as many opportunities for new figures as the German cotillon, and the demonstration lasted two hours. Ivan remained to the end, although Angela preserved her cold silence. When they had to join in the waltz circle she leaned on his shoulder, her fingers pressed his, her breath touched his face; when she returned to her place she resumed her coldness, and kept her head steadily averted.

When the cotillon was over Edmund brought Ivan the news that this long dance had cost him a thousand gulden. Ivan shrugged his shoulders, as if the loss didn't concern him.

"Wonderful man!" thought Edmund. Presently he said to his cousin:

"It seems that you kept Ritter Magnet all to yourself, my pretty cousin."

Angela raised her white shoulder to him, while she said, angrily:

"This man has bored me for a long time."

From the moment that these words were spoken by the queen of fashion a marked change took place in the opinion of the world as to Ivan's merits. He was no longer considered a capital fellow, but was looked upon as a pushing *parvenu*. Angela said nothing more, but this one sentence conveyed much. There are men of low origin whose own vanity misinterprets the true meaning of the condescension shown to them by those above them in station, and by so doing make terrible mistakes which must be punished. Such bold *parvenus* must be taught to curb their wishes. Ivan was counted as one of these. The foolish man had imagined that a highborn lady, a Bondavara, because she was patriotic, would, forsooth, stoop to such as he; he had mistaken her graciousness for the encouragement she might give to one of her own class. He must be ostracized, and that speedily.

The signal had been given by those words of the countess's: "He has for a long time bored me." The first means taken under such circumstances is to make the offender ridiculous. This can be done in different ways. The victim remarks that his weak points are held up, that he is never left in peace, that he is perpetually placed in situations which are arranged to make him a laughing-stock. Not that any one is rude enough to laugh at him openly; on the contrary, they are most polite to him, but it is a politeness that provokes laughter. He soon finds that no one is his friend, no one makes any intimacy with him, although no one actually insults him; but if he is a man of any intelligence he soon feels that he is not one of the society, and that his best part will be to take his hat and go.

This happened now to Ivan, but his habitual phlegm did not desert him; he understood the situation, and was determined to stand his ground to the bitter end. He was invited to take part in an amateur opera, made up of most aristocratic personages; it was done on purpose to subject him to a mortification. He was given the *rôle* of the "King." He made a sensation; his voice was a fine, melodious bass. Angela was the "Elvira"; Salista, "Ernani"; but the "King" was the favorite.

"The devil is in the man," growled the marquis. "He has been an actor, I'll bet."

On another occasion he was invited to a fox-hunt at Count Stefan's splendid hunting-seat near Pesth. The *élite* of the country round gathered at these hunts, which took place in the beginning of the season. It was arranged that Ivan should be mounted on a fiery Arabian. This was considered a great joke. It would be such fun to see the quiet book-worm in the saddle; he would have to cling on, for the Arabian would hardly allow his owner to ride. It would be rare sport. But here was another disappointment; Ivan sat the fiery racer as if he had grown in the saddle. When Salista saw him mounted, he muttered between his teeth:

"The devil is in the fellow. I would take a bet he has been a hussar."

Countess Angela took part in the first run at Count Stefan's. She sat her horse splendidly; she was quite at home in the field.

About ten sportsmen drew the first cover; the hounds had the fox out of the bushes, and the cavalcade rode after Renard, who took his course over a slope of a hill, which was divided by a cleft in the rock, at the bottom of which ran a mountain stream. The fox took refuge in this cleft; he probably thought he might find there an empty fox-hole, into which he might sneak. In any case he might escape by the skin of his teeth, as the horses could not venture to follow him. It was a chance, for if the dogs hunted him out of the burrow he could make tracks by the right-hand side. The hunt was on the left.

"Forward!" cried the daring Countess Angela, and put her horse to leap the cleft.

It was a breakneck jump. How many will risk their lives to follow her? When she reached the other side she turned and looked back. Ivan was beside her. The dogs pursued the fox, who had taken to the stream; the rest of the hunt galloped along the left side of the chasm. Angela thought as little about them as they did of her. In every one's mind there was only one idea—the fox. The countess rode at the very edge of the chasm, taking no heed of the dizzy height she was on and the dangerous depths into which one false step of her horse might precipitate her. She followed poor Renard, who was seeking an outlet, distracted as he was by his pursuers. Suddenly he rushed out through the riders on the left bank and took to the woods.

"After him! Tally ho!" resounded along the hillside, and soon fox, dogs, and horsemen were lost to

Angela's sight. At once she turned her horse's bridle; she made for a short-cut through the mountain, over which she meant to jump her horse, and so join the hunt without loss of time. She never looked back to see if Ivan followed her, but galloped up the steep mountain-side, sitting her horse in splendid style. At the turn of the path a hare suddenly broke from the cover under the horse's feet. The animal shied, and swerved violently to one side, throwing the countess out of the saddle. In the fall the long skirt of her habit got entangled in the saddle and kept her fastened to the horse. Her head hung, with all her hair streaming on the ground. The frightened horse ran towards the crevice; if he dragged his rider down its side her head would be battered to pieces by the trunks of the trees. Ivan fortunately caught his bridle in time. He freed the foolhardy rider from the saddle; she was unconscious. Ivan laid her upon the soft turf, and pillowed her head upon the stump of a moss-grown tree. Then he saw how the fall had disarranged her dress. The malachite buttons had come off the body of her habit, and the bodice was treacherously open. Ivan drew from his necktie his breast-pin, and with it closed the countess's corselet.

When Angela came to herself she was alone. Both the horses were tied to a tree by their bridles. In the distance through the gathering mist she saw a man coming towards her from the valley below. It was Ivan, who had gone to fill his hunting-flask with water. The countess rose at once to her feet; she needed no help. Ivan offered her the water; she thanked him, but said she was quite herself. Ivan threw the water away.

"I think it would be well if you were to return to the castle."

"I will do so."

"It is not far. I know a short way through the wood. We can lead the horses."

"Very well," returned the countess, submissively. But when she looked at her dress and saw how it was fastened a hot blush covered her face. When she was in the shade of the wood she turned to Ivan, and said, suddenly, "Have you ever heard of Julia Gonzaga?"

"No, countess."

"She was the Chatelaine of Fondi. Barbarossa had surprised Fondi in the night and carried off Julia. A noble knight came to her rescue, and she escaped with him from the freebooter. It was in the night, and she had to ride barefooted, for she had just risen from her couch. Do you know how she rewarded her deliverer? She stabbed him through the heart with the first dagger that came to her hand."

"And she did right," returned Ivan. "A strange man should not have seen her naked feet."

"And the man?" asked Angela.

"Ah, poor fellow! he had the misfortune of enjoying too much happiness."

CHAPTER XIII

ONLY A TRIFLE

THE fox was taken. Out of the far distance a triumphant "Halali!" was heard, and then the horn sounded to collect the scattered members of the hunt. Countess Angela and her escort were by this time at the border of the wood. Ivan sounded his horn in answer to the summons, and to show the others that they were already on their way home. They arrived at the castle a quarter of an hour before the rest of the company. Then they separated, and did not meet again until suppertime. The huntsmen spent the interval talking over the day's exploits, and the ladies were occupied with their toilettes.

Countess Angela told her aunt what had happened. She was incapable of any sort of deceit. Lies, which come so easily to the lips of some women, were impossible to her. If she did not tell a thing she kept silent; but to speak what was not true—never! But what if Ivan related to the men what had occurred? It was so much the habit to talk over the day's sport, and make a jest of everything. Why should he not make capital of such an adventure — a rescued lady — a beauty in *déshabille?*

When supper-time came it struck every one that the countess had a constrained manner, and closer observers noticed that she avoided looking at Ivan. She was dressed all in black, which was, perhaps, the reason that she was so pale. She was silent and preoccupied; she was wondering if they all knew what Ivan knew. The gentlemen tried to amuse her. They were full of the day's run, how the fox had doubled, how they thought they would never catch him, how they regretted that the countess had not been present, how unfortunate it was that she had been on the opposite side of the mountain, but that it was far better for her to have lost the run than to have ventured to leap the crevice. That would, indeed, have been madness; an accident would certainly have been the result. No one alluded to the fact that she had met an ugly one; but, then, wellbred people never do allude to anything unpleasant, which, though otherwise agreeable, has this drawback, that one never knows how much or how little they know.

It was a remark of her cousin Edmund that convinced Angela eventually that Ivan had kept his own counsel as to her accident.

"Did Behrend accompany you to the house?" he asked. (No one now called him Ritter Magnet, nor were there any familiar jokes with him).

"Yes."

"And his escort was not agreeable to you?"

"What makes you say that?" inquired Angela, hastily.

"From Ivan's manner; he seems terribly down in his luck. He hasn't a word to say to a dog, and he avoids looking at you. Don't you remark it? You have, I think, made the place too hot for him; he won't stay longer. Have I guessed right?"

"Yes, quite right."

"Shall I give him a hint to go?"

"Do, for my sake; but without harshness. I will not have him offended."

"Do you think I am such a bungler? I have an excellent plan to get him away quietly."

"You must tell me what it is. I am not vexed with the man, only he bores me. Do you understand? I won't have him driven away by any of you; but if he goes by his own free choice, I should be glad if he were at the antipodes."

"Well, I have no objection to tell you what I mean to do. This man is a scholar, a philosopher, as you know. He holds very different opinions from us who live in the world. For one thing, he abhors duelling. Don't spoil your pretty face by frowning. I am not going to call him out, neither is any one else, so far as I know; that would be a stupid joke. But this evening, in the smoking-room, Salista and I will get up a dispute about some trifle or another; the end of it will be a challenge. I will ask Behrend and Geza to be my seconds. Now, what will happen? If Behrend refuses, which is most likely, he will have to withdraw from our party—that is the etiquette—and we will have nothing more to say to him. If, on the contrary, he accepts, then the other seconds will manage to fall out about the arrangements of our meeting—Salista's and mine—and the regular consequence of such a falling out is that the seconds challenge one another; then our philosopher packs up his traps, thanks us for our hospitality, goes back to brew his gas. He doesn't fight, not he; for I hold that, although it is within the bounds of possibility that even a philosopher, if deeply insulted, may have recourse to his pistol to punish the offender, yet, when it is a matter of pure, worldly etiquette, it is only your born gentleman who will stand up in a duel."

"But suppose he does consent to fight this duel?"

"Then my plot has failed. We should then have a sort of court-martial, and it would have to decide that no offence was meant and none given. We would all shake hands, and the little comedy would be at an end."

Angela yawned, as if weary of the subject. "Do as you like," she said. "But take care. This man can show his teeth; he can bite."

"Leave that to me."

That evening at supper the conversation was purposely turned on duelling, for the purpose of convincing Angela that Ivan's views on the subject were sound as regarded his own safety. The opportunity offered, for the latest event in fashionable life was a duel, in which the only son of a well-known and distinguished family had lost his life for some silly dispute about a trifle.

"I hold the duel to be not merely a mistake, but a crime," said Ivan. "It is flying in the face of God to take the law into our own hands. The *Te Deum* which the conqueror sings over his murderous act is a disgrace; it cries to Heaven for vengeance. The appeal to weapons as satisfaction is likewise an offence against society, for it hinders the possibility of telling the truth. The man who tells us our faults openly to our face is a benefactor, but by the present laws of society we are bound to challenge him, and to kill him if we can; we have no other course, so it must be false compliments or the duello."

Edmund continued the discussion. "I take a different view of the matter," he said. "If duelling were not a law of society it would be in a sense a denial of God's mercy, for if you look at it in this way it cannot be denied that one man is weak, another man strong, and that this is a decree of Providence. The result of this difference in many instances would be that the weaker would be the slave of the stronger, who could box his ears, insult him, and all the law would give him would be, perhaps, a couple of pounds. This chasm between the law of God and the law of man is filled by the pistol-ball, which puts the strong and the weak on the same level. The pistol is not a judge, for it often decides the cause unjustly. Nevertheless, this unwritten law, and the respect, not to say fear, it infuses, has a salutary effect, and makes it impossible for the bully to tyrannize over a man of more education but less physical strength.

"But that it should be so is a crime of society," answered Ivan. "A false sentiment of honor has dictated this law. The world has no right to make such a rule; it should honor those equally, be they poor or rich, well-born or humble, who keep the law of the land as it is constituted. But what does society do? If a gentleman gets a box on the ear from another, and does not immediately demand satisfaction for the insult, and, *nolens volens*, make himself a target to be shot at by perhaps a better marksman than himself, what happens? He is at once dishonored; society ostracizes him. The world, if it pretend to any justice in the matter, should reform this absurd principle, and punish the man who has given the first offence. Then society, and not a leaden ball, would be judge."

"That is all very fine in theory, my dear sir; but I ask you, as a man of honor, to put yourself in the position in which, for some reason or another, you find it necessary to have satisfaction for an affront."

"I could not imagine myself placed in any such position," Ivan answered, quietly. "I offend no one intentionally, and should I do so inadvertently, I would at once apologize. I give no man the opportunity to asperse my honor, and if he were foolish enough to do so I would call upon those who know, and I should deem myself indeed unfortunate if they did not clear me of any such accusation."

"But suppose the honor of some one near and dear to you were attacked?"

"I have no one who stands to me in that close relationship."

This last remark cut short the discussion. Nevertheless, before many hours had passed the Marquis Salista proved to Ivan that there was one person whose good name was dear to him.

It was at supper, and Angela was present. The marquis was entertaining her with anecdotes of the revolution, in which he had taken part. He was bragging fearfully that when he was lieutenant of the cuirassiers he performed prodigies. At the battle of Izsasseg, with only a handful of men, he routed the entire regiment of Lehel Hussars, and at Alt Gzoney he cut the Wilhelm Hussars to pieces, and didn't spare a man.

Not a feature in Ivan's face moved. He listened silently to these wonderful tales. Angela at last grew weary of all this boasting and glorification of the Austrians over the degraded Hungarians; she turned to Ivan, and put to him a direct question:

"Is this all true?"

Ivan shrugged his shoulders. "What can I, a poor miner who lives underground, know of what goes on on the surface of the great earth?"

Angela need not have anxiety about him. He is a philosopher, and there is no fear he will go too near the fire.

After supper the company separated; Count Stefan, with Countess Theudelinde and some other ladies, went into the drawing-room. The moon shone through the bow-windows. The countess played the piano, and Angela came and spoke to Ivan.

"Here is your pin," she said. "You know the old superstition — a present of sharp-pointed instruments dissolves friendship, and those who wish to be friends never give them?"

"But," answered Ivan, smiling, "the superstition provides an antidote which breaks the spell. Both friends must laugh over the present."

"Ah, that is why you laughed when I spoke of the iron goads. There, take back your pin, and let us laugh for superstition's sake!"

And they laughed together, because it was a superstition so to do. Then Angela went out on the balcony, and took counsel from the soft air of the summer's evening; she leaned over the balustrade, waiting for Count Edmund, who had promised to bring her the first news of how the plot had worked.

The gentlemen stayed late in the smoking-room; the night is their time for enjoying themselves, so Angela had a long vigil. The moon had long disappeared behind the high tops of the poplar-trees before Angela heard Edmund's step coming through the drawing-room to the bow-window. The ladies were still playing the piano; they could talk unreservedly.

"Well, what has happened?" asked Angela.

Edmund was agitated. "Our trifle has turned out a rank piece of folly," he said, crossly.

"How?"

"I should not tell you, Angela, but the situation is such that it would be wrong to conceal anything from you. We had it all arranged just as I told you. When we were in the smoking-room we began to play our practical joke. Some one said how pleased you seemed to be with Hungary—"

"Oh, how stupid of you!" said Angela, angrily.

"I know now it was a stupid thing to do. I wish I had seen it before; but it always happens the knowledge comes too late."

"What business had you, or any one, to mention my name? I gave no permission to have it done."

"I know, I know; but in men's society, unfortunately, no one asks a lady's permission to mention her name. It was only a joke. It had been settled among us that I, being your cousin, should protest against this chatter in connection with your name; then Salista was to say that he knew well that what kept you in Pesth was the fine eyes of a certain gentleman, that I was to get angry, and forbid him to say any more, and that then we should get up the mock duel."

Angela was trembling with anger, but, anxious to hear more, she controlled herself with difficulty.

"I never heard such a childish joke," she said. "It was a college trick."

"It would have been good for us all if it had ended like a college trick. When I told you that we had prepared a trick you approved of it, Angela; you know you did. None of us thought for a moment that it would end as it has done. Behrend was sitting at the chess-table; Salista was opposite to him, leaning against the chimney-piece. After Salista had said the words, 'I know that a certain pair of eyes keeps Countess Angela in Pesth,' and before I had time to make the answer agreed upon, Ivan threw down the gauntlet. 'That is a lie!' he said."

"Ah!" cried Angela, while an electric thrill ran through her veins.

"We all sprang to our feet; the joke had ended badly. Salista grew pale; he had not counted upon this. 'Sir,' he said to Behrend, 'take back that word of yours; it is a word that in my life no man has said to me.'"

"And Behrend?" asked Angela, seizing Edmund's hand.

"Behrend stood up from the table, and answered quietly, in a cold voice, 'It is possible that up to the present you have given no occasion for this reproach to be cast in your face; but to-night I repeat that you have lied.' Then he left the room. I ran after him to try and smooth down matters. I met him in the hall. He turned to me and said, quietly, 'My dear friend, you know what must now happen. I beg that you will ask Count Geza in my name, and that you and he will be my seconds. You will communicate to me what has been settled; all is in your hands.' In this way he invited me to play the part which I had destined for him. Now he is the duellist, and I am the second. I tried to drive him into a corner. I represented to him that it was not his right to throw down the gauntlet for the Countess Angela. He answered, 'It is the right and the duty of every gentleman to protect the lady whose guest he is.' This answer, from a chivalrous point of view, is perfectly correct, but it sounds strangely from the lips of the man who a couple of hours ago told us there was no one in the world for whose good name he would fight a duel."

Angela sank back in her chair. "Oh, what terrible folly it has all been!" she wailed. "No, no, this duel cannot be! I shall prevent it!"

"I wish you would tell me what means you intend to take to prevent it."

"I will at once speak with Ivan Behrend—this moment; do you hear?"

"Unfortunately, that is impossible. When he left me he gave the order to put his horses to. There, you hear those wheels? That is his carriage. Geza has gone with him, and we four are to follow him presently. One cannot arrange this sort of thing in a strange house; that is done only on the stage. The principals must wait in their own houses to hear what we have decided to do."

"But, my God! I will not let it be done; do you hear? I will speak to Uncle Stefan."

"I have told you everything, so that our sudden departure should not surprise you; but I can tell you exactly what Count Stefan will say—that no fuss must be made; let the whole thing be done quickly and quietly. The seconds, too, must act with great prudence, and not irritate the principals by much delay."

"What do you mean by saying the seconds should act with prudence?"

"So far as depends upon them they must determine the issue of the duel, and either soften or accentuate the conditions according to circumstances. In this case we will soften. Your name will not appear as the cause of the challenge. We will induce Behrend to say that he used the word 'lie' in connection with Salista's expressions concerning the Hungarian troops. This plausible ground for a challenge will be accepted as sufficient by both sides, and in this way your name need never be mentioned."

"But I do not care! What does that matter? If any one is killed for my sake—"

"Compose yourself, my dear cousin; the seconds will be prudent. We shall place them thirty feet apart, and give them worn-out pistols with which, at half the distance, the aim would be uncertain; then we shall not allow them to take aim more than a minute, and you may be certain if they were both as thick as an elephant and protected like robin red-breasts they couldn't be safer; they may fire away for hours and never hit one another. Now, my dear child, be sensible, I beg of you. When you have a husband he will have many an affair of this kind upon his hands, and all for your beautiful eyes. But I must be going, the carriage is at the door, and we start at daylight."

And Edmund took himself off with a hasty good-bye.

This little joke had spoiled all the sport. The loss of six men made it impossible to continue hunting the next day; therefore every one resolved to return to Pesth in the morning. The night was disturbed. The companion of the Countess Angela, who slept in her room, told every one that her mistress had hardly slept a wink, that she was constantly getting up and lighting the candle, saying that it must be daylight and time to set off for the city.

The next morning, at ten o'clock, when all the guests had left, and Countess Theudelinde and her suite were already in Pesth, Countess Angela went to her room, and walked up and down restlessly until about eleven o'clock, when Count Edmund was announced.

He came in pale and disturbed, and Angela, who tried to read his face, concluded that something had happened.

"In God's name, what is it?" she asked. "Who is hurt?"

"No one," replied Edmund, dryly; "but the affair is in a worse state than it was."

"Has the duel taken place?"

"Yes and no. It has begun, but is not finished."

"I do not understand."

"I own it is something quite new. I have never known such a thing in my experience. If you wish, I will tell you all about it."

"Oh, for Heaven's sake, do!"

"As agreed, I called at Behrend's house at six o'clock to fetch him; Geza went on with the doctor. When we got to Lassloosky, Salista was just getting out of his carriage. Ivan lifted his cap and wished him good-morning; he probably did not know that this is not usual. The principals never greet one another. Salista did not return his bow, although he might have done so, seeing that Ivan was evidently ignorant of the proper etiquette. From Lassloosky we all drove together to Leopold's Field, where we got out of the carriages and went on foot through the forest. When we reached the appointed place, a clearing in the wood, we stopped, and the seconds on both sides asked the principals, according to precedent, whether they would not make up their difference. Both sides refused. Upon which we measured the distance, marked the barrier with our pocket-handkerchiefs, and loaded the pistols. When this was over, the principals, who had been pulling blades of grass and standing about, took their places. We handed them their pistols; the signal was given by Geza clapping his hands. Salista made two steps forward and shot. Just as I expected, he did not hit his man. Ivan called out in a loud voice, 'To the barrier!' and Salista advanced to where the white pocket-handkerchief lay, while Ivan went to his barrier. Then he said, addressing Salista, 'You did not return my salutation, but if I hit your head-piece you will have to take off your cap to me.' He then took aim; the half-minute during which he held his pistol showed us his nerve was perfect. The pistol went off, and Salista stood opposite his adversary bareheaded; his helmet lay two perches behind him, with the gold rose torn from its front."

"Ah!" cried Angela.

"This man shoots as well as Robin Hood. We loaded the pistols again, because, according to the agreement, they were to have three shots each."

"Three shots!" exclaimed Angela.

"Yes. We all agreed it was better to have the affair on a proper footing, so far as the conditions went. Thirty steps is a great distance; besides, the pistols were bad. In addition, both men were wrapped up to the chin; one had a black coat, the other a dark gray military cloak—colors bad for hitting; and both had their shirt-collars concealed. There was not a point about either that would serve for a target. But the cap business had changed the nature of the whole affair, and made much bad blood. It proved, for one thing, that Behrend was a first-rate shot, and this put Salista's military spirit on its metal. The barriers were withdrawn for the second shot. Salista took off his gray cloak, tied back his hussar jacket, so that his red waistcoat and white shirt stood out clear, and instead of standing, as is usual in a duel, with one side to your adversary, he presented to him a full front, and this with red and white, the best colors, as every one knows, for a mark. Yes, and while we were loading the pistols, what do you think he did? But Salista is a madman when he is roused! He took his cigar-case out of his pocket, and lighted one to show his indifference. For the second time it was his turn to begin. He took much more pains than the first time; in fact, he was such a time taking aim that we had to call to him to shoot. Again he missed. The leaves of the branches under which Ivan stood fell upon his head; the ball had gone into the tree."

Angela shuddered.

"Ivan now addressed his opponent. 'Sir,' he said, 'it is not fitting that at such a supreme moment as this you should smoke a cigar.' Salista made no answer, but stood fronting Behrend; his face was slightly turned to one side, and he blew clouds of smoke into the air. Ivan raised his pistol for a second, took deliberate aim, then a sharp report, and Salista's cigar flew from his mouth into space."

An involuntary smile spread over Angela's lips, but it was gone in an instant, and her face resumed its immovable expression, as if cut out of stone.

Count Edmund went on. "In a fury Salista threw his pistol upon the ground. 'The devil take me,' he cried, stamping with rage, 'if I shoot any more with this man! He is Beelzebub in person. He has shot the cap from my head, the cigar from my mouth, and the third time he will shoot the spurs from my boots. He shoots all round me; he is like a Chinese juggler. I will not shoot any more with him; that's flat!' His seconds in vain tried to persuade him; he would not listen to them; he was furious; he would hear nothing. He wasn't going to be such a fool as to stand up there to be a mark for a second William Tell, who would not only shoot the apple from his head, but aim right at his heart. If they wanted to have a fair fight, with all his heart—but let it be with swords; then one would see who was the best man. We all talked to him, told him not to play the fool, that he must stand his adversary's fire no matter where he was shot, in his spur or his head. The duellist has no power to refuse; he is in the hands of his seconds. At last Behrend got curious to know what the row was about; he called to me and Geza, and we had to tell him that Salista would not stand another shot, but had demanded that the duel should be decided by swords. To our surprise Ivan answered, coolly, 'With all my heart. Give us the sabres.' 'Do you consent?' 'I consent to fight with scythes if he wishes.' So it was agreed. Salista's seconds heard this discussion with great satisfaction; they were very much put out by his outbreak, it being quite unusual to change the weapons in a duel; and there would have been a regular scandal if Ivan had used his right of refusing any such alteration in the conditions under which the duel was to be fought."

"And you have allowed such an innovation to be made?" said Angela, looking at her cousin with contracted eyebrows.

"Certainly, when the challenger has agreed to it."

"It was shameful of you!" Angela continued, with suppressed tears in her voice — "ungenerous to allow such an unequal fight. One man has practised fencing all his life; it is his profession; the other has never had a sword in his hand."

"The fight will be drawn at the first blood," said Edmund, in a soothing voice.

"But you had no right to agree to such a bloodthirsty idea; you have overstepped your duty as second. You should have said to Salista's seconds that the affair should conclude then or never."

"That is quite true; and we should have done so, only Behrend chose to interfere."

"You should not have allowed it; you could have stopped it. When does the duel take place?"

"As we had no swords we could not fight this morning. It is against the law to have a duel in the afternoon, therefore we have postponed the second meeting until to-morrow at daylight."

"Before daylight to-morrow I will put a stop to the duel."

"How so?"

"I shall speak to Behrend; I shall explain everything to him."

"If you tell him that this affair has arisen out of a joke, the result will be that, instead of fighting a duel with one man, Behrend will have six duels on his hands."

"I will tell him in such a way that he will not ask to fight with any of you."

"Then you will have ruined Salista."

"How so? What has he to do with it?"

"If this half-finished *rencontre* gets wind, and it reaches the ears of the authorities that an officer refused his adversary's third fire, Salista will have to leave his regiment, he will be received nowhere, and he would have to go back to the pope's army as zouave."

"For my part, I don't care if he becomes the devil's zouave! What do I care about him? Let him go to the Sultan of Dahomey. He is only fit to be the general of his army. For my part, he may go quite to the bad; he is half-way there already. But who cares what happens to him? *I* don't. Your duty is clear; you should protect your man. Isn't that so?"

Edmund looked with astonishment at the excitement into which the countess had thrown herself; she was trembling, and her eyes gleamed with passion.

"This is quite a new view of the affair," he said. "If you look upon it in this light, I must agree that we have been wrong, and you most certainly right. I shall go at once and look for Geza; we will both repair to Behrend, and tell him our opinion."

He bowed low before his cousin, and left. In an hour he returned. He found Angela in the same place.

"Well, what is done? Is it all settled?"

"Listen. Geza and I went to Ivan. I explained to him that we considered it our duty not to infringe the conditions laid down in such matters, and that we were resolved not to allow the duel with swords to proceed. He pressed both our hands warmly. 'I thank you,' he said, 'for the friendship you have shown me, and since your convictions will not allow you to stand by me in this affair, I shall not try to persuade you. I shall go to the nearest barracks, the Karls Kaserne, and I shall tell the first two officers I may meet that I am engaged in an affair of honor to be fought with swords, that I am a stranger in the town, and that I throw myself upon their kindness to be my seconds.'"

Angela, with a despairing gesture, clasped her hands together.

"You said the truth," continued Edmund, "when you prophesied that this man would show his teeth. He has the grip of a bull-dog when he gets an idea. We told him that Salista was a celebrated swordsman. He took it quite coolly. 'If the devil himself was my adversary, I should look him in the face,' was all he said."

Angela sat down and hid her face in her hands.

"We had no other course than to assure him, so far as our services went, he was free to make use of us. So it was settled. We go for him to-morrow at daybreak. How it will all end, God only knows!"

With these words Edmund took himself away. Angela never noticed he had left the room.

That night she never lay down. All through the long hours of the night she walked to and fro in her room.

When fatigue forced her to sit down for a moment she could not rest. Once only the thought that was in her mind found expression in words:

"I have treated him as Julia Gonzaga treated the man who saved her life."

When daylight broke she threw herself, dressed as she was, upon her bed. The maid next morning found the pillow, in which she had buried her face, wet with tears.

CHAPTER XIV

THIRTY-THREE PARTS

It must certainly be said of our philosopher that he was acting somewhat inconsistently. He had left his home and property, where he had lived a simple country life amid his own people, happy in the study of those mysterious powers—fire and water; he had abandoned all his scientific pursuits to belong to a world to which he was, and must ever be, a stranger, feeling more or less like a fish upon dry land. Even his science he had turned into a farce, so bringing it into disgrace. He had lent himself to lectures and tableaux, to singing operas, and dancing Hungarian cotillons, to hunting foxes at breakneck speed, to rescuing beautiful ladies, mixing himself up therewhile in the affairs of noble families, to fighting duels with officers for the sake of lovely countesses, and running the risk of being sabred by an intemperate savage! It was no wonder that, reviewing all this, Ivan should say to himself, "Good heavens, what an ass I have made, and am making, of myself! What have I to do with all the nonsense that goes on in this fashionable world of Pesth? Above all, what is it to me whether Countess Angela is at war with her grandfather, whether she goes to Vienna, or whether he comes to Pesth? Why is it necessary for me to remain here, leading such an uncongenial life, apparently without any object?—and, although I have an object, yet if this were known to the world I should be considered an even greater fool than I am at present deemed to be."

Now, as Ivan's reflections have been made public, it is only proper that the reason of his apparently objectless conduct should be laid before the reader of these pages, so that he or she may be in a position to judge whether he was a fool or a wise man, or something between the two—a man of sentiment and feeling, who does what his heart commands him to do. With some natures the heart cannot be silenced; it has its rights. We may remember that when the Abbé Samuel paid his first visit to Ivan, he found that gentleman in the act of writing a refusal to the Countess Theudelinde's invitation; that he was, in fact, upon the point of returning to Bondavara, and that the arrival of a letter changed all his plans, and was the cause of his remaining in Pesth. This letter came from Vienna; the writer was a certain pianist whose name had been for some years mentioned among the first class of artists—Arpad Belenyi.

Nearly fourteen years before our story began Ivan had lived for a long time in the house of the Belenyis. We shall know later what he did there. Arpad was at that time a child of five years old; he was already counted a prodigy, and could play long pieces upon the piano. At that time warlike and patriotic marches were all the fashion. One day the bread-winner of the family, the father, died suddenly. The widow was in despair, especially for her orphaned boy. Ivan consoled her with the promise that he would look after him, and provide for his education.

On account of certain circumstances, some months after, however, Ivan had to leave the family Belenyi somewhat suddenly, and it seemed doubtful if he should ever see them again. Ivan at parting gave all the money he could spare to the widow, and told her to get Arpad a good musical education, such as would fit him for an artistic career. The boy, he thought, would attain eminence, and make a livelihood by his art. And here let it be clearly understood that Ivan was neither a friend of Belenyi nor the lover of Madame Belenyi; neither was he connected with the family in any way, nor was he in duty bound to do as he did. For years the Belenyis heard nothing from Ivan, nor he from them. Once, on his inquiring about them, he was told that in consequence of a lawsuit they had lost their house, had left the town, and that neither mother nor son had since been heard of. Then, after another spell of years, Arpad Belenyi's name began to be mentioned in different newspapers, always as a young and astonishingly clever artist. From this time Ivan took in regularly a musical paper or magazine, and so followed attentively his adopted son's career. The latter, however, knew nothing of his kind benefactor until, later, Ivan's name also appeared in the papers. His discourse at the Academy led to his being traced by his adopted son, who at once wrote him a letter, beginning with the words, " My dear father." It was a letter full of simple, boyish sentiments, through which broke at intervals the natural fun and playful humor of the artist. He told Ivan everything concerning himself ; how he had travelled in many countries, accompanied always by his mother, to whom he had always to give an account of his actions as near the truth as possibly could be. He had already given concerts before crowned heads, and had received several orders which he was allowed to wear only on Sundays ; the other days of the week they were locked up by his mother. He had earned a good deal of money, but he was not permitted to spend much.

Mamma gave him every day a five-shilling piece for pocket-money; the rest she put by to buy back her little house which "old Raize" had robbed her of. He, therefore, to make more money, gave music-lessons and played accompaniments for artists. This was well paid, particularly of late, when he had fallen in with a little artist, a new singer, who paid splendidly. She was said to be the wife of Felix Kaulmann, the rich banker.

When he came to this passage Ivan's heart began to beat. He laid down the letter, then took it up again, and read it with renewed attention.

"This girl is a mixture of Muse and Mænad," wrote Arpad. "Now she is a petulant child, the next minute a wild Amazon; a born artist, full of genius, yet she is not likely ever to rise above mediocrity. She is full of intelligence and life, and with this often as stupid as a donkey. There is no doubt she could attain an unenviable notoriety, but she shrinks from it, for although she conducts herself like a courtesan, I would take my oath she is in reality as innocent as the child she really is. She is very trying to me, full of mischief and petulance, and this because I treat her to no soft manners, but scold her well for being so naughty. If you could only see, dear papa, what a splendid master I am, always serious, no frivolity allowed! Now I have photographed myself for you, have I not? Do not think, however, that I would have scrawled all over my paper this monologue about my pupil, as if I had nothing better or wiser to write about. I have done so because the subject has a certain interest for you. You must know this curious little angel confides in me as if I were her confessor. Sometimes she chatters all through her lesson, telling me where she has been, what she has done, everything that has happened to her; and she often tells me things which, if I were in her place, I would not talk about. Have a little patience, my dear good papa. This lady has thirty-three different *rôles*, all of them of different kinds. They are not, strictly speaking, stage parts, but monologues, which are composed expressly for her. These scenes we rehearse together; I play her accompaniment, while she sings and acts.

"I am coming now to the kernel of the nut. I am going to crack it for you. Here are the names of the actress's thirty-three parts—'Loreley,' 'Cleopatra,' 'The Queen of the Sun,' 'The Greek Slave,' 'The Bacchante,' 'Nourmahal,' 'The Bride,' 'The Matron's Cap,' 'The Bayadère,' 'Claudia Laeta, the Vestal,' 'Amalasontha,' 'Magdalene,' 'Ninon,' 'La Somnambula,' 'Medea,' 'Salome,' 'The Houris,' 'The Despair of Hero,' 'The Phrygian Cap,' 'Turandot,' 'The Peasant Girl,' 'The Mother,' 'Jeanne la Folle,' 'Ophelia,' 'Judith,' 'Zuleika Potiphar,' 'The Market Woman,' 'The Grisette,' 'The Creole,' 'Lucretia,' 'The Will-o'-the-Wisp,' 'Julia Gonzaga.'

"The thirty-third part I do not know; we have not as yet rehearsed it. But why the deuce does she learn all these parts, for she never treads the boards? The report is that the reason why this lady's talent is so much cultivated is that she is engaged to sing at the Opera-house. This seems even more strange, and I, for one, am slow to believe it. A banker like Kaulmann, who is a millionaire, and whose wife pays for her apartment four thousand florins! Besides, she would have to give her singing-master, who has got her the engagement, six thousand; to the leader of the orchestra, two thousand; four thousand to the newspapers to puff her; another three thousand to the *claqueurs;* and something else to the men who throw the wreaths and flowers. There would remain for her about a thousand florins;

that would hardly pay for her scents. So you see the absurdity of the whole thing. Where are we now? This pretty creature, who wishes also to be a famous artist, has several lovers who can easily pay their court to madame, seeing that she and her husband live in separate apartments. This is only natural; the banker could not have his mind, which is occupied with important speculations, disturbed by constant *solfeggi*. There are several persons in Vienna who bear the title of the 'Mæcenas of Art'; they are gentlemen of high position, who have great weight in the departmental government, and whose voices are heard in all social and official capacities. These have been allowed the privilege of being present during the rehearsals of the thirty-two monologues; the thirty-third has not as yet been played before any one. In all this I can assure you everything is conducted with the greatest propriety. I am always present, also the husband, who remains so long as the comedy continues. Among the company are representatives of the highest nobility, counts, princes, senators, and ministers. They are good sort of people, and call one another Fritz, Nazi, Muke, etc. Among others we have two princes, who come every time we have a rehearsal—the Prince Mari and the Prince Baldi; the names they received on baptism being Waldemar and Theobald. Yesterday Eveline—for so is my pupil named—was not inclined to work, and without my asking her what ailed her, with her usual frankness she came out with her annoyance.

"'Only fancy,' she said; 'that odious Prince Waldemar, when he was in my opera-box last night, threatened that if I did not let him come to our next rehearsal he would ruin Lixi.' (Lixi is short for Felix, her husband's name.)

"'Why don't you admit him?' I asked. 'He is not worse than the other jackanapes who come here.'

"'Because I cannot endure him. I told Lixi what Prince Waldemar had said, and Lixi answered that he would ruin the prince. At the same time he gave me to understand that Prince Theobald must be invited to the rehearsal.'

"'All right,' said I; 'he is a fine old gentleman. You can have no objection to him; he is old enough to be your grandfather.'

"The young wife bit her lips, and, with a frown on her lovely face, said:

"'I have to ask him to do something. What do you think it is? Oh, you could never guess! It is to give his signature that he will consent to a certain affair which will cost him nothing, but which will help Lixi greatly. You know that Lixi has a grand speculation on hand, a gigantic coal company, which is to start the business with I don't know how many millions of money; but the place where the coal-mines are situated, the Bondavara property, belongs to Prince Theobald and his sister. The countess has already given her consent, but without his ratification the shares would not be taken up at the exchange. Prince Waldemar is working against us, and therefore I am to win over the old prince to our side. Lixi says it will be very easy to get round him just at the present moment, because his granddaughter, Countess Angela, of whom he is very fond, has quarrelled with him and left him. The poor old man is very sad and lonely, and Lixi says whoever cheers him up will be able to do anything with him; and,' she added, with a wise look, 'we are not deceiving him, for the Bondavara coal is the finest in the world.'

"I burst out laughing; I could not help it. Then she pulled my hair and said:

"'Why do you laugh, you ridiculous donkey? I think I must be a judge of coal, for I worked as day-laborer for ten years in the mines of Herr Behrend.'

"At these words my astonishment was so great that I jumped up from my seat.

"'You may stare your eyes out of your head,' she said, laughing at my amazement, 'but it is quite true. I used to shove the coal-wagons, and barefoot into the bargain.'

"'Gracious lady, believe me, I did not jump up from astonishment; I was surprised to hear you name Ivan Behrend. What do you know of him? Pray tell me.'

"'He was the owner of the coal-mines in Bondavara, near which Felix is going to open works upon an enormous scale. He was my master; God bless him, wherever he goes!'

"Now, dear papa, I have come to the heart of the business, after, it must be owned, an unconscionably long prelude. With my weak intellect I have thought out the whole thing. Here is my kind friend, my adopted father, the owner of a mine in Bondavara, and beside him men with I don't know how many millions at their backs are going to form a coal company. It would be a good thing to let him know, that he may act in time; it may be good for him, but it would seem to me that it may also be very bad. Here the air is full of speculation; you see, I am already slightly bitten. Let me know how and in what manner the affair affects you and your interests. I shall write to you what goes on here, for I shall be behind the scenes; this little fool tells me everything."

The receipt of this letter had decided Ivan to accept

the Countess Theudelinde's invitation to give a romantic reading at her house, and to enter into the society of Pesth. He wrote to Arpad, and begged him to give him every day an exact account of what he heard through Evila of the progress of the coal-mine company.

From this time Ivan received regularly every week two or three letters from Vienna.

"The old prince nibbles at the bait. Kaulmann has brought him to the rehearsal of the new piece. Eveline sings and acts enchantingly; that is, when she is within four walls, and has only a few people for audience. If she acted like this on the stage she would be a celebrated actress in no time; but so soon as she comes before the footlights stage-fright seizes upon her, she trembles, forgets everything, stands there like a stick, and, worst of all, sings quite false. These rehearsals have been given on the pretext that the prince should have an opportunity of judging of her talent, so that he may influence those in power to give her an engagement at the opera. I know what their real object is. The prince is a real connoisseur in music, and he understands not alone art, but artists. He knows that there is a price set upon such black diamonds as sparkle in Eveline's eyes. There is the additional incentive that Prince Waldemar is desperately in love with this woman, and Prince Theobald, for certain reasons, will do anything to prevent her falling into his hands. He would even go the length of taking her himself sooner than such a misadventure should happen.

"A short time since Prince Waldemar met me, and offered me one hundred ducats for every leaf of the album in which are the portraits of Madame Kaulmann in her character costumes. You must know, of late, each day that we rehearse one of the monologues at the piano a photographer is present and takes the artist in her costume. Everything must be finished in the house, and not more than four pictures are allowed to be executed; one of these is for Prince Theobald, one is kept by herself, one she presents to me, and the fourth is for my friend Felix. The negative is then broken. I would not sell my photographs to Prince Waldemar, but I send them to you as they follow one another. Mamma does not like to see such pictures in my room."

Ivan received with each letter a photograph; each portrait represented Evila as a lovely creation in a most graceful pose. Arpad had not the least idea what a hell of different passions were raised in Ivan's breast as he looked at the beautiful image of the woman he had and still loved.

In the first portrait she was represented as "Loreley" the fairy, who, in the whirlpool of the Rhine, sings her magic song and combs her hair with a golden comb, while her left shoulder rises from the waves, which partially conceal her form. Her eyes gaze invitingly at the fisherman, whom she entices to his ruin. In the second photograph she appeared as "Cleopatra" at Tarsus, where she is displaying all her charms to seduce her conqueror and make him her slave; a rich portrait, in which the lascivious queen is represented laden with splendid dresses and jewels, while the expression of the beautiful face was an admirable mixture of pride, dignity, and weakness. The third photograph presented the sun-queen, "Atahualpa," the wife of the last Inca. Her look was haughty and sublime; the sublimity of the expression diverts attention from the uncovered arms, white as marble, round as an infant's, which are raised to heaven, offering as a sacrifice a human heart. Her face mirrored the coldness of heaven itself. The fourth, as the "Greek Slave"; she represented the tortured beauty, who in vain tries to break the chains of shame in which she is bound—a lovely marble statue, equal in conception to one by Thorwaldsen or Pradier. The fifth was the "Bacchante," from one of the Roman bas-reliefs, which represents the procession of Bacchus. A wild, bold, dissolute conception; showing accessories of surprising drapery, panther skins, cups, etc., an ideal debauch; limbs in wild movement. The sixth portrait was of a bride; a white lace dress, upon her head a white garland, her figure concealed by a white veil, on her face an expression of soft emotion at the approaching realization of her happiness, in her eyes tears, on her lips a tremulous smile. With what wonderful charm she stretches out her hand to receive the betrothal ring! The eighth portrayed a young woman who for the first time puts the matron's cap upon her head. Pride, shame, and conscious triumph are all in her face. She feels that the cap upon her head is a well-deserved crown—a crown for which she has sacrificed a garland.

Ivan contemplated this picture for a long time; his heart was full of the bitterness of disappointed love. His adopted son's present had been somewhat unfortunate.

The ninth photograph represented Evila as a "Bayadère," in the artistic dress of the Indian dancer, striking the tambourine over her head. Round her slight figure a shawl embroidered in gold was wound in careless folds, on her neck a chain of gold coins, her small feet bare, and strings of pearls up to the knee.

In the tenth portrait she appeared as "Claudia Laeta," the vestal virgin, at the moment when she is led to the stake because she has refused the solicitations of Caracalla; on her face an expression of horror, of virginal modesty. With one hand she tries to cover her head with her cloak to escape from the gaze of the multitude.

How is it possible for one woman to play so many parts? Arpad accompanied these pictures with diffuse explanations, which were so many arrows in the heart of Ivan. The result of all this posturing was, he said, becoming every day clearer.

"The prince is more and more fascinated; he is falling deeper and deeper into the net spread for him. After each rehearsal he declares that a real treasure has been concealed, which has been a loss to art that must be at once remedied."

But such treasures are very costly, especially when a man has reached the age of sixty-eight, close on seventy, and has a marriageable granddaughter; then it is necessary to look very closely into his check-book to see if it would be possible to provide for the grandchild and at the same time satisfy the caprices of a beautiful young woman.

Not long ago Prince Theobald had built a splendid palace in the Maximilian Strasse; it was destined for the Countess Angela, in the case that she agreed to her grandfather's wish as to her marriage. The palace was furnished with the utmost magnificence. The countess, however, had thought otherwise. She broke off her marriage with Sondersheim; she had good reasons, no doubt, but she need not have openly defied her grandfather. It was unwise of her so to do, for Evila was weaving her spell closer round the old man's heart, and Angela had best be prudent, and return speedily to Vienna, else the palace in the Maximilian Strasse will be presented, without a shadow of doubt, to Madame Kaulmann.

Arpad's letters had made Ivan acquainted with the

ins and outs of the whole affair; through them he had learned that the woman he had loved had become the wife of another man, and was likely to be the mistress of a third. The first blow he could bear with a certain resignation; he wished her all happiness; but that she should sink up to the neck in shame, led thither by the act of her own husband, was a bitter thought! No, that she should be saved from, if Ivan could compass her deliverance. For this end he remained in Pesth. Hence it seemed to him he could pull the strings of this complex drama, and defeat the conspiracy against Evila's honor; for this purpose he went into a world that he despised, affected a manner of life totally inconsistent with his ideas, and cultivated a friendship with the Countess Angela, that his influence might induce her to play the part of the good angel.

Was he a fool to sacrifice his own feelings for a woman who had inflicted upon him the severest mortification a man can endure? Those whose hearts are dominated by cold prudence will judge his folly perhaps rightly; those who have hearts that feel for others will acknowledge that he did well in obeying its dictates, and from his own point of view, perhaps, he acted for his own ultimate advantage.

If Prince Theobald is induced to consent to the lease of his property to the Bondavara Company, Ivan's little coal-mine is ruined. Good if he can, while working for another, help himself. A man of business is always a speculator; therefore we say to the warm-hearted and compassionate that Ivan acted a part to save Evila from shame, and to the cold-hearted and unfeeling that it was all in the way of business, to save, if he could, his little all from the monster company ready to devour it bodily.

Arpad continued to send the photographs. They were

of all kinds, tragic and comic. "Medea," with her murderous revenge and jealousy; the daughter of Herod, with her voluptuous dance to gain the saint's head; the cruelty of "Judith," the wild laughter of "Jeanne la Folle," the devotion of a holy nun, the coquettish tricks of a *grisette*, a languid Creole, a supernatural "Will-o'-the-Wisp"—these were the principal representations in which Ivan found rather studied effort at catching an artistic effect than natural instinct or expression. This was the school of Madame Grissac, to whom Felix had intrusted Evila's education. Two portraits that came at the end produced upon Ivan a painful impression. One represented a mother by the cradle of her child, the other a peasant girl, a coal-carrier, with her hair plaited down her back, and a red frock tucked up above her ankles. It pained Ivan deeply that she should profane these two sacred subjects. Why take a mother's love to be made a vehicle to create an old man's admiration? And the girl with the red frock! Ah, that was unpardonable! He could not forgive her for having wounded him to the very heart.

One day the artist wrote to Ivan—

"My good patron, Felix Kaulmann, is an out-and-out scoundrel. Up to the present he generally attends the rehearsals when the prince is present. Yesterday Prince Theobald seemed quite excited, so much so that Kaulmann was struck by it. To his question the prince said that he was very happy. He had received a letter from his granddaughter, the Countess Angela. She wrote in the most friendly manner. She told him that she had met a certain Ivan Behrend, who had the courage to give her a regular scolding, and had told her to her face what was the duty of the Hungarian magnates towards their country, a duty in which they were wanting, and which

Prince Theobald would fulfil if he left Vienna and came to reside in Pesth, in which case the countess would agree to a reconciliation. The old prince seemed so happy at the idea of seeing his child again! Kaulmann, however, looked very black, blacker still when the prince said he would consider the matter; but that, as the countess had taken a fancy to Pesth, he thought he would go there. Inwardly Felix gnashed his teeth with rage, outwardly he expressed great satisfaction that the countess had at last broken the ice; it was a good sign that she was getting tired of her obstinacy. But if he were in the prince's situation he would try and persuade the countess to come to Vienna, instead of going himself to Pesth. The prince listened to this suggestion; he fell into the trap, and will not go at once to Pesth, but will try to bring back the countess. In the meantime we are to have the two last rehearsals. The thirty-second is the representation of 'Julia Gonzaga,' whose story you will find in any library. The most interesting part of this scene is the toilette of the heroine, who appears in a night-dress made of muslin, with her feet naked. In spite of this rather risky costume the lady's virtue was irreproachable, for in her hand she held a dagger, and threatened to kill any one who ventured to look at her feet. As I wrote to you, Kaulmann has always been present at these rehearsals, but from this one of 'Julia Gonzaga' he is obliged to absent himself, as he has to go away for a few days. I believe that my office should be called *garde des dames*. As it happens, however, on this occasion I, too, am unavoidably prevented from being present. When I went home and showed mamma the enclosed photograph she shuddered, and positively forbade me to assist at a rehearsal in which a woman appeared in such a costume. I must plead illness or any other cause, but stay at home I must. I thought over several lies, but at last I decided that I would tell my gracious pupil the truth; so I did.

"'Listen,' I said. 'My mother will not allow me to accompany you if you sing barefoot. If it is really the point of the piece that 'Julia' must present herself without stockings on her feet, then I must deny myself the pleasure of playing on the piano.'

"The silly child laughed very much, and said she would get somebody else. She may do as she likes; I don't care. Mamma is perfectly right in forbidding me to go, and I think that I have done perfectly right to tell my pupil why I refuse to accompany her."

This letter depressed Ivan. For a long time he looked at the photograph, considering it from every point of view. Evila in a dress the thin material of which showed every motion of her plastic limbs; in one hand she gathered the folds across her breast, her eyes had a murderous glare in their violet depths, her long and beautiful hair fell to her feet; in her right hand she pointed a dagger towards a motionless form which lay at her feet covered by a rug. This was the second time that Ivan had heard the story from a lady.

The next day he received another letter from Arpad; he found it on his return from the first meeting with Salista.

"Eveline," wrote the artist, "performed her tableau before the prince without the accompaniment of the piano and without the company of her husband. She looked so lovely that all the prince's good principles melted away like snow before the sun. He took her hand and kissed it; then the murderous look disappeared from her sweet eyes; she broke out into a ripple of laughter.

"'Prince, do you not see that I have a knife in my hand?'

"'I can take it from you.'

"The young girl laughed again; and we all know how easy it is to take anything from a smiling woman.

"At this moment there resounded through the room an echo of Eveline's laugh; that is to say, if you can call a frog's croak an echo of a nightingale's song. Out of the conservatory, which ornaments one side of the room, there came a crippled dwarf, who supported himself upon crutches. His long head was sunk between his high shoulders, and his white, satyr-like face was distorted by an odious grin as he dragged himself between the prince and his inamorata.

"'Prince, we are not alone,' laughed Eveline, freeing her hand from the clasp of the astonished nobleman.

"'In Heaven's name, who is this splendid specimen of a toad?' he cried, with an air of disgust.

"'This is my only beloved little brother,' cried Eveline, putting her arms round the little monster, and covering him with kisses while she stroked his head. 'My dear, only little brother, my all, my dearest; my ugly, cross, quarrelsome little tyrant, who comes to me whenever he likes.'

"'A horrible creature!' said the prince. 'The hobgoblins who kept watch over the gate of the Witch of Endor were cherubims as compared with this monster. I beg of you, Eveline, not to kiss his face, as it takes away forever the pleasure one would have in kissing so lovely a mouth.'

"Eveline made no answer, but, suddenly turning away, she threw a burnoose round her shoulders, put her tiny feet into a pair of slippers, and said, demurely:

"'Prince, the thirty-second rehearsal is over, and

there only remains the thirty-third to complete the course.'

"The prince asked what the title of this last should be, and Eveline whispered in his ear that he would know the next day but one.

"'And how many more will know it?'

"'No one but you.'

"'Not this Caliban?'

"'Certainly not.'

"The prince took his leave in an ecstasy, firmly convinced that at the last representation he would have Eveline all to himself. Eveline needed a day to prepare herself.

"The scene was repeated to me by the cripple, who likes me very much, and comes nearly every evening to share my supper; for although everything possible for his comfort is provided by Eveline, he is never happy unless he begs from some one. If he were a prince, I do believe the creature would get out of his carriage to ask for alms. He finds such a wonderful pleasure in begging. For a stick of sugar-barley he will tell me everything. What pleased him most was the prince's remark about his being a splendid specimen of a toad. He imitated for me how he crept out of the conservatory on his crutches, and how he laughed when he saw the gentleman wanted to take the knife from his sister. You will hear from me again the day after to-morrow."

The day after to-morrow! These words to a man who might be lying stark and stiff by that time! They gave Ivan a sudden chill; but he said to himself he would not die easily, he would fight for his life.

That night he dreamed a curious dream, in which he saw two "Julia Gonzagas," who both wanted to kill him, and yet he had deserved nothing but good at their hands.

So goes the world!

CHAPTER XV

TWO POINTS

A DUEL with swords has this distinct advantage over a duel with pistols: you need have no concealment concerning it; the day before it is spoken of as an interesting wager would be. In former times it happened rarely that a duel with swords had a fatal ending, and therefore it is surrounded with none of the mystery that attends the more serious affair; for the seconds, likewise, there is far less responsibility. If a principal gets severely hurt, the attending surgeon declares that the sufferer has not died of the wound, but that there was some trouble in the organism which would have probably killed him within the next forty-eight hours. And who, nowadays, would make a fuss over a man who was doomed to die in forty-eight hours?

The duel which was to take place between the Marquis Salista and Ivan was spoken of at the club with indifference, as a thing that had a foregone conclusion. Salista spoke most of it himself, and at six o'clock the evening before stood at the chimney-piece and entertained a select group of friends, among whom were the four seconds, with his ideas on the subject.

The golden youth of Pesth, being in the habit of having constant fencing-bouts at the different gymnasiums, know well who is the most skilful fencer, and are therefore able to predicate, accurately enough in many cases, what the result will be. Salista had the reputation of being a first-rate swordsman; he had already fought several duels, and always been the victor; he had one particular stroke, a master-stroke, which few fencers could parry; it was a quick thrust in the stomach, which, passing round the point of his adversary's sword, ripped up his abdomen. If the other intercepted the thrust, he was likely to get out of time, so that his face, being left uncovered, was exposed to a well-delivered thrust which would spoil his beauty, if it did not have more dangerous consequences. Some men would have felt that the circumstances connected with the preceding duel required explanation, that the refusal to stand your adversary's fire had a doubtful sound. For a similar offence others had been rigorously punished by having to leave Vienna for some weeks, and being sometimes kept in Coventry even longer. Salista was, however, a privileged person; his courage was not called in question. He was, moreover, a cool hand, and carried off his difficult position with the most astounding *aplomb*. As he now stood upon the rug he talked with a good deal of swagger as to what would happen on the morrow.

"We shall see what stuff this Admirable Crichton is made of. Sword-exercise is not like pistol-shooting; there can be no mathematics. We will ask him how he construes the under-cut when the sabre takes his legs from under him."

Count Geza rebuked the boaster. "You must remember," he said, "that Ivan acted towards you in the most chivalrous manner when he accepted the sword instead of the pistol, and you must also consider that he is a man of learning, very much thought of, and likely to be of service in his generation."

"Very good. You needn't be afraid, I shall not kill

him; I shall only slice a piece off his nose, that he may carry home a souvenir of Pesth. A scholar like him will not care if his beauty is spoiled; science is not sniffed up like snuff, and his nose is no use for looking through the telescope at the stars."

Here Edmund interfered, and protested hotly against any injury being done to the nose of his principal. At last the marquis had to content himself with a slice off his ear; but Edmund still remonstrated.

"You should be satisfied with a cut on his hand," he said; "the whole matter is not worth more."

Count Stefan here made a suggestion in his quiet way.

"My good Salista, what if this coal-heaver were to cut *you* down?"

"What!" blustered the marquis, standing with long legs apart in front of the chimney-piece. "To show you what I think of him, I will give him two points; I will let him have two cuts at me on my arm, and then I will cut him down. You shall see! You can make your bets. Who holds the wager?" So he went on boasting until the discussion came to an end. His last question was whether the seconds would be quick enough to interfere before he made a cripple of their great scholar.

On the following day the two parties met. The large ball-room in the hotel had been thought the most suitable place, as it was generally hired for such occasions. The seconds had chalked the floor with pulverized chalk to prevent the combatants from slipping. In an adjoining room both the principals had to strip to the waist; then they were led into the room. There was no necessity to draw lots as to the placing of the men, as the room was panelled all round with looking-glasses. Before they were given the sabres the following conditions were read out:

"First blood. Stabbing is not allowed."

Salista protested. He would not hear of first blood. The duel should go on until one of the combatants declared himself no longer able to fight. Every one tried to persuade him to be more moderate, but he would not give in.

"Give us the swords!" cried Ivan, out of all patience. "I am getting a chill, half-naked as I am."

This interruption decided the matter. The paces were measured, the principals placed in position, and their swords handed to them.

Both were naked to their waists. Salista exhibited Herculean muscles, Ivan had a well-developed form. He had certainly not so much flesh as his adversary, but was bony, had long arms, and a vaulted chest. The fight began in the usual manner. Both men held the points of their swords towards each other, had the left hand drawn back, and their heads protected by their arms. Now and again they crossed their swords dexterously, trying to find a place for a good thrust, and striking one another softly. Each stared into his adversary's eyes, seeking to read his intentions. Salista essayed to give his adversary a thrust which would injure his face. This was very difficult, for the face is always protected by the arm. Ivan, on his side, endeavored to give his opponent the double thrust. This requires extraordinary agility; but he succeeded. He tore the top muscle of Salista's right arm the whole way down. That this blow does not bleed at once is explained by the cellular texture of the muscles.

"Forward!" cried Salista. "No blood!"

He now gave up all efforts at injuring his adversary in the face, and resorted to his well-known trick, the belly-thrust, which is difficult to parry, and if it hits is often deadly in its effect. If it is not parried, the effect is certain; and if it is, the giver can, if he is a good swordsman, hit his adversary a terrible cut over the head. Ivan did not parry, good or bad. Salista had not forgotten that the duelling-sword is shorter than the cavalry practise-sword; but he forgot, or rather didn't know, that his adversary had arms of unusual length. This is, therefore, what happened. Ivan did not attempt to parry the belly-thrust; he raised his arm, and let the sword-point of his opponent pass at a distance of two lines over his body, while he aimed straight at the other's arm, cutting him crossways in the same place where he had before cut lengthways.

These were the two points. Through this cross-cut the difference of strength between the two men was equalized. This last defeat filled Salista with fury. With the roar of a wild beast he threw himself upon his adversary, and with all his strength made two cuts at the head. He cut as a butcher cuts with his axe; it was a miracle that both swords didn't break in two, for, according to rule, Ivan received both thrusts upon the handle of his sword, and before the other could give him a third he gave him quickly a thrust in front with such strength and precision that it came with full force on the head and face of the marquis. It was lucky that the sword was light, otherwise he would have split his skull in two. Salista reeled under the blow, then raised his left arm to protect his head, tottered sideways, and fell down, supporting himself upon the handle of his sword. His seconds ran to him to raise him up and lead him away. Ivan stood with his sword-point lowered, his face apathetic, as if turned to marble. His seconds congratulated him.

"Are the gentlemen content?" he asked.

"I dare swear they are," returned Count Edmund. "Nothing could have turned out better; the affair is at an end."

With these words they conducted Ivan into the next room to dress himself.

When he returned to the hall he found that his adversary had recovered consciousness; the two doctors were with him, one binding up his head, the other his arm.

According to the usual etiquette, Ivan went to him.

"Forgive me, comrade," he said.

Salista gave him his left hand, and said, cordially, "It is not worth talking about; but it was a splendid fight. The other two don't count, because I had said I would give you 'two points;' the third—ah, that was a cut! But I shall be all right in a week."

Ivan asked the doctors if the wounds were dangerous, but Salista answered for them.

"Soldier's luck," he said. "I have given similar cuts a hundred times; now it is my turn, and I don't complain. Only one thing troubles me. Neither arnica nor ice-bandages can do me any good; but *you* who have caused this suffering can mitigate it. Confess, now, that you have been in the army."

"Without doubt," returned Ivan. "During the War of Freedom I was lieutenant of hussars."

"May the devil fetch you! Why didn't you tell us before? In what regiment did you serve?"

"In the Wilhelm Hussars. Therefore I am the sole survivor and witness of that memorable exploit of yours, when you cut us to pieces."

Everybody burst out laughing. No one laughed more than the wounded man. The doctors reminded him that he must not laugh, else the bandage over his face would get disturbed.

"Very good," said Salista. "I shall laugh only on one side of my face. Comrade, God bless you! I shall not think any more of the cut now that I know it was the work of a soldier, and not of a civilian. Come, kiss me on the other cheek, the one you have left me whole and entire. So, my brother. I cannot give you my right hand, for you have given me a cross-cut there that will show a scar for many a day. It was first-rate, that cut, a regular hussar cut, and, therefore, I don't in the least mind it."

And the combatants kissed one another.

The next moment the wounds began to bleed afresh, and Salista fainted from loss of blood. Ivan held his head upon his knees while the doctors bound up the veins; then he helped to carry him to the carriage.

Every one said, "What a capital fellow!"

CHAPTER XVI

GOOD-BYE

THE friends and acquaintances of both parties were assembled at Count Stefan's to hear the result of the duel. The seconds on both sides had promised to come and give the earliest news. All the *habitués* of society were waiting; there was suppressed excitement; bets were made upon which should be wounded, and whether Salista would give a heavy wound or only a slight scratch to his adversary. Count Stefan had the courage to bet ten to one that Salista would get a scratch; he also risked " even money " that the marquis would be the only one wounded. That Ivan would escape with a whole skin no one else for an instant imagined. If they had done so they might have offered a hundred to one, and even at that no one of the party would have taken the bet.

The outposts planted themselves at the windows, to be the first to see the carriage with the seconds. When a cab drove up, they shouted to the others :

"Edmund and Geza have arrived!"

"Then I have won my bet," said Count Stefan; "the seconds of the man who is least hurt get away first."

Count Edmund went to the countess's apartment to let her know what had happened, while Geza ascended to Count Stefan's rooms. He rushed in with the triumphant air a victorious second should have.

"He has put him to the sword."

"Who? Who? Ivan? Salista?" cried the company, surrounding the messenger in their excitement.

"Ivan has put the marquis."

An "A-ah!" was the incredulous rejoinder of the others.

"But I tell you he has," repeated the young count; "he has cut him into a jelly."

"And Ivan?"

"He is as untouched as I am."

"Ah, you are making fun of us."

"It is no subject for fun. Ask Salista."

"But where is Ivan?"

"He will be here immediately, and will convince the unbelievers, who will find no wounds into which they can poke their fingers. He went home with the doctors, for Salista had two, who have at last succeeded in stitching him together."

Then he related to them circumstantially all that had happened. For those who did not clearly understand, he demonstrated with the help of two walking-sticks the course the duel took. He came to the double-cut.

"In this way Ivan parried the stomach-thrust and gave the fore-cut—the final *a tempo contre coup*. The performer of these wonderful exploits had not even turned a hair."

"Why, he is a miracle!"

"No such thing," protested Count Geza. "He has been in the army—captain in the hussars." (He advanced him a grade, but captain sounds better than lieutenant.) "He fought all through the revolution; he was nineteen times in action, and fought with the Cossacks besides. He has also received a good-service medal."

All this the count imagined might be the fact, although he had certainly not heard a word of such a history from Ivan. Once a man has scored one success, he is credited with twenty more.

"Truly a wonderful man!" said Baron Oscar. "For three months he has been among us every day, and has never mentioned his soldiering experiences."

"Now we have really landed him upon us, like a Sindbad that can never be shaken off," remarked Baron Edward. "We wanted to be rid of him, and instead we have raised him into the saddle. He will never dismount; he is saddled on us forever. No one would dare now to speak to him."

"Good God of Saxony!" cried Baron Oscar, "how the man will carry his nose in the air! There will be no standing him, for the women will, of course, make the deuce of a fuss about him, and men must have a certain respect for him. *Sacré bleu!* A man who can shoot and fence like this fellow! But I would bet anything that it was a mere accident."

"I think quite the contrary," remarked Count Stefan, "and I very much fear that Ivan will leave us all cooling our heels here, and not show his face. He will never cross any of our thresholds again."

"Oh, he wouldn't be such a confounded fool! I bet you a hundred to one."

"First pay me the bet you have lost."

Baron Oscar put his hand in his pocket, but before he drew out his pocket-book a happy thought struck him.

"But how if Geza and his brother second were playing off a joke? They may have concocted this story. Perhaps the truth is that at the last moment the quarrel was made up and there was no duel, and that they have both come from a luncheon where no blood, but plenty of champagne, flowed."

"If you don't believe me, then drive to Salista. My cab is at the door. Go and convince yourself."

The baron rushed off. On the staircase he met Count Edmund coming up from the ladies. He asked where Oscar was rushing in such haste.

"He doesn't believe Geza's story."

"That is just the way the ladies have treated me; they won't believe me. They say, 'If nothing has happened to Ivan, where is he?' The Countess Theudelinde sheds tears like a river; she execrates us all, and declares we have killed her hero. The cuckoo only knows which of the two ladies is the most in love with him. Up to this I thought I knew, but now I am all in the dark."

Baron Oscar returned at this moment. He didn't say a word, but took out his pocket-book and paid Count Stefan his bet. It was a very convincing answer.

"Well, how is Salista?" asked several voices together.

"He is terribly disfigured."

On this every one took out their purses and paid their lost bets; they did it with very sour faces. If only Ritter Magnet had been disfigured!

Just then Ivan was announced. The sour faces changed with marvellous rapidity into friendly smiles. He was greeted warmly; every one wanted to shake hands with him. He was the hero of the hour, but he looked tired and very serious. Count Stefan was the last to press his hand.

"I rejoice," he said, "to see you uninjured."

Two young fellows said to one another, "Old Stefan may very well rejoice; he has made a good thing of the handicap, and cleared us out jollily." But in spite of their losses, they, too, congratulated the victor.

Every one seemed pleased except, perhaps, Ivan. "I thank you all," he said, in his grave voice, "for your warm sympathy; and I thank you, count, in particular, for your cordial reception, and for the friendship which you have accorded to me. I shall always preserve a grateful remembrance of your kindness. I beg of you to bear me likewise in your recollection, for I have come now to take leave. I am returning to my home to-morrow."

The count winked with his left eye at Baron Oscar, as who should say, "Did I not tell you so?" But he spoke no word to induce Ivan to rescind his resolution. He pressed his hand warmly as he said:

"Be assured that I have a sincere esteem for you, and wherever we may meet again always consider me as an old friend. God bless you!"

Baron Oscar made much more fuss. He held Ivan with both hands on his arm.

"My dear friend, we cannot allow this. Such a good fellow as you have proved yourself to be cannot slip away from us in this manner—just at the moment, too, when you are going to be the lion of the season. You sha'n't escape; you belong to us."

Ivan laughed; gentle sarcasm, half pain, half irony, totally unmixed with bitterness, was in the laugh. Then he answered this burst of friendship:

"I thank you, comrade, for the honor you do me, but I am not fit to be Governor of Barataria; it is far better for me to be at home. I go to get my 'grison' saddled, and I ride away."

(Any one who is conversant with "Don Quixote" will remember the skit upon the island of Barataria, and the affecting meeting between the ass and his master.)

When he had finished speaking, Ivan made a deep

bow to the company and left the room. Count Stefan followed him, and, in spite of his protestations, accompanied him down the stairs to Theudelinde's door. He was much moved by Ivan's last words.

When he returned he found the entire company still in a very uncomfortable frame of mind, discussing the scene that had just happened with much annoyance.

"Who has told him the joke about the island of Barataria?" asked Baron Oscar.

Each one gave his word of honor that he had not betrayed confidence.

"Then may the devil fly away with me if I don't believe it was the abbé."

But Count Stefan shook his head. "No, my friends," he said, "believe me, no one has told Behrend anything. He is a man of acute penetration, and he has read you like a book without appearing to take notice."

Geza, however, swore that the priest had blabbed.

We swear to nothing, but think it right to mention that a few days previous the Abbé Samuel had received a letter from Vienna with the words, "What are you about? You are ruining the whole thing. That ass Behrend is bringing about a reconciliation between the countess and the old prince. Get him out of Pesth, for he is working dead against us.—FELIX."

"At all events, we have pleased my pretty cousin," remarked Count Edmund. "She wanted him to be sent about his business, and we have done it."

"Oh, is that so?" And Count Stefan smiled sardonically. "*Cherchez la femme,* as Talleyrand said. But I know the dear, capricious sex. When Ivan tells the ladies down-stairs that he is leaving, there will be a reaction, and your pretty cousin will cry out, 'Then we shall go together!'"

The others laughed incredulously; only Edmund assumed the air of Pontius Pilate.

"I should not be surprised," he said. "*Enfin*, there would be nothing disgraceful in the affair. The fellow is a gentleman; he was a soldier, and is of good birth. His land joins the Bondavara property; his income is something under two hundred thousand florins. Angela is heiress to twenty millions; but then, if our well-beloved uncle, Prince Theobald, lives another ten years and carries on as he is doing, it may result that Ivan and Angela may be on the same platform as regards their fortunes. So far as rank is in question, if the government continues to play the game they are playing with our rights and privileges, and if under the new parliamentary *régime* the peasant's coat is to ascend the tribune, then I shall ask to be *raised* to the peasantry."

The Countesses Theudelinde and Angela received Ivan in their private sitting-room—a mark of close intimacy. He came in with a constrained air; his face was pale, and the emotion he could not suppress gave softness to his usually stern expression. Theudelinde came to meet him with outstretched hands. When she drew near she took his in her clasp, and pressed his fingers warmly. Her lips trembled, and with difficulty she kept the tears which filled her eyes from coursing down her cheeks. She could not speak, but simply nodded to Ivan to take his place before a small table, upon which a splendid bouquet stood. Theudelinde sat on the sofa, Angela beside her. The young countess was simply dressed; she had not even a flower in her hair. She was grave, and hardly raised her eyes to Ivan.

It was Theudelinde who broke the rather embarrassing silence.

"We have been in terrible trouble about you," she said. "You cannot imagine what tortures of anxiety we have gone through during these two days."

Angela's eyes were on the carpet; she was included in the "we."

"I cannot forgive myself, countess, for the share I have had in causing you pain. I can only do penance for my fault, and to-morrow I am going into banishment at Bondathal."

"Ah!" Theudelinde's voice expressed surprise. "You are going to leave us? What are you going to do in Bondathal?"

"I will return to my business, which I have too long neglected."

"And do you like to live in Bondathal?"

"I am tranquil there."

"Have you relatives?"

"I have none."

"You have a household?"

"So far as I can, I do everything for myself."

"You have surely friends and acquaintances who form a pleasant circle around you?"

"I have only my workmen and my machines."

"You live there a hermit's life?"

"No, countess, for a hermit lives alone, while I have my books and my work; I am never alone."

The countess's face assumed almost a solemn expression.

"Herr von Behrend, give me your hand, and stay here."

Ivan got up, and bowed low before her. "The kind feeling which has prompted your words, as well as the honor you have done me, shall never be forgotten by me. It is a proof to me of your great goodness, and I beg of you to accept my heartfelt thanks."

"Then you will remain? How long?"

"Until to-morrow morning."

"Ah," cried the countess, with a petulant air, "when I ask you to stay!"

Her disappointment was so transparent, her annoyance so sincere, that it was impossible not to feel sorry for her. Theudelinde looked at Angela as if she expected her to come to her help; but Angela never raised her eyes, shaded by their long lashes, while her fingers plucked nervously at the petals of a marguerite, as if she were consulting that well-known oracle.

"Countess," said Ivan, still standing, and with his hand on the back of his chair, "when I answer a friendly invitation such as yours with an apparently uncivil refusal to remain, as you so kindly wish me to do, I feel that it is incumbent on me to give you my true reason for withdrawing myself from your society. I cannot say to you what I would to a mere acquaintance; I cannot make such excuses as 'that I have business at home; that I have been too long here; that I shall return soon.' To you I must confess that I go away because no inducement would prevail on me to remain, and that when I go I mean never to return. Countess, this is not my world; here I *could* not live. I have spent three months here; I have been a daily guest in the best circles; I have lived with members of the highest and most cultivated society, have studied closely their manner of life. I quite agree that these people have every right to live in what manner they choose; but I, who have been accustomed to a totally different manner of life, who have been taught to consider existence from a different point of view, to reverence the higher aims and obey its finer instincts, *I* should be acting a lie and violating my own principles were I to remain in such an atmosphere and live after such a fashion. Here, in this exalted rank, you are all solitary rings, while we in the lower order hang together as links of one chain. You are totally independent one of the other, therefore you follow each one his own inclinations. With us the pressure of life knits us more closely together, and we call egotism and generosity by different names from what you do. I am, therefore, not fit for your circle. I am ashamed to be haughty towards those upon whom you look down, and I cannot bend before those whom you delight to honor. I do not recognize the gods whom you adore, neither can I mock at *my* God, and ignore Him as you do. In this world of yours there is a malicious demon who transforms all that is good in man's nature, and who prompts him to laugh and deny every inclination to virtue. Who tells his friend or neighbor the truth to his face, and who cares for any one who is not present? Dear friends race together over hill and dale; but suppose one makes a false step and breaks his neck, good-bye to him, the dear friend is gone. Another does not break his neck in the race, but he dissipates all his fortune; those who are running with him never say to him, 'Step out of the course; you are going to the bottom.' All at once he stumbles, and his fortune and the honors of his ancestors lie tumbled in the dust. Good-bye to him; his name is struck out of the club-list; that dear friend is no more. It is true we knew yesterday and the day before yesterday that he would surely get a bad fall, but no one else knew of it, so we rode with our dear friend to the last. Now all the world is aware of his tumble in the dust, therefore we know him no more. If any one wishes to go on his own way, and live a rational life to himself, oh, then, he is a coward, a miser, a carpet knight! And how do the women fare in this world of yours? What about domestic life, and the sweet joys of the home? What tragedies are enacted inside those splendid mansions, and outside what fun is made of them by friends and acquaintances! What refinement in sin! what idolatry of false joys! And when these are over, what *ennui* of life, what endless weariness! No, countess, this life is not for me. I should be poisoned in such an atmosphere. You can bear it, you grace it by your presence; but for me, I should go mad were I to remain. Therefore I go, and all that is now left is to ask your forgiveness for my bold words. I acknowledge my indiscretion; I have spoken bitterly of society, and yet I stand on its parquet floor. I have been ungrateful; I have given expression to my antipathies in the presence of those who have shown tolerance towards my faults and my awkward manners; who have accompanied me to the door of the circle where I have often played a ridiculous part, and, notwithstanding, have never been laughed at before my face. But, countess, the words I have uttered I have felt, so to speak, constrained by your goodness to say. You have, with extraordinary kindness, asked me to remain, and I would prove to you that I am forced to leave by a power stronger than myself."

During Ivan's rather lengthy address Countess Theudelinde had risen to her feet. Her eyes began to light up, her face to wear a glorified expression, her lips to move as if she repeated each word he said; and when he had spoken the concluding sentence she seized both his hands, while she stammered out:

"You speak the truth—the truth—nothing but the truth; you speak as I spoke forty years ago, when *I* left the world as you are doing now! The world is ever the same; it does not change." Here she wrung her hands passionately. "Go home," she sobbed out; "go back to your solitude, hide yourself under the earth, conceal yourself in your mine, God will be with you wherever you are—everywhere! God bless you! God bless you!"

She did not remark that Angela had also risen from her seat, and as Ivan took his leave she made a step forward, and said, in a firm, decided voice:

"If you go away, you do not go alone, for I shall go with you." Her whole face glowed as she spoke these words.

Ivan was master of the situation. Standing upon this giddy height, he did not for that reason lose his balance. With wonderful presence of mind he answered the excited girl:

"You will do well, countess. To-morrow is your grandfather's birthday, and early to-morrow you can be with him. He is ready to clasp you in his arms."

Angela grew white as a marble statue. She sank back in her armchair; the leaves she had plucked from the flower lay scattered at her feet. Ivan bowed to her respectfully, kissed the hand of Countess Theudelinde, and quitted the room.

Ah, there are men who never forget their first and only love!

Not long after Ivan had left, Count Edmund dropped in to see the ladies. He appeared to come by accident, but he was dying with curiosity. Countess Angela was more amiable than usual. When he was leaving, she said to her cousin:

"Go to Salista, and tell him that I have inquired for him."

Count Edmund was courtier enough to conceal the

astonishment he most certainly felt, but as he went down the stairs he began to hum Figaro's song from the *Barber of Seville*:

> "The falseness of women
> One never can know,
> One never can know!"

Countess Angela wrote that same evening to her grandfather. Ivan was right in saying the next day was his birthday, and this was her birthday greeting:

"I am not coming home. Adieu."

For two days every one in Pesth spoke of Ivan and his duel with Salista; the third day he was forgotten. Good-bye to him!

CHAPTER XVII

THE LAST REHEARSAL

On the morning of his birthday Prince Theobald received a letter. It was from his only grandchild, and ended with the word "Adieu."

The prince's birthday had been always a festival. From Angela's childhood up to the last anniversary of the day she had each year given him a remembrance. On this day it had been a bitter gift.

Among his treasures the old man kept a particular casket, handsomely fitted with gold mountings, in which he preserved these birthday offerings. There was the wreath Angela had given him when she was nine years old; the scrawl she had written in her childish handwriting on a sheet of Bristol-board; the bit of embroidery, worked in pearls and gold, which later she had done for him with her own hand. To these gifts the prince, with a deep sigh, added her last letter, with its cold farewell.

Prince Theobald was easily moved to anger, while his heart was sensitive to affection. When he reflected calmly he found he had every right to exact obedience from his granddaughter. Angela owed a duty to him, to his position, to the princely house from which she sprang. If, indeed, her heart stood in the way of agreeing to his wishes, one might, perhaps, excuse her; but Angela, he knew, loved no one. Why, therefore, should she seek to defy him for a mere foolish whim? Prince Theobald went to Eveline's last rehearsal with his mind in a tumult of annoyance and excitement; his blood circulated wildly. He could send a strange answer to her farewell. Yes, and he would!

When he reached Eveline's house the servant admitted him as a favored *habitué*, without a word, and left him in the drawing-room while he went to announce him to his mistress. The prince looked round him; it was the room where Eveline usually gave her representations. The rose-colored curtains were drawn, one corner was filled with greenhouse exotics, the air was perfumed with the scent of the flowers. In another corner two turtle-doves cooed melodiously, while from behind a little *bosquet* a nightingale sang its soft stave of love, sorrow, and triumph. One could hardly imagine one's self in an ordinary drawing-room; it was more like the throne of a nymph, or fairy, in the depth of a wood.

The prince seated himself upon a sofa, and, taking up an album which lay upon the table, he turned over the leaves. It was a collection of photographs of Eveline in her different parts. He went through it from cover to cover, examining each tempting and seductive portrait carefully, and as he did so there rose before his memory the casket in which Angela's letters and embroidery were preserved. His thoughts were so absorbed in these recollections that, with a start, he found himself at the last page in the book before him. He roused himself to look at the beautiful figure in a common stuff frock. How captivating, how simple, how lovely!

The nightingale sang, the doves cooed, the air grew heavy with the scent of the pomegranates. The prince wondered in what form of enchantment would his hostess appear. And now there fell on his ear, coming from a distance, a forgotten tune. Once he had heard it, long ago; but the air he remembered. It moved him strangely. It was a simple volkslied, the same with which the nurse was wont to rock the cradle of Angela when she was a baby—a Slav tune. The text was unknown to him.

After a few minutes the song ceased, the door of Eveline's dressing-room opened, and she came in—and how? In what new and captivating costume did she appear?

She wore a simple white-and-black dress of crape cloth; her hair was smoothly combed back from her young face, and hung down in a long plait; a white lace collar was round her throat.

Softly, modestly, and yet with the confidence of a child, she drew near to the prince, and when she was close to him she handed him a little sachet of white satin, upon which was embroidered the kneeling figure of a child. Then raising her eyes, full of tears, to his face, she said, in a low voice, which trembled with emotion:

"My lord, will you accept this little birthday gift from me? May Heaven preserve your days."

This scene was so devoid of all acting, it was so full of feeling and sincerity, that Prince Theobald, thrown off his guard, forgot himself, and, instead of the formal "madame," said:

"My child—"

At these words the young girl, sobbing wildly, threw herself into his arms.

"Oh, prince," she cried, "do not recall those words; call me your child. There is on this earth no creature more desolate, more unhappy than I am."

Prince Theobald laid his hand kindly upon the fair

head of the sobbing girl and kissed her gently on the forehead.

"Be it so," he said. "Look up and smile, Eveline. I am in earnest. You are almost a child, and you shall be one to me. I will be your father—no, your grandfather. Fathers love their children sometimes, but not always; but grandfathers never fail in loving their grandchildren. You shall be my little granddaughter. When I am sad you will cheer me with your gay chatter; you will read or sing to me when I cannot sleep; you will care for me and nurse me when I am ill. I shall adopt you as my child. I shall take care of you, and provide you with all that you want. In return you will obey me; you will listen to me; you will bear with an old man's whims and his petulant temper; you will try and please me. I promise you that you shall be treated well. You shall be mistress over all that I have; you shall have everything suitable to the position of my daughter; but I must exact the obedience of a child."

Eveline answered by kissing her benefactor's hand.

"Are you pleased at my proposal? Do you think you will be happy?"

Eveline laughed in childish delight. She danced about the room in her joy, and fell down at the prince's feet, crying out:

"Oh, my dear, dear grandpapa!"

Prince Theobald threw himself back on the sofa and burst into a harsh, bitter laugh.

Eveline drew back, hurt and frightened by the horrid discord in the laugh.

"I am not laughing at you, my dear," said the prince, kindly. "Come, my pretty granddaughter, and sit beside me." (He had laughed at the answer he could now make to Angela's farewell.) He stroked Eveline's hair tenderly. "Now we must talk seriously. Listen to what I have to say, for my words are commands. In *our* family there is only one master, whom all obey. First of all, there is your husband to be considered. It seems to me he takes the responsibilities of his position lightly. Still, he must give his consent to my adoption of you. I don't apprehend, however, any difficulty in obtaining it; you may leave that to me. After that you will take up your residence in my palace in the Maximilian Strasse. It shall be yours on one condition—that you receive no visitors without previously consulting me. Kaulmann is included in this condition. You must have no intercourse with him, except on matters of business. Will it pain you to be separated from him?"

"I could not be pained by that. We have always lived apart."

The prince pressed her hand kindly. "Poor child!" he said. "Your husband is a scoundrel. He has treated you as one of his speculations, and has attained his end. One thing, however, you receive from him—his name. He cannot take that from you. By-and-by you will learn what an inestimable advantage it is to a woman to bear her husband's name. It is a passport; but I do not think Kaulmann meant it in that light. Well, let us talk no more of him, but of your future. I shall procure for you an engagement at the Opera-house. You must have a certain position before the world, by whom the secret tie between us would not be understood. The title of actress is like the mantle of a queen; it gives you the *entrée* to the *salons* of a certain artistic world. Your future shall be my care. You have talent; if you study you will succeed. You must rise to the head of your profession, so that when I die you will be able to support yourself."

"If I could only get over my stage-fright!" said Eveline, sadly.

"You will when you get accustomed to the footlights. You will learn by experience that in this world, and especially on the stage, every one is taken at his own valuation. Any one who makes little of himself goes cheap. Above all, you must be most careful how you choose your friends. This is important, and on this point you must allow me to judge for you. If you feel a preference for any one person you must tell me with frankness, and I shall know whether it will be a safe friendship for you."

"Oh, prince," cried Eveline, "I shall be guided in all things by you!"

"My child, do not promise too much. Engagements made in a moment of enthusiasm or sentiment are speedily forgotten; but there is one promise I would have from you. There is one man whom you must give your word to me that you will *never* receive—that you will never break the seal of a letter that comes from him; that you will never accept a present from him, never take up a bouquet he may throw you, never notice his applause. This man must not exist for you; you must take as little notice of him as if he were a crossing-sweeper. This man is Prince Waldemar."

"Oh, sir, I already hate him. I shudder at his approach."

"I am glad to hear it. He deserves every good woman's hatred; but he is rich, young, handsome. He raves of you. Women are flattered by the love of such as he; and circumstances may arise to alter your ideas. Wealth has a wonderful attraction, and poverty is a great temptation. The time must come when I shall no longer be here. You must swear to me that when I am dead or removed from you you will keep your oath to accept nothing from Prince Waldemar."

"I swear it to you by what is most sacred—the memory of my dead mother."

"Now allow me to kiss your forehead. I am going to Kaulmann to make the necessary arrangements. I thank you for your remembrance of my birthday. Your little present has made me rich. I came here in a very perturbed state of mind; I go away with a tranquil heart. I shall always be grateful to you. God bless you!"

Some days later Eveline removed to Prince Theobald's palace in the Maximilian Strasse, where she was surrounded by every splendor and luxury.

The world supposed—and we must acknowledge there was reason for the supposition—that Kaulmann's wife was the Prince's mistress. The prince imagined that he would frighten the Countess Angela and bring her to reason, and Eveline thought she was fulfilling her duty as a wife when she obeyed her contemptible husband by sacrificing her good name to further his ambitious schemes.

At this time, and as the result of Eveline's obedience, the Joint-Stock Mining Company received the assent of Prince Theobald Bondavary to the contract already signed by his sister, Countess Theudelinde.

And in this manner the Bondavara property passed away from the last two possessors. If Countess Angela had followed Ivan Behrend's advice this would not have happened, and the property would have been hers.

Why was the Countess Angela so obstinate? Why

did she behave so foolishly as regarded her own interests, so ungratefully towards her kind grandfather? A word must be said in her defence. This Prince Sondersheim, whom Prince Theobald wished his granddaughter to take as her husband, was the same Prince Waldemar of whom mention has already been made. Prince Theobald knew his character well. We have heard what he said to Eveline. The world had the worst opinion of him, and Angela knew what the world thought of her future husband.

Was it any wonder she refused to give herself to such a man? Could she act otherwise than she did? Women are the best judges on this point. Men cannot witness against themselves.

CHAPTER XVIII

FINANCIAL WISDOM

The Bondavara Joint-Stock Company was about to issue its prospectus; the speculation had been advertised largely, and now it only waited the necessary capital of ten millions to start the railway which was to put the finest coal-mines in the kingdom within the reach of the markets of the great cities. The speculation did not, however, attract the public. Who knows about the value of the mine? said one. Who believes what the papers say? We all know that trick. The gudgeons held off, and did not rise to the bait offered.

One day Felix Kaulmann brought one of the directors to see Ivan Behrend, and while these two were in conversation he noticed, lying on the table, a piece of coal from the Bondavara mine, upon which was distinctly visible the outline of a plant about the size of a finger.

"Is this the impression of an antediluvian bird's claw?" he asked.

"No," returned Ivan; "it is a petrified plant."

"Ah, I am making a collection of petrifactions."

"Then take that to add to it," said Ivan, carelessly.

Felix carried away the piece of coal in his pocket.

Shortly before the prospectus was issued there appeared in one of the best-known scientific journals an illustration and article descriptive of the petrified *bird's foot* which had been found in the Bondavara mine. The article was signed "Doctor Felicius."

All the *savants* were excited. "We must see this impression!" they cried.

The discoverer had given to the creature, whose footmark had remained unalterably impressed upon the tender (!) coal, the learned name of *Protornithos lithanthracoides*.

"Ho, ho!" exclaimed the united bodies of geologists, physiologists, professors, philosophers, artisans, and artesian-well borers, "that is indeed a long word!"

One set of learned men declared the thing to be possible, another denied its possibility.

And why was it not possible? Because at the period of coal-formations neither birds nor any one of the mammalia could exist, or did exist, in the bowels of the earth. There we find only traces of plants, of mussels, of fish sometimes.

And why is it credible? Because in these days we make discoveries every day. Humboldt declared that in the antediluvian world no apes had ever lived, for the reason that the fossil of an ape had never been found. Since then one fossil ape has been discovered in England, in France three of the Ourang species.

By degrees the strife raged in every newspaper; it was taken up in English, French, German, and American publications. At last it was proposed that the matter should be referred to a commission of five well-known professors, to whom the petrifaction should be submitted, and who should decide the question in dispute. Doctor Felicius offered one thousand ducats to the one who would prove that his bird's claw was not a bird's claw.

The tribunal of the five learned judges examined the

petrifaction with microscopical attention, and after a long sitting brought in a unanimous verdict that the impression was not made by the claw of a Protornithos, but was that of a leaf belonging to the plant *Annularia longefolia;* in fact, there could be no question of the bird species, as the specimen of coal produced was not brown coal, but the *purest* black, in which coal formation it was not possible for even a bird to exist.

Doctor Felix Kaulmann quietly paid the thousand ducats, and thanked the whole republic of professors for the service they had rendered to the Bondavara coal; such an advertisement could not have been obtained at an expense of forty thousand ducats. Let people say that the Protornithos was a humbug—who cares? The reputation of the Bondavara coal was firmly established on the best scientific grounds.

The period had now arrived when the undertaking should be floated at the exchange. This, perhaps, is the greatest science on earth. The stock-exchange has its good and its bad days. Sometimes it is full of electricity, the sheep frolic in the meadow; at other times they hang their heads and will not touch the beautiful grass. Sometimes they come bleating to the shepherd to beg that he will shear them, for their wool presses too heavily on them; another day they butt their heads together and will not listen to their leader. Again, and no one can tell why, when the bell-wether begins to run, all the rest of the flock run after him; neither the shepherd nor his dog can stop them. The science lies in knowing when there is good weather on the stock-exchange. On a favorable day men are in such excellent humor—there is so much gold in every pocket, everything goes well—that even a company for the excavation and alienation of the icebergs would find bidders.

On a bad day the best and safest speculation would get not a single offer.

It was on one of the good days that the Bondavara Coal Company made its *début* at the Vienna Stock-exchange. It caught on, and by the day on which the subscriptions should be paid into the Bank of Kaulmann came round it was necessary to have a military cordon drawn across the street, to allow the stream of people to pass through in any sort of order. The subscribers had, in fact, collected before the doors early in the morning; those who were strong trusted to their own strength to make way for themselves by elbow force. In the crush battered hats and torn coats were matters of small consequence; verbal insults and personal injuries, such as pushing and squeezing, were treated as nothing. The windows of the bank which looked on the street were burst open, and some excited individual called out:

"I subscribe ten thousand, a hundred thousand, a million!"

When at last six o'clock struck, and the doors of the bank were closed, a stentorian voice called from the balcony to the crowd below:

"The subscription is closed!"

What a disappointment for those who had not been able to get their money in in time! They went away dejected men.

The Bondavara mine had indeed "caught on." Instead of ten millions, eight hundred and twenty thousand millions had been subscribed. Did the subscribers really possess all that money? Certainly not. Each one deposited the tenth portion of the sum subscribed as a guarantee, and this only on paper; actual money the company did not as yet touch. Those who made part of the vast crowd, who tore the coats from one another's backs, were not blessed with a superfluity of money, neither had they the slightest interest in the production of coal, but to-day it is fine weather on the exchange; the Bondavara Company's bonds stand at par. Every one wanted to make this small profit; that done they care no more for the bonds or the company.

It is, however, a fact that trees do not grow in heaven. Prince Waldemar was at the head of the countermine, and he was one of the cleverest, most astute men "on 'change."

To understand the business the reader should be himself a speculator. It is carried on something after this fashion. Those who want to buy in are oftentimes men of straw; they merely want shares to sell them at once to the first bidder. As a natural consequence, this lowers the value; there is a fall, sometimes a total collapse. If the investment is a sound one it recovers vitality, and the shares go up again. There is, however, a way to guard against this trick. Almost every company has a syndicate, whose office is to ascertain whether the applicants for shares are men of straw or not. Pending the inquiry, the time is made use of to employ certain agents, to whom a free gift is made of, say, five hundred shares. These men immediately set up a tremendous uproar; they drive up the shares, they tear the certificates out of one another's hands, screaming out the high rate at which they are buying. But the general market sees no shares pass; the experienced ones know that this is all a well-acted farce, and that any one who has ready-money need only go to the fountain-head and buy as many shares as he wants at par. On the other hand, the bears are waiting their time to rush in and cause such a depreciation as will

17

run down the shares to almost nothing. When they have got them at this low figure they may allow them to rise again.

The only one who loses in this cruel game is the small capitalist, who has ventured, poor soul, on ice, and who has sacrificed his little all at the shrine of the golden calf, taken his carefully hoarded store, his hard-earned salary out of his drawer, and has cast it upon these unprofitable waters, tempted by the tales of high interest, and the like. All of a sudden the bears have rushed in, the mine has exploded, his hopes are blown into air, vanished like a dream; his shares are so much waste-paper. He goes home certainly a sadder if not a wiser man. Well for him if he is not a begger. This is how they manage matters on the stock-exchange.

CHAPTER XIX

FILTHY LUCRE

In the town of X—— there is a street called Greek Street. It is a circle, or crescent, of pretty houses, which at one time were erected and peopled by Greek merchants. In the middle of the street stands a church with a façade of marble and a splendid gilt tower, whose bells are the most tuneful in the whole town. It is said that when those bells were cast the Greeks threw, with both hands, silver coins into the liquid metal.

Old Francis Csanta was now the last of the race. Once he had been a jovial fellow, a careless, free liver, towards ladies a gallant cavalier, among men a desperate gambler. With years he became silent, moody, miserly, avoided the company of his fellow man or woman, and was a hater of music and all pleasure. The more he indulged in solitude the worse his peculiarities grew. So soon as one of his former friends, or relations, or boon companions died, he bought the house in which they had lived. By degrees the whole street belonged to him; only one house remained, and that next door to his own. This had been occupied by a connection of his who had left one daughter. Strangely enough, she had not followed the general custom of celibacy, but had married, and was the wife of a music-master, who enjoyed the Magyar name of Belenyi. This pair had in due course a son born to them, to whom they gave the name of Arpad.

This vexed old Csanta sorely. Why should the last remaining Greek girl have married—above all, married a music-master? Why should there be a son? Why should that son be baptized Arpad? And why should these annoying circumstances take place under his very nose? The house, too, was an offence; the only house in the street that did not belong to him. The church was his; no one went in except himself; the clergyman said mass for him only. He was the patron, the congregation, the curator, the vestryman, the supporter; he filled every office; he was everything. When he was dead the church would be closed, the grass would grow upon the threshold.

The generation in the next house showed no sign of dying; the boy Arpad was as lively as an eel. At the age of five he threw his ball over the roof, and it fell into the old Greek's garden, who there and then confiscated it. The lad gave him much more annoyance.

About this time evil days came to the country. The Hungarians and the Austrians killed one another. The reason of their so doing is hard to find. Historians of the present day say that it was all child's play, and that the cause lay in the refusal of the Hungarian sepoys—who are Mohammedans—to bite off cartridges which had been prepared with the fat of swine—the German method. Or did this happen in India? Nowadays it is all uncertain; mostly what is known about it comes through the songs of the poets, and who believes them?

What interests us in this old story is that it has to do with Ivan Behrend, and how he came to dwell in the Belenyi's house. It so happened that he was one of the regiment who repulsed an assault on the town, and in consequence he was billeted on the music-master and his wife. He was well liked. He was young then, and had good spirits. One day the poor musician, coming home through the streets, was struck by a shell, and brought into his house dead. Such things happen occasionally in time of war. Little Arpad was an orphan, and then it was that Ivan adopted him as his son. A short time after this Ivan laid down his arms and retired into private life. Why he did so, and where he went, is quite immaterial. Before he went Ivan gave the widow Belenyi all the gold he had with him, so that with this money Arpad's musical education might be paid for. He did not care for the gold, and he could not have employed it better. If he had taken it with him, who knows into what worthless hands it would have fallen?

He hadn't been long gone when a Hungarian government official stood in the market-place of X——, and, to the accompaniment of much drumming, gave out the government order that all German bank-notes should be brought to the great square, and there made into a funeral-pile and set fire to. Any one refusing to obey this order should be dealt with accordingly. Every one knew what this meant, and all who didn't wish *to be dealt with* hastened to bring their bank-notes, which were then and there burned.

The widow Belenyi had her little savings, a few hundred gulden. What should she do? It went hard with her to see her money thrown into the fire. She went to her rich neighbor and besought him to help her, and to change her money into Hungarian bank-notes. The old Greek at first refused to listen, but by-and-by he relented and did as she wished. He even did more, for after a week had passed he came to her and said:

"I will no longer keep the money which your father

lent to me at the rate of six per cent. Here it is for you—ten thousand gulden; take it, and make what you can of it." As he spoke he paid her the whole sum in Hungarian bank-notes.

A week later another commandant arrived in the town; this one was a German. The next morning more drumming was heard in the market-place, and the order was given that all who possessed Hungarian bank-notes must give them up to have them burned. Those who refused would be shot or hanged.

The poor widow ran weeping to her neighbor, and asked what she should do. The whole sum he had given her lay in her drawer untouched. If it were taken from her she and her child must beg or starve. Why had he given her this money? Why had he changed her German notes if he knew that this was going to happen?

"How could I know it?" shrieked Csanta; and, still screaming, he went on to lament over himself. "If you are beggared, so am I—ten thousand times more beggared than any one. I haven't a copper coin in the house. I don't know how I can pay even for a bit of meat. I shall have a hundred thousand bank-notes burned. I am ruined! I am a beggar!"

And he fell to cursing both Germans and Hungarians, until the widow Belenyi implored him not to shriek so loud, else he would be heard, and, God help us all! hanged.

"Let them hear, then! Let them hang me! I don't care. I shall go to the market-place and tell them to their faces they are robbers, and if they won't hang me I'll hang myself. I am only considering whether I shall suspend myself from the pump-handle or from the steeple of the tower."

The widow besought him, for Heaven's sake, not to do such a terrible deed.

"And what's to become of me? Am I to go round with a hat and beg for a penny? Here, these are my last halfpence."

He drew a few coins from his pocket, and began to weep piteously; his tears flowed in streams. The poor woman tried her best to console him. She begged him not to despair; the butcher and the baker knew him, and would trust him. She was tempted to offer him a piece of twenty groschen.

"Oh, you will soon see!" sobbed the old man. "Come to-morrow morning early, and you will see me hanging from a hook in the passage. I couldn't survive this!"

What could she do? The poor soul carried her Hungarian bank-notes to the commander, and saw them consumed in the market-place.

Oh, it was a laughable joke! To this day when people talk of it their eyes fill with tears.

For the widow, and many like her, there followed months and years of grinding poverty. She had lost all the capital saved for her by her father; there remained nothing but the house. The front rooms she let as a shop, and in the back she lived and eked out her miserable income as best she could.

For a long time she looked with a frightened gaze at her neighbor's passage, expecting to see the old man hanging from an iron hook; but she was spared this sight. The old man had no notion of ending his days. He had certainly lost a few thousand gulden, but these were only the chaff; the corn was safe. He had a secret hiding-place to which he could have access by a secret passage underneath his house; the cellar was, in fact, underneath the water. A mason from Vienna had built it for him, and the people of the town knew nothing of it. The cellar was full of casks, and every cask was full of silver; the old man's cellar concealed a treasure. By means of secret machinery constructed in his bedroom the owner was able by touching a spring to open a sluice concealed in the bed of the stream, and thus in a few minutes to submerge his cave. No robber could have penetrated there. All the gold and silver pieces which came into Csanta's hand found their way to this subterranean hiding-place, and never saw the light of day again.

Meantime his neighbor, the widow, suffered the grip of poverty; she sewed her fingers to the bone to keep things together and to earn their daily bread. The gold pieces Ivan had given she wouldn't have touched even to save herself from starvation; they were used for the purpose for which he gave them—for Arpad's musical education, and musical instruction was so dear. The child was a genius.

But living grew dearer, work harder to get. The widow was forced to get a loan upon the house; she asked her neighbor, and he gave it readily. The loan grew and grew until it reached a good sum of money, and then Csanta asked it back. Frau Belenyi was not able to refund, and the old man instituted proceedings, and as he was the only mortgagee he got it for one-quarter its real value. The amount over and above the debt and the costs were handed to the widow, and there was nothing left but to leave. Madame Belenyi took her son to Vienna, to begin in earnest his artistic education.

The old Greek possessed the whole street; there was no one left to annoy him in his immediate neighborhood; he suffered neither from children, dogs, or birds.

And his treasure increased more and more. The casks which filled the cellar that lay beneath the water were filled to overflowing, and the contents were always silver.

One day Csanta received a visit. It was an old acquaintance, a banker from Vienna, whose father had been a friend of the old man's, and at whose counting-house he could always get exchange for his bank-notes and other little accommodations. The visitor was Felix Kaulmann.

"To what circumstance do I owe the honor? What good news do you bring me?"

"My worthy friend, I shall not make any preamble. Time is precious to you, as it is to me, and therefore I go straight to the point. By the authorization of the Prince of Bondavara I have been placed at the head of a joint-stock company, who have just started some gigantic coal-works, whose capital has risen from ten millions to eight hundred and twenty millions."

"That is eighty-two millions more than you would require."

"The money is the least part. What I stand in need of is well-known men for the administration, for the result of the whole undertaking rests upon the zeal, the capability, the intelligence of the governing body."

"Well, such men are not difficult to find if there is a prospect of a good dividend."

"The dividend is not to be despised. The bonus to each member of the administration will be, yearly, five or six thousand gulden."

"Really? What a nice income!—a stroke of luck for those who are chosen."

"Well, I have chosen you for a member, my worthy friend."

"An honor, a great honor for me; but how much must I put down before I am admitted?"

"Neither before nor after shall you be asked to put down anything. The only condition is that every member of the administration must hold one thousand shares."

"That means paying in a deal of money, my young friend."

"I didn't say a word of paying in; I only spoke of holding."

"But, my young friend, although I am only a provincial merchant in a small way, I know that, so far as money is in question, to subscribe is another word for payment."

"With this exception—if both subscriptions equalize one another. Ah, I see you do not like even a question of subscribing. Well, listen. We will suppose that you take one thousand shares in my coal company, and at the same time I give you an undertaking to take over one thousand shares at par from *you;* in this way we are even, and neither of us loses a shilling."

"Hem! But what is the necessity for such a joke?"

"I will be frank with you. The world has its eyes fixed upon the actions of important men; if these stir in any affair, the others stir likewise. If on 'change it is known that you, my worthy friend, have bought a thousand shares, a hundred small speculators will immediately invest in shares. In this way you secure to yourself a sinecure which will give you five or six thousand gulden, and I will secure for my undertaking a splendid future. Now, have I not spoken the truth?"

"H'm! I will consider the affair. Meet me to-morrow at the restaurant."

Csanta spent all the morning in the restaurant; he

listened to all that was said of the Bondavara speculation, and came to the conclusion that he would risk nothing, since all danger was covered by Kaulmann's bond. When Felix arrived he had made up his mind.

"Good! I shall draw the shares; but none of them shall hang round my neck, for I don't like paper. Paper is only paper, and silver is always silver."

"Don't be afraid, my friend; I shall retain all shares for myself. I deposit the caution for you, and I pay the instalments."

Felix completely satisfied the old Greek as to his upright intentions in the matter of the shares, and left in his hands the undertaking in which he pledged himself to take them over at par.

Now began the manœuvre behind the scenes. The agents, the makers of books, the brokers rushed in; the Bondavara shares rose rapidly. The syndicate had, all this time, never given a share into any one's hand. The bears had not yet begun to dance. Herr Csanta had become a student of the newspapers. True, his eyes never left one column, but that contained for him the tree of all knowledge; it spoke golden truth. With amazement he read how every day the value of the Bondavara shares increased. The profit grew higher and higher; it went up in leaps and bounds; sixteen, eighteen, at last twenty gulden over par. Those who had put down two hundred thousand gulden had won in two weeks twenty thousand gulden. A splendid speculation, indeed, in less than a fortnight to make a fortune! Compare the case of an honest, hard-working usurer like himself. What difficulties he had to go through to extract twenty per cent. out of his miserable clients! The work was hardly worth the gain; the fatigue of trapping some silly idiot, the odium and hatred incurred by exacting his rights from some miserable beggar with a family, or taking the pillow from under the head of a dying man; these things go against the grain, but they must be done if you want to fill your cellar with silver coins. And here a wretched, good-for-nothing speculator, by merely a stroke of the pen, makes in two short weeks a fortune. Luck is not evenly meted out to mortals.

The time had come when Felix Kaulmann could demand from Csanta the thousand shares upon which he could now make a profit of twenty thousand gulden. No honest man could allow such an iniquitous robbery of his rights, or, at least, not without making a struggle. It is only a fool who allows himself to be made a tool of. A man may steal for himself; to rob the widow and the orphan to fill another man's purse, that is wicked and immoral.

When Felix Kaulmann came again to the town of X——, the old Greek received him with great ceremony and seeming cordiality.

"I hope you bring good news, my dear young friend," he said, clasping Kaulmann's hand in his.

"I have come about that little business of the shares," returned Felix, with the air of a man of business. "You remember our agreement?"

"What shares do you mean? Oh, the Bondavara! Is it pressing?"

"Yes, for the first instalment of interest is now due; two gulden each bond, which, as the shares are in my name, will make an addition to my savings."

"Oh, so you intend to call in the shares?"

"But that was our agreement."

"And if I do not wish to surrender more than five hundred?"

Kaulmann drew in his lips. "Well, I suppose I should be content."

"And if I do not wish to surrender any of the shares?"

Kaulmann looked at him uneasily. "Sir," he said, "I thought I was dealing with an honest man. Besides, you forget I gave you a written agreement."

"My friend, my good young friend, that is true. You gave me a written agreement signed with your name, which covenanted that you were obliged to take these shares from me at par; but I gave you no signed document, and there is nothing that can force me to hand you over these shares. There you have the whole thing in a nutshell."

"But, my good sir," repeated the banker, taking hold of the lapels of the old Greek's coat, "listen to me. Don't you know that it is one of the laws in the Chamber of Commerce that there is no need of written indenture? If I take shares from you I have only to make a note in my pocket-book. Surely you know that this is the law on 'change?"

"What do I know of the laws they make there? I never set my foot in the place."

Kaulmann made an effort to laugh. "I must confess I have never been so sold by any one. I have found my master. Will you give me none of the shares?"

"Not half a one."

"Very good. Then you must count out the sum-total agreed upon."

"Certainly. I shall pay down the money."

"I mean the whole sum. Do you understand?"

"Undoubtedly. Don't be afraid; the money is ready; this house is bail for more than that amount. If needs be I can pay you in gold, if needs be in silver."

"Well," cried Kaulmann, bringing his clinched fist

down on the table, "I would never have believed that in this little town I should have been so sold."

Csanta suspected that were he to fail in paying his first instalment his shares might be annulled. He therefore lost no time in placing the first thirty-five per cent. into the bank. But this was not an easy task. To transport seventy thousand silver gulden to Vienna would necessitate a conveyance, and not only a conveyance, but an escort of gendarmes, and this paraphernalia would make people stare. Well, let them stare!

When the old man descended into his cellar and looked at the casks which contained the necessary sum, his heart beat, his limbs trembled. These casks contained the treasure he had garnered up ; his solid capital. It was foolish, he knew, still he could not help tears coming to his eyes as he chose seven casks from the twenty which should be the first to go. He wept as he spoke to these children of his heart.

"You shall have no cause to reproach me, you who remain here," he said ; "those that are now leaving you shall soon return. They are going on a safe journey, not on a wild, venturous sea, where there would be danger of shipwreck, but on a safe railroad, to increase and multiply. Once I have the shares in my hand, they shall not stay a night in my possession. I shall sell them at once, and get back my silver. The profits, too, I shall change into silver. Instead of seven casks I shall return with nine."

In this way did the old Greek miser comfort himself for the temporary loss of his silver pieces. He counted them that night when the day's work was done, and then set about arranging the transport of his treasure to Vienna.

The day before Csanta had decided upon this step the "bears" had begun to explode their mine. It was, however, only a trial; they wanted merely to show their teeth. Specie was in demand; if silver goes up, paper securities fall. The seven casks from Csanta's cellar arrived opportunely. Two wagons laden with leaden casks, and guarded by gendarmes with drawn sabres as they went slowly through the streets, attracted the attention of passers-by. When it came to be known that these casks were full of silver, and that all this silver was to be paid as the first instalment of some Bondavara shares, there was considerable excitement. Peru and Brazil were opening their floodgates. The firm of Kaulmann very naturally made as much as possible of the event, as being a feather in their commercial cap. The delivery arrived, as it happened, during the absence of the chief cashier, which involved an immense amount of running hither and thither in search of him, as it was necessary Csanta should receive his receipt. In the afternoon the shares were handed over and the silver was counted. All this made much stir and business in the Kaulmann Bank. Kaulmann intrusted the conduct of the affair to his most capable clerk. He instructed him how to act in regard to the matter, and added that if the old Greek gave him a gratuity, he was to kiss his hand, and to place himself altogether at his service. This man's name was Spitzhase.

Later in the day Spitzhase brought Csanta his account, regularly drawn up, together with the shares, and begged to inform his excellency " that he had brought seven hundred gulden more than was necessary, for the reason that since yesterday silver had risen one per cent."

" H'm !" thought Csanta, " this is an honest fellow; I

shall give him a gratuity." And he gave him a bank-note of twenty gulden.

Spitzhase overpowered him with thanks; then took his hand, and kissed it.

"H'm!" thought Csanta, "I have given him too much; perhaps five gulden would have been sufficient." Aloud, he said:

"I made a mistake. Give me that note back; I will give you another." And he gave him a bank-note of the value of five gulden.

Spitzhase thanked him warmly, and kissed his hand.

"H'm! this is really a good fellow — quite after my heart. Give me back those five gulden; here is another note. I made a mistake." And he handed him a note of fifty gulden.

Spitzhase kissed both his hands, and showered blessings upon him. Csanta was now convinced that he had made this man his friend for life.

"If I had brought the silver to-morrow, I should have got more," he said, reflectively.

"No, you may believe me, to-day was the right moment; to-morrow silver will fall two per cent."

"How do you know?"

"Oh, I am acquainted with the weather on the stock-exchange."

"You are? Then why don't you speculate if you know so well the ins and outs?"

"Because one must have money, and I have none. I can only dabble in trifling matters."

"Are you well known on 'change?"

"I spend all my time there, except when I am asleep."

"Then take me to the stock-exchange. I should like to look about me."

Csanta meant, as soon as he could find a suitable purchaser, to sell his Bondavara shares.

"One can go in the evening?" he asked, as they went along.

"That is the most lively time, particularly on a day like this."

Csanta was now introduced into the Temple of Mammon. Even outside the door he could hear a strange noise and tumult of voices, and as he stepped inside his head almost reeled at the strange spectacle. The large hall was stuffed full of men, who circulated in a narrow circle. Each one spoke, or rather shrieked, as if all were quarrelling. They gesticulated with their hands, holding up pieces of paper in the air, making signs and figures on their fingers, and screaming out names and making offers until the noise was deafening.

Spitzhase, who was perfectly at home, led Csanta through the throng. The old merchant was indignant at the manner in which he was pushed and driven about, no one even begging pardon for his rudeness. He would have liked to know what was meant by the words so constantly repeated, "I give!" "I take!" His attention, however, was at once riveted by another word which seemed to be in every man's mouth, and which gradually became plainer: "Puntafar! Puntafar!" It dawned upon him that it must be Bondavar. He stopped and timidly asked one of those who were shrieking, "Who wants 'Puntafar'? What is the price at which the Bondavara shares are selling?"

"Thirty over par."

Csanta's eyes blazed. "It is impossible; it cannot be!" he said. "Yesterday they were at twenty."

"That was yesterday. To-day they are thirty. If you want to buy to-morrow you will have to pay thirty-five. The whole world is buying the scrip. A rich nabob from India has brought all his silver here, and bought Puntafar shares. The Dey of Morocco and a Russian prince, who both own silver mines, have each ordered ten thousand shares. Even the little folk, who have only a few hundreds, are tearing the shares out of one another's hands; they won't have anything but Puntafar. What will you take?"

Csanta had very little idea that he united in his own person the East Indian nabob, the Dey of Morocco, and the Russian prince, as likewise that it was he who had caused this uproar. Far from such an idea crossing his mind, he believed that this man was making game of him.

"Oh, sir," he said, "thirty gulden exchange is too much. I can give you a thousand Bondavara shares at five-and-twenty."

These words caused such a tumult as hardly ever had been heard on 'change. Every one crowded round Csanta; he was set upon from all sides—behind, before, at his side, on his back—he was fairly mobbed. People fought with one another over his head, and flourished their fists in his face.

"Who is he? Who is he? A bear, a conspirator, a thief, an agent! Out with him! Bonnet him! Pitch him out! Twenty-five, will he take? Give him twenty-five blows on his back and tear his coat in pieces!"

Spitzhase could hardly manage to get him out. He was in a deplorable condition when he issued forth, his hat smashed, his clothes all awry, his face pale, his breath short. Once in the open air his rescuer began to scold him.

"What the devil did you do that for? Just at the moment when the cabal was silenced and trampled in the dust, to come forward as one of them to run down your own shares!"

"I did not want to run them down; I only wanted to ascertain if it was really the case that such an advance on the price could be realized."

"Oh, that's the way with you," returned Spitzhase, in an aggrieved tone. "Well, I can tell you the exchange is not a good place to try jokes in. It was all quite authentic. The Bondavara scrip is as sound as ready-money. To-day it is thirty for scrip, eight-and-twenty for gold; to-morrow it will be thirty-two, and so on—always getting higher. If I had the money I would put in my last farthing. I know what I know, and I have studied the weather on 'change, but what I have learned from Kaulmann I cannot tell; my lips are sealed."

Upon this Csanta pressed the clerk very hard. "You can tell me," he said; "I am already in the boat. What have you heard?"

"Well," said Spitzhase, lowering his voice and looking round cautiously, "what you say is true; you are a large holder of stock, so perhaps I may give you this hint. *Puntafar has not reached its highest point yet.* Oho! they are very tricky who hold over. I am in the secret, and there is a plan, the details of which I durst not reveal, which will give such an impulse as will drive the shares still higher. In six months one impulse will be given, in another six months another. Oh, the world will open its eyes and its ears; but what I say to you, you will see! In a year's time Puntafar will be at one hundred over par."

"A hundred!" repeated Csanta, falling back against the wall in his astonishment. But he soon recovered himself. He was angry with Spitzhase for treating him as if he were a fool.

"I tell you what you are," he said; "you are a great boaster. Leave me; I shall get home by myself." And he dismissed Spitzhase angrily.

The next morning his first word was to ask the waiter for the papers. His eyes eagerly sought the exchange column, and there, just as Spitzhase had prophesied, silver currency had dropped two per cent. Bondavara stood at thirty to thirty-two florins, and what is written is gospel truth.

"Not one shall I sell!" cried Csanta, clapping his hands.

And then he got up and dressed himself. Here was a stroke of luck. It was like a fairy-tale; a man had only to leave the window open at night and next morning his pockets are full of gold.

He was swallowing his breakfast when Spitzhase was ushered in, his face beaming with triumph.

"Now, what did I tell you?" he cried, as he laid down the paper before Csanta, pointing with his finger to the exchange column.

The old Greek said not a word of having read the good news; he nodded his head as he answered, with great composure:

"Is it really true? Well, that is satisfactory."

"I rather think so; by the evening they will be up to thirty-two. Oh, if I had only some money!"

"Well, here is another note for you. Go and buy yourself a share. There, don't kiss my hand. I cannot allow it." But he did allow it.

"Don't sell the share," he went on; "keep it for yourself. When the next instalment comes due I will pay it for you. For God's sake, don't kiss my hand again! I will do more than that for you. If you kiss my hand every time I shall have no hands left. Remember that I shall expect you to show your gratitude in a more tangible manner. You must let me know the first thing if the head of your bank is going to try any tricks with the bonds. You will be sure to give me the first news as to when I should sell. Do you understand me? Good! Now that you have a share yourself you have an interest in the matter, and if we sell our shares are we not entitled to a commission?"

Spitzhase kissed every finger of the old man's hand.

"I implore one thing of you, master," he said; "don't betray me to Kaulmann. If he found out that I betrayed his secrets to any one he would dismiss me on the spot."

"Don't be afraid. You have to do with an honorable gentleman," returned the Greek, with an air of dignity.

The honorable gentleman believed that he had won over the honest clerk to betray the secrets of the honorable banker, his employer. It was an honorable game all round. We shall see which of the honorable gentlemen played it best.

CHAPTER XX

NO, EVELINE!

IT was high time Ivan returned to his coal-mine; he was needed there. While he was fighting duels in Pesth, strange things were happening in Bondathal. Not far from his workmen's colony there arose enormous buildings with almost miraculous quickness. As often happens when no difficulty is made as to price, the only question asked is, how soon shall the work be finished? The shares had not yet been issued, and the company had already spent in the interest of the undertaking a million of money. Everything was pressed forward at fever-heat. Here was a new invention for making tiles by machinery, there a donkey-engine supplied the materials for building the walls. The earthworks were in a most advanced condition, the chimneys smoked, the roofs were covered, a whole street was already built, a new town was rising as if by magic.

Of all this activity Ivan had been kept in ignorance by his assistant, Rauné, who had, likewise, been silent as to another disturbing element which had made its appearance for the first time among the workmen, and which disputed the palm with "choke-damp" and "foul air," and was quite as fatal as either. This new element was "a strike." A portion of Ivan's workmen struck for higher wages, otherwise they would join the new coal-mine, which was called "The Gentleman's Colony." It offered nearly double the wages, certainly more than the half again, of what Ivan paid. This happened after Raune had explained to the men that he had accepted the office of director, which had been offered to him by the new company, and he naturally wished to take with him the best and cleverest among Ivan's men, so that they, too, might profit by the higher wages. Who could resist such advantageous offers? Miners are like all other men; they have their price.

Ivan now gnawed the bitter bread of self-reproach. He saw the folly he had committed in taking into his service and admitting into the secrets of the business the paid director of a company created to bring about his own ruin.

A scientific man is not a good business man. While he was making investigations as to the probability of animal life existing in the antediluvian strata of coal-mines, he was blind to the danger of a rival company close to his own factory. Nay, more; he had allowed himself to be hoodwinked by an inferior intelligence, and had fallen into the trap set for him by his old friend Felix. Ivan was philosopher enough to accommodate himself to circumstances. There was little use, he told himself, in crying over spilt milk; he had broad shoulders, and they should, if it were possible, push the wheel of fortune. But though he said this, he had little hope of succeeding.

On his return, and when he got, as he thought, to the bottom of the evil, he called his workmen together.

"Comrades," he said, "a great undertaking has risen up beside us; the company of the new coal-mines offers you wages which I give you my word of honor it is impossible to pay without considerable loss to themselves. Up to the present I have worked my mines with a certain amount of profit; I offer you to-day, in addition to your usual wages, a share out of this profit. For the future we shall divide with one another what we earn. At the end of the year I shall lay my accounts before you; one of your number, chosen by yourselves, shall examine and audit them, and according to the wages of each man and the work he has done he shall receive his share. If you agree to this fair offer I shall continue the work. If, however, you think it better for your interests to take the higher wages offered by the company, I shall not enter into competition with men who have millions to spend; it would be a folly on my part. I shall, therefore, sell them my mine, and you may then be certain of one thing, that when they have both mines in their own hands, and find that no rivalry is possible, the rate of wages will be lowered. To those who stand by me I offer a contract *for life;* the profits of this mine, so long as I live, shall be divided between myself and my workmen."

This was an excellent stroke, especially as the company could not imitate it. More than half the men closed with Ivan's offer, and undertook to remain with him. A great number, however, influenced by paid agents, who were sent about to stir them up, went over to the "Gentleman's Colony."

Those who remained had a great deal to suffer from the ones who left. Not a Sunday passed without fights taking place between the two parties.

Ivan soon heard that his powerful rival had found a way of checkmating him. His customers, to whom he sent large consignments not only of coal but also of copper and iron bars, wrote to him that the new Bondavara Coal Company had offered the same class of goods at fifty per cent. less, and that therefore, unless he was prepared to make a similar reduction, they could not deal with him. Fifty per cent. higher wages and fifty per cent. less profit means working for nothing. Rauné had Ivan's business in the hollow of his hand; he could ruin it, and he meant to do so. Ivan saw this quite clearly, but he did not lose heart. He wrote to all his former customers that it was not possible to give either the coal or the iron a farthing cheaper, not if it hung round his neck as a dead weight. The consequence was his coal and his iron accumulated in his warehouses; scarcely a wagon with his name was to be seen in the streets of Bondathal. He had to work the mine and the foundry for himself alone.

For the men who had remained true to him there was, indeed, a bad outlook. Their former comrades jeered at them in the open street. "Where is the profit?" was a popular cry. Ivan tried to quiet the disappointed men; he asked them to wait patiently. By the end of the year, he prophesied, they would be on the right side. To give things for nothing was not trade, and if the company chose to do it he wasn't going to follow such a suicidal example.

The great buildings of the new colony being now completed, the directors of the company announced that they would hold high festival in honor of the opening of the undertaking. The principals, directors, managers, shareholders were to come from Vienna and be entertained at a banquet. The largest room in the factory was fitted up as a dining-room, the tables being laid for workmen as well as for the distinguished company of strangers. It was widely circulated that the prince was coming. The company had chosen him as their president. Both the princes were patrons of commercial and industrial undertakings, but Prince Theobald possessed an extraordinary financial talent; any speculation he engaged in was a sound and sure one, so it was said, as also that he had taken a million shares in the new company. It was so far true that Kaulmann had offered him this million, which was to increase the value of the Bondavara property, but it is needless to remark that the million of shares had no tangible existence. Previous to the inaugural ceremony a religious service was to take place, and, as was only fitting, this was to be conducted by the eminent Abbé Samuel. Before such distinguished guests it would hardly be in keeping to have a man such as pastor Mohak, although it was true that he slaved all through the year among the people.

The guests came from the castle, where they had arrived the previous day. They drove into the town in splendid coaches. That of Prince Theobald came first, with his armorial bearings emblazoned on the panels. Behind two footmen with dazzling liveries of scarlet and gold. On the box the coachman with a powdered wig and three-cornered hat. The coach drew up at the church door, the footmen jumped down and opened the carriage door. There alighted first an old gentleman with white hair, a clean-shaven, soft, friendly face, and a very distinguished air. He gave his hand to a splendidly dressed lady in a velvet and lace costume, who descended from the equipage with graceful nonchalance. The crowd saw her violet velvet boots and embroidered silk stockings.

"What a great lady!" cried the boors to one another. "She must be a princess, for all the gentlemen at the church door received her hat in hand."

Only one man in a rough workman's coat called out: "Evila!"

It was Peter Saffran who had recognized her.

The lady heard the exclamation, and turned a laughing face to the crowd outside.

"No," she said; "it is *Eveline.*"

She bowed her head sweetly as she crossed the threshold of the church.

Eveline's vanity had brought her to Bondathal; she wanted to show her silk stockings to her former companions, who had seen her in wooden shoes with no stockings, except on occasions. It was the vanity of the peasant girl—not pride, take notice, but mere vanity. She did not look down upon her friends, as some upstarts do; she wanted to do good to every one of them. She was ready to give them money, to earn their grateful thanks, particularly to those who had been kind to her in the old days; to those especially she wished to prove that, although she had risen to a high position, she had never forgotten how much she owed to them. She would now, in her turn, do them good. Eveline had looked forward to seeing her former bridegroom. Most probably he had long since consoled himself for her loss, and had married another. A present of money would make *him* happy. She had also counted on meeting Ivan. She had the most grateful remembrance of his goodness, and she was glad to think she had it in her power to prove her gratitude by deeds. She could not give him a present, but she could tell him of the dangers that threatened his property from the large undertaking of the company, and she promised herself to use all her influence to make the best terms for Ivan in case he would consent to arrange matters with his gigantic rival.

Yes, it was indeed the vain desire of doing good that had brought Eveline to Bondathal. She had arranged how and where she would have her first meeting with Ivan.

The notabilities and proprietors of the neighborhood had been invited in the name of the prince to the banquet, which was to inaugurate the opening of the works. No one could refuse such an invitation. It was true that when Eveline had proposed to the Abbé Samuel that he should undertake the office of intermediary, and call on his learned colleague Behrend, and bring him with him to the banquet, the abbé had exclaimed not for all the world would he venture to propose such a thing as that Behrend should wait upon their excellencies. And when he said this he knew very well what he was saying.

To return to the church door. As Peter Saffran stood stock-still, gazing after the vanishing figure of his former betrothed, he felt some one tap him on the shoulder; turning round, he saw standing behind him Felix Kaulmann. Peter's face went deadly white, partly with fear, more from inward rage. Felix, however, laughed carelessly, with the indifference of a great man, to what was, in his opinion, only a good joke.

"Good-day, fellow. Mind you come to the dinner," he said, as he followed the prince into the church.

Peter Saffran remained gaping at the noble gentlemen as they got out of their carriages, and when the crowd began to move into the church he followed in the stream. He made his way into the darkest corner, before the shrine of a saint, knelt down, with both his hands laid upon the wall and his head upon his folded arms, and there he made a vow—an awful, terrible vow. Those who saw him in his kneeling attitude, with bent head, imagined he had been struck at last by grace, and was repenting of his sins. When he had finished his prayer, or his curse, he got up quickly, and, without waiting for the end of the splendid ceremonial, hastened out of the church, casting a wild look behind him as he went, for he imagined that the saint in the shrine was pointing her finger at him and calling out, "Take him prisoner! He is a murderer!"

The church service being over, the distinguished company drove to the company's colony, and went over the works. They drove under triumphal arches which were erected in the streets, and were received by a deputation of workmen. The best orator made a speech, which would have been very eloquent only he stuck fast in the middle. The young girl who recited some verses was more happy in her delivery, and her youngest sister presented a bouquet to Eveline, who kissed the child.

"Ah! you are little Marie. Don't you know me?"

The child, however, was too frightened at this beautiful lady to make her an answer.

The guests visited the buildings under the guidance of Herr Rauné, who spared them nothing—the factory, the machinery, the iron-works. They were terribly tired of it all, and glad to get into the large rooms which had been temporarily arranged as the banqueting-hall. Here they were received by two bands playing Rakoczy's "March." To the banquet came a crowd of guests alike invited and uninvited—gentlemen, peasants, clergymen, and Bohemians. Eveline, however, looked in vain for her former master. Ivan was not among the guests. He had not even sent an excuse. What an uncouth man! and yet, perhaps, he had reason. If you drink beforehand to the skin of the bear, the bear has every right to decline being present at the feast. Peter Saffran, however, came; he was treated as the chief guest, and given the first place at the workman's table. This struck even his obtuse senses. Looking round he saw he was the only representative of the Bondathal mine.

The banquet lasted far on into the evening. Gentlemen and workmen were exceedingly merry. Towards the close of the feast Felix sent for Peter. He presented him to the prince.

"Here is the brave miner of whom I have told your excellency."

Saffran felt the blood rush to his face.

"Well, my good friend," continued Felix, "how has the world treated you since I last saw you? Are you still afraid of 'the doctor'? There's a plaster for you; it will heal any remains of your former injuries." So saying, he took out of his pocket-book a note for a hundred gulden and put it into Peter's hand. "No," he added, "don't thank me, but thank the kind lady there, who remembered you."

He pointed to Eveline, and Peter kissed her hand, or, rather, her beautiful mauve glove.

What a transformation in the man-eater! He had grown obedient and gentle.

"That good lady," continued Felix, "wishes you well. At her request his excellency, Prince Theobald, has given you the post of overseer in the new company's colony, at the yearly salary of a thousand gulden. What do you say to that?"

What could he say? He kissed the hand of his excellency.

Kaulmann filled a large goblet to the brim with foaming champagne and handed it to Peter.

"Toss that off," he said. "But first drink to the long life of his excellency, our generous prince."

"And to the health of this dear lady," added the prince, gallantly, at which the trumpets sounded shrilly, and Peter Saffran, the prince, the banker, and Eveline drank to one another.

This scene delighted the working-men. Here was no pride, the gentlemen clinking glasses with the common miner. This was the right spirit.

Peter Saffran, meantime, was wondering within himself which of the two gentlemen was Eveline's husband, and in what relation did the other stand to her? He emptied his glass and put it down again, but it did not occur to him to put the question to either of the three, therefore it remained unanswered.

The festival closed with a splendid display of fireworks. The sparks from the Catherine wheels fell in a shower of molten gold into Ivan's mine.

The following morning Saffran came to Behrend and informed him that he had taken service with the company.

"You also?" said Ivan, bitterly. "Well, go!"

Peter was paler than ever. He had expected reproaches for his treachery, but as none came he suddenly burst out with what had been for some time in his mind.

"Why did you *that time* call your friend a doctor?"

"Because he is one. He is a doctor of law."

Saffran raised his finger in a threatening manner. "Nevertheless, it was very wrong of you to call him *that time* a doctor." And then he turned on his heel and went his way.

Ivan's strength of mind was more and more put to the proof. Each day brought fresh defections. His best men left him to go over to his enemy, who, like some horrid monster, raised large furnaces which crushed the very life out of his smaller chimneys. His business friends fell away from him. They looked upon him as an obstinate fool, carrying on such an unequal fight; but the darker the outlook the stronger grew his determination to see the affair to the bitter end. He would not leave his old home, his own little territory; he would carry on the unequal, perhaps the fruitless, task of opposing his apparently triumphant adversary.

In the depth of his misfortune one true, reliable friend remained to him, and saved him from utter despair. This friend was the multiplication-table. Before he began to calculate he put these questions to himself, as if he were some one else:

"Is this colony a company of commercial men? No, a company of speculators. A joint-stock company? No, it is a game of chance. Is it a factory? No, a tower of Babel." Then he went on to consider this point. "Two and two make four, and, turn it how you like, it makes nothing *but* four; and if all the kings and emperors in Europe, with decrees and ukases, were to tell their individual subjects that two and two make five, and if the pope fulminated a bull to enjoin on all true believers that two and two make five, and if even the best financial authority was to declare that we should count two and two as five, all these—kings, emperors, popes, and accountants—would not alter the fact that two and two make four. These generous shareholders of the Bondavara Company are working against a well-known fact. The new company builds, creates, invents, contracts, buys, and sells without taking any heed of the primary rule of arithmetic; therefore it is clear that the company is not working for the future, but merely for present gain. Therefore, I will live down this swindle."

At the end of the year the company gave their shareholders a surprise. The Bondavara shares began to fluctuate between thirty-five and forty florins exchange, although the date of the payment of second instalments of capital was at hand. At such times all the early bonds are handed in. Csanta thought this would be a good time for him to bring in his shares and to get his silver back. He was contemplating a visit to the bank when he received a private note from Spitzhase, putting him on his guard not to fall into such a mistake as to sell. "This very day the board of directors had met, and a resolution had been carried unanimously that at the next general meeting the shareholders should be surprised by getting a bonus of twenty per cent., upon which the shares would at once rise higher. This was a profound secret, but he could not allow his good friend to remain in ignorance."

And at the next general meeting the commercial world heard the same story. The first two months of the Bondavara Coal Company had been such a signal success that, besides the usual rate of interest, the directors were enabled to offer upon each share a bonus of six florins, which amounted (with the usual rate) to thirty-five per cent., an unheard-of profit in two months.

When Ivan read this in the newspaper he burst into a loud laugh. He knew, no one better, what amount of profit the factory had made, but it is easy to manipulate accounts so that the ledger presents these remarkable results. What do the unbusiness-like, credulous shareholders understand of such matters? The board of directors know very well how matters really stand; but they have their own ends to serve. The outside world may bleed; what is that to them? There is no court-martial in the stock-exchange, and no justice for the injured.

Csanta did not sell his shares. He paid his second

instalment in silver pieces, rejoiced over the bonus, and blessed Spitzhase for preventing him from selling his bonds at thirty-five. They had now risen to forty florins, and continued to rise.

Ivan watched this diabolical swindle with calmness. He said to himself:

"How long will the game last?"

CHAPTER XXI

RESPECT FOR HALINA CLOTH

It was a singular coincidence that in the same moment that Ivan said to himself, "How long will this game last?" Prince Waldemar, meeting Felix Kaulmann, beaming with triumph, at the exchange, put to him the question, " How long, do you think, will this comedy last?"

"The third act is still wanting," replied the banker.

"Yes, the third instalment. Then I shall hoist you on your own petard."

"We will see about that."

The bears could not imagine what Kaulmann had in his head. That he had a plan was certain; what it was no one knew but the Abbé Samuel and Prince Theobald.

The third act was not the instalment; it was the Bondavara Railway. This question bristled with difficulties. The government was irritated against Hungary, and in their irritation would not listen to any proposals as to railways and the like. Even the country party was sulky. Let the country go to the devil; what did they care? And no doubt they had justification for their righteous indignation. Every Hungarian who wore "broadcloth" was against them. The body of officials, the middle class, the intelligence of the country, preferred to lay down place and to give up government patronage sooner than submit to the chimeras which the cabinet at Vienna indulged in by way of government. Good! So far as officials went, men were easily got to fill the places the others had resigned, for when a good table is spread, needless to say, guests are not hard to find. The hired troop pocketed their salary, took the oath, stuffed their pockets, but did nothing to promote the government measures. Between the men who had resigned and the newly appointed officials there was only this difference: that one set openly declared they would do nothing; the others pretended to do something, but found it impossible to accomplish anything. They tried to shove, but the cart would not move an inch. From those who wore cloth among the middle classes the government had to expect nothing, that was evident. Formerly those who wore silk and satin acted as a sort of counterpoise—the high and mighty, and the magnates, the lawyers, and the priests—but now all these held aloof. The primate remonstrated, the bishops advised the nobility, the higher classes collected in Pesth and talked treason.

Flectere si nequeo superos—

Let us turn now to the Halina cloth. Halina cloth is, as every one knows, the commonest description of cloth, only worn by the poorer classes. This cloth was suddenly adopted in the capital of the Austrian empire. This was no capricious freak of fashion set in motion by some high lady who "imagined" her elegance could give dignity to the roughest material; this was another affair altogether, inaugurated by the legislative body of the kingdom, who were all clothed in Halina. Well, what has any one to say against this? Why not? Are we not democrats? It is true that these right-minded men hardly understood a word of the language in which the legislative debates were carried on, but this had the inestimable advantage that they could make no long speeches, and therefore could in no way impede the course of business. Neither did they possess any knowledge of the laws of nations, the rights of citizens, the complicated details of finance, nor the construction of budgets: and this pastoral innocence entitled them to universal respect and confidence, for it placed them above suspicion. No one could suspect these honorable deputies of siding with the government because they held government appointments.

We repeat that the introducer of Halina cloth to be worn by the legislative assembly was a man of talent. But in Hungary, also, the fashion should be adopted. Were there not one hundred and eight seats in the legislative assembly ready for so many excellent men? These should not be left vacant. To fill these seats, however, there was one lever necessary, and that was the influence of the clerical party.

The clergy in Hungary were such poor creatures, so ignorant and uneducated, that they actually preferred to remain faithful to the traditions of Radoczy than to adopt the new-fangled ideas promulgated at Vienna. Even such an insignificant pastor as Herr Mahok returned the decree which had been sent to him from headquarters, with directions to read it on Sundays to his flock, saying that it was a mistake; he was not the village crier. If the government wished to issue a protocol, let it be done in the market-place, by order of the judge of the district, and accompanied by the drum and trumpet. The pulpit was not the place for government protocols. The like refusal came from every pastor in Hungary, and in face of this flat rebellion the ministers resolved that the power of the clerical party should be broken.

"Now is the time to act," said Felix Kaulmann to the Abbé Samuel.

The primate had been in Vienna; he had been refused an audience; he had fallen into disgrace. The Bishop of Siebenburg had been elevated to the primate's seat, and given all its honors and dignities. The clerical party in Hungary was doomed. Against it the sword was drawn; the moment was approaching when it would be cut in two.

The Bondavara Railway was the *gradus ad Parnassum*. If it succeeded, if it was worked properly, the house of Kaulmann would rank with that of the Pereires and Strousbergs; then, also, the pontifical loan upon the Church property in Hungary could be effected. All this with one blow! Rank in the world, power in the country, influence in the empire, success in the money-market, and the triumph of the Church.

The Abbé Samuel had begun his ambitious career. The first task was to introduce the hundred and eight Hungarian wearers of Halina cloth into the legislative body, and thus to secure the Bondavara Railway, the title of bishop, and a seat in the House of Peers. These three things lay in the hollow of his hand, for he had three strings ready to pull, which would set in motion the statesman, the financier, and the influence of woman.

On one Saturday Ivan, to his surprise, received a visit from Rauné, who, in a few words, stated the matter which had brought him. The proprietors and inhabitants of the different parts of Bondathal wished to send a deputation to Vienna, to lay before the government and Parliament their request that the means of communication between their mountainous territory and the other parts of the empire should be put on a better footing. This matter interested Ivan equally with the rest, and therefore it would be desirable that he and his workmen should attend the mass-meeting which would be held on the next day.

Ivan at once refused all co-operation. "We live," he said, "under exceptional laws, which forbid political meetings. This mass-meeting has a political object, and therefore I refuse to disobey the law."

In spite of this protest the assembly took place next day, and the Abbé Samuel made a brilliant speech. His dignified appearance imposed respect, his proposal was intelligible and for the general good; its usefulness could not be gainsaid. To insure its popularity the astute abbé took care not to introduce into his speech the hated word "Reichstag." The resolution was carried unanimously that a deputation of twelve men should be chosen to proceed at once to Vienna, and there present the wishes of the people. The twelve delegates were then chosen by the abbé, and his choice was received with loud shouts of approbation. The Bondavara shareholders came forward with unexampled generosity, and presented each member of the deputation not only the price of the journey, but a cloak made of Halina cloth, a hat, and a pair of boots. Twelve new suits! That was worth going to Vienna for. Still, it went against the grain. A peasant is suspicious; they don't care to crack nuts with gentlemen; they mistrust presents that most probably will be dearly bought. If any man in a black coat had made the proposal it would have encountered vigorous opposition, but a priest, a distinguished priest, his advice can safely be followed; there is nothing to be afraid of when he is at the head of the deputation. All will go well, even although they may have to undertake heavy responsibilities which may some day involve loss. But what loss? Ah! time will tell. Once on a time twelve men went to Vienna, and sold the rights of their fellow-countrymen to the devil. God knows what might happen, only that the priest is with them; there is the plank of safety.

Nevertheless, the twelve men had to swear, man to man, before they put on the new suits, upon their souls, that they would deny that they could write. They were to sign nothing, and if they were asked if such a one in Bondathal had houses and fields, and, above all, sons, they were not to give any answer.

The deputation started in a couple of days after the meeting, under the guidance of the abbé. Peter Saffran went also. He had been named one of the twelve, for he was specially wanted in Vienna.

A day or so later Ivan was cited before the military officer commanding the district; he was accused of having acted against the law by causing the "Reichstag" to be lowered in the eyes of the people, of having kept the people, especially his own workmen, from taking part in legal demonstrations, of having insulted members of the legislature, and of having allied himself with secret societies. He was cautioned to avoid anything of the sort in future. The next time things would be more serious; he was at liberty to go this time unpunished.

Ivan knew perfectly well from what quarter this denunciation had come. To destroy his business utterly it would be necessary to place its owner for a year in confinement; his innocence would then be established, and he would be allowed to go scot-free. In the meantime his property would be ruined. It was lucky for Ivan that on this occasion the jailer's wife was ill. It would have been necessary to remove her from the rooms which were set apart for prisoners under suspicion, and so Ivan was allowed to go his way.

Ah, it was a great day when the twelve men from Bondathal, in the twelve new suits of Halina cloth, arrived in the metropolis. Here they are! Here are the Hungarians, the indomitable sons of the soil. A deputation to the Reichsrath, an acknowledgment of the February patent, the first pioneers! They deserve three times three.

All the newspapers hastened to congratulate them; the leading articles of all political shades were full of this new and remarkable demonstration.

The minister gave the deputation a private audience, where the abbé set forth their demand in a well-expressed speech, laying great stress upon the fact that it was the people themselves who wished to free their country from its present condition, having learned to distinguish their real benefactors from those false prophets who wished to condemn them to a baneful and ruinous inactivity. The abbé dwelt expressly upon the great intelligence of the men who formed the deputation. In return his excellency the minister pressed the hand of the abbé, and assured him that the bishopric would soon be vacant, and that it would be his care to see that a loyal prelate should fill the seat. His excellency then entered into conversation with the members of the deputation, and as none of them understood a word of his language, they were much pleased with what he said. His excellency, having been told by the abbé that Peter Saffran was the most distinguished of the party, took especial notice of him. He pressed his hand, while he expressed a hope that the members of the deputation would attend the morning sitting;

places would be reserved in the gallery—for the present in *the gallery*.

Peter promised for his fellow-members. He could speak German as well as French; he had picked up both languages during his ship experiences.

All this time the minister had said nothing as to the grant to the Bondathal Railway, and that was the principal thing.

At the next sitting of the Reichsrath the front row of the gallery was reserved for the distinguished guests. They sat in arm-chairs, leaning their elbows on the cushions, and letting their round hats hang over the rails.

His excellency the minister gave a discourse which lasted over an hour. The opposition maintained that during his speech his excellency had glanced fifty-two times at the gallery, to see the effect he was producing upon the Hungarians. One fell asleep, and let his hat fall into the hall. The hat fell upon one of the deputies, and awoke him from a sweet doze.

For three days this trivial circumstance gave food to the government papers; then it became the absolute property of the accredited wit or fun journals, which put into the mouths of the Hungarians all manner of things which they had never said. Never mind; those excellent men couldn't read German, so it didn't matter. They stuck fast to their arm-chairs in the gallery as long as the sitting lasted; they were more comfortable than their beds.

The last evening of their stay they were taken to the theatre. Not to the Burg Theatre—that would not do for them—but to the Treumann Theatre, where a piece was playing suitable for them, with plenty of fun, singing, dancing, laughing; and the great joke of all was that the principal part was to be played by the beautiful

Eveline, Frau von Kaulmann. Will Peter Saffran recognize her?

It had not been possible to get an engagement at the Opera-house for Eveline, for there was an Italian season running. When it finished there would be a prospect of an engagement for her if she first learned the routine of acting at some less important theatre, and grew accustomed to the footlights. Therefore, she played *en amateur* on the boards of the Treumann Theatre. Her natural gifts and her extraordinary beauty caused a sensation. The *jeunesse dorée* went mad over this new favorite of the hour. The piece which was played in honor of the peasants was one of Offenbach's frivolous operas, in which the ladies appear in the very scantiest of costumes. The noble portion of the audience enjoy these displays more than do the poorer; it did not, at all events, amuse the simple folk in Halina cloth. The ballet, with the lightly clothed nymphs, their coquettish movements, their seductive smiles, their bold display of limbs, and their short petticoats, was not to the taste of the Bondavara miners. It was true that the girls in the coal-pit wore no petticoats to speak of, but then they were working. Who thought anything of that? Chivalry belongs to the peasant as much as to the gentleman; the former indeed practise the motto, "Honi soit qui mal y pense" more than do their better-educated superiors. But now as Eveline entered they felt ashamed. She came on as a fairy or goddess, concealed in gold-colored clouds; the clouds were, however, transparent. Peter glowed with rage to think all the world could penetrate this slight transparency; he burned with jealous fury as Eveline smiled, coquetted, cast glances here, there, and was stared at through a hundred opera-glasses. Peter forgot that this was only a stage, and that the fairies who played their parts upon it for an hour or so were many of them most virtuous women, excellent wives and daughters; for what happens on the stage is only play, not actuality. The former bridegroom did not reason in this wise. You see, he was an uneducated peasant in coarse Halina cloth, and his ignorant mind was filled with horror, disgust, rage. That she should allow herself to be kissed, to be made love to—shame! No, my good Peter, it was no shame, but a great honor. Out of the boxes bouquets and wreaths fell on the stage; there was hardly a place where she could put her feet; it was all flowers. The house resounded with applause. This was not shame, but honor—certainly not of the same kind that would be offered to a saint or a good woman; it was more the worship offered to an idol, and most women like to be worshipped as idols.

Peter told himself all the sex are alike, and comforted himself with the thought that not one of his companions would recognize Eveline. But Peter took a sore heart back to his inn.

In the hall he met the abbé, and asked him, "When are we going back?"

"Are you weary of Vienna, Peter?"

"I am."

"Have a little patience. To-morrow we must pay a visit to a charming lady."

"What have we to do with charming ladies?"

"Don't ask the why or the wherefore. If we want to attain our end we must leave no means untried. We must beg this lady to interest herself for us. One word from her to his excellency the minister will do more than if we said a whole litany."

"Very good; then we had better see her."

CHAPTER XXII

TWO SUPPLIANTS

The next day, at eleven o'clock, Abbé Samuel came to fetch his followers, and conduct them to the house of the influential lady whose one word had more weight with his excellency than the most carefully arranged speeches of priests and orators.

The carriage stopped before a splendid palace; a porter in a magnificent scarlet livery, with a bear-skin cap, answered the bell, and between a double row of marble pillars they ascended the steps. The staircase was also of marble, covered with a soft, thick carpet. The school-master at home, if he had a bit of this stuff, would have made a fine coat of it. Up the staircase were such beautiful statues that the poor peasants would have liked to kneel to kiss their hands. The staircase was roofed in with glass and heated with hot air, so that the lovely hot-house plants and costly china groups suffered no injury from the cold air. In the anteroom servants wearing silver epaulettes conducted the visitors into the drawing-room. The sight almost took away their breath. There was no wall to be seen; it was panelled in the most sumptuous silk brocade; the curtains of the same texture had gold rods, and splendid pictures in rich frames hung on the silk panels. The upper portion of the windows was of stained glass, such as is seen in cathedrals, and opposite the windows was a large fireplace of white marble, upon whose mantelpiece stood a wonderful clock, with a beautiful figure which moved in time to the melodious tick. The furniture was all of mahogany. From the ceiling, upon which the arabesques in gold were a feast to the eye, there hung a lustre with a hundred lights, whose thousand glass drops sent out all the prismatic colors of the rainbow.

The good peasants of Bondathal had hardly time to take in the wonders of this fairy palace when a gentleman in a black coat and a spotless white tie came out of an adjoining room. This grand personage, whom they imagined to be the master of the house, turned out to be an equally important person—the groom of the chambers. He informed them that his mistress was in the next room, and ready to receive them.

There was no door to this inner apartment, only curtains of heavy damask, such as church banners are made of. This second drawing-room was still more wonderful than the first. The walls were panelled in dove-colored silk. From the ceiling to the floor there were enormous mirrors set in china frames, and between each mirror were *consoles* with marble statuettes representing dancing nymphs. The stone floor was covered with a soft carpet, into which the foot sank as into summer grass. The fireplace was of black marble, with a silver grating. The furniture was of the Versailles pattern; tables and chairs, arm-chairs and footstools, of delicate coloring; chairs of Sèvres, with feet and elbow rests ornamented with delicate flower-garlands and charming Watteau figures. Every piece of furniture was a masterpiece. Upon the centre-table and *consoles* were Japanese vases of different and most elegant shapes. In one of the windows an aquarium had been constructed full of gold-fish and sea-anemones.

The poor peasants did not notice all these beautiful objects; their attention was fixed upon their own reflections in the long glasses, and which in their ignorance they imagined were other deputations, headed by another abbé wearing a gold cross. But even this strange spectacle was lost sight of in their amazement at the beauty of the great lady who now came forward to receive them. She was a lovely vision. Her dress of violet silk was covered with the most costly lace, her black hair fell in curls over her shoulders; her face was so beautiful, so fascinating, so dignified, that every man in the deputation was ready to fall at her feet.

Peter Saffran was the only one who recognized her; it was Eveline, his promised bride.

Now the abbé, bowing low, addressed her in most respectful language, as he laid before her the desire of the deputation, that she would accord her powerful protection to the Bondathal population. The lady answered most graciously, and promised that, as far as possible, she would exert her influence. She was heart and soul in the matter, for she added, smiling:

"I am myself a child of Bondathal."

At these words the deputation exchanged glances, and every one thought she must be the daughter or wife of one of the Bondavara magnates. Only Saffran was gloomy.

"What is she?" he thought. "Only last night she was singing, dancing, and acting; her beauty was displayed to the eyes of a crowd, who looked at her through opera-glasses, while I had to cover my eyes with my hat so as not to look on her degradation, and here to-day she is a sort of queen, promising us her influence with cabinet ministers. What is the truth? Was last night a comedy, or is to-day a clever farce played by her and the priest?"

You see, Peter Saffran had been in the Fiji Islands, and he remembered how amazed the savages had been when the white man washed the black from his hands, and showed their natural color; only here it was the whole body that was in question.

The abbé, who seemed highly pleased with the success of his interview, now gave those behind him a sign to move on, and bowed respectfully to the lady, who whispered a few words in his ear.

The abbé stopped Peter Saffran as he was leaving the room, and said, in a low voice:

"You are to remain; this kind lady wishes to speak with you."

Saffran felt the blood rush to his head. He almost tottered, and as he returned to the room he could hardly move. But Eveline hastened to him, holding out both her hands. She had taken off her gloves, and he felt the soft, velvety clasp of her fingers as she pressed his horny hand in hers; he heard in his ear the sweet, fresh ring of her voice, to which he had often listened.

"Ah, Peter, say a word to me—a kind word;" and she patted him two or three times on the back. "Are you still angry with me? There, Peter, don't be vexed any more. Stay and dine with me, and we shall drink to our reconciliation."

And she put her arm into his, and stroked his cheek with her delicate little hand, which looked as if it had never known what hardship was.

Eveline had kept religiously to her promise of always informing Prince Theobald when she expected guests, and the prince reserved to himself the right of a veto if he did not approve of their reception, for there were among the *dilettante*, and even among apparently most respectable gentlemen, certain individuals who should not have the *entrée* to the drawing-room of a lady who is not living under her husband's roof.

The prince liked pleasant society, and, if he approved of the company, enjoyed himself all the more that Eveline did the honors for him.

On this particular day Eveline had told the prince she expected two visitors. One was Peter Saffran.

The prince laughed. "Poor fellow!" he said, "treat him well; it will do him good." But when he heard his excellency the minister was coming he frowned heavily. "What is this?" he asked. "What brings *him* to see *you?*"

"Why! Is he a woman-hater?"

"On the contrary, he is a scoundrel, only he wears a hypocrite's cloak. Great men who are at the helm and guide public affairs have their weaknesses, but they dare not sin openly. A man in his position might as soon become a member of the Jockey Club as visit a beautiful actress, unless he had some ostensible reason to give for so doing."

"But he has a reason, and a very good one. I asked him to make the appointment."

"*You invited him here!*" The prince's face grew more cloudy.

"That is to say, I asked him to give me a private audience, and his secretary wrote to say his excellency would prefer to come here."

"And for what purpose do you require an audience?"

"Felix desired me to ask for it."

"Ah, it was Kaulmann's doing! Wherefore?"

"He wants these documents to be signed."

Eveline showed the prince a folded parchment.

The prince glanced at it and shook his head. "And does his excellency know that this is the reason why you asked for an audience?"

Eveline burst into a laugh. "Oh dear, no! When his secretary first wrote he asked why I required an audience; I answered it was about my engagement at the Opera, and then he said he would come. He knows nothing of this," she added, touching the papers in her hand.

"And Kaulmann told you to do this?"

"Yes."

"Then Kaulmann is a refined villain. Do as he has told you; but you may take my word that your husband deceives himself if he imagines you can snare a savage with a silken net. You can receive your guest, but I do not think you will succeed in your scheme."

Eveline put her hand upon Peter Saffran's, and led him into another room, where there was a wonderful display of silver, and thence, through a private door, into a fourth apartment, the walls of which were wainscoted with dark wood; the ceiling, too, was supported by cross-beams of wood, and finished with painted shell-work.

No one was in the room. Eveline sat down on the sofa, and made Peter sit beside her.

"Listen, Peter," she said, laying her hand on the rough sleeve of his Halina-cloth coat. "It was the will of God that I should separate from you. It grieved me very much to leave you, because, you know, we had been called in church three times. But, then, you could not bear my little brother; you were cruel to him, and you beat me. I don't bear you any malice now. I have forgotten and forgiven, but at the time I was very angry with you, not so much because you ill-treated me, but I followed you that night to the cottage in the wood. I was quite ready to forgive and forget, only I looked through the window, and I saw you dancing with Ezifra Mauczi. I saw you kiss her, and I was angry in downright earnest."

Peter gnashed his teeth. He felt the tables were turned against him, and he could say nothing. It would be very different if it were his wife who accused him of such things; he would know how to treat a jealous, scolding wife; but he couldn't take this beautiful lady by the hair, and drag her round the room, and beat her on the head until she begged for pardon.

"But, as I said," continued Eveline, smiling again, "we are not going to talk about bygones. It was all God's will, and for the best. We would have been a most unhappy couple, for I am passionate and jealous, and you would have given me cause. Now you can do as you like, and I have the happiness of doing good. I like to help as many people as possible, and every day twenty poor creatures are fed in my house. Oh, I do more than that; I get heaps of things done for the poor! I speak a good word for them, and get them helped by rich people. Also, I mean to be a benefactress to your valley; thousands and thousands of people will bless my name for what I shall do for them. Is it not a happiness to be able to help others?"

Eveline paused for an answer. Peter felt he ought to say something, if it was only to show that he had not become dumb.

"And does all this money come from the Bondavara Company?" he asked.

Eveline blushed scarlet. How was she to answer such a question?

"Not altogether. I earn a good deal by my art; for every performance I receive five hundred gulden."

"Five hundred gulden!" thought Peter. "That explains a great deal. A good salary indeed! A woman might spare some of her clothing to earn so much money. It is money got by work, and not such hard work as carrying coals. She had to show her legs for that also. But all said and done, it was money honestly earned."

Peter's face began to clear.

"There, you look more like yourself. Don't look wicked again," pleaded Eveline; "and when you go back home tell every one that you have seen me, and that we had a great talk together, and are good friends again. If at any time you know of any one in want, send me a line, and, if it is in my power, I will gladly help them. You must marry, if you are not already married. No? Well, then, you must choose a good girl, Peter. There is Panna, she is just the wife for you, and she was always a friend of mine, or there is Amaza, she liked you, I know, and she is an excellent housekeeper; only, don't marry Mauczi; you would be very unhappy with her; she is a bad girl. And in case you do marry, Peter, here are my wedding-presents for your wife; and remember, I advise you to marry Panna. Here are a pair of ear-rings, a necklace, and a brooch; and to you I give, as a remembrance of myself, this gold watch. See, Peter, my likeness is on the back. Think of me sometimes when you are very happy."

When she said these words Eveline's eyes overflowed, and her lips trembled convulsively. Peter saw it, and drew the conclusion that with all her splendor she was not happy. One thought now took possession of him. He gave no heed to the bridal presents. Whether they were of gold or lead was all one to him, no one should ever see them; but what he thought was:

"She has a good heart, she is generous, she gives with an open hand; but I do not care for her gifts. If she will only kiss me once I will bless her. What is a kiss to her? An alms, one out of the numbers she gives to those fellows on the stage, with their smeared, painted faces."

Poor fool! he didn't know that stage kisses are only mock kisses, just as stage champagne is only lemonade or pure water. Peter believed that one kiss from Eveline would satisfy his thirst; it would assuage the pangs of regret, of jealousy, or rage that had consumed him since the previous night. All would vanish when he would touch her cold, fresh lips. And, after all, had they not been betrothed to one another—all but man and wife? Who could object? Only he didn't know how to express what was in his mind.

"And now let us eat together, Peter," said Eveline, kindly. "I am certain that you are tired of all the good things you get every day; you are satiated with the Vienna cookery. Wait, and I shall cook you something myself—your favorite dish, Peter, which you often said no one cooked so well as I did. I shall make you some porridge."

Peter was electrified. A smile broke out all over his face, either at the mention of his favorite dish, or at the thought that his hostess would herself prepare it. But how is she to cook? There is no hearth, no cooking-vessels.

"Everything will be here," said Eveline, laughing joyously. "I shall change my dress; I cannot cook in this."

She ran off as she spoke, and returned in two minutes.

Actresses learn how to dress quickly. She now wore a white embroidered maid's frock, and a little cap on her head. She called no one to help her, but laid a cloth on the oak table, filled a silver kettle with water, set it to boil on a spirit-lamp. She turned up the sleeves of her dress to the elbows, and shook with a light hand the meal into the boiling water; then she turned the mixture deftly with a silver spoon round and round until it became thick. Then she took the kettle by the handle, emptied it on to a glazed clay plate—yes, actually a clay plate!—and poured some cream over the mixture. She fetched two wooden spoons, one for Peter, one for herself.

"Let us eat off the one plate, Peter."

And they ate this porridge off one plate. Peter felt a strange moisture fill his eyes; he had not wept since he was a child. The porridge was excellent; all the cooks in Vienna put together couldn't have given him a meal so much to his mind. There was wine on the table, but no glasses.

Peasants never drink during meals; but when they had finished Eveline fetched a clay jug and asked Peter to drink, after, as is the custom, she had taken a draught.

"Drink this, Peter; it is your old favorite."

There was mead in the jug—a very innocent sort of drink—and Peter thought it was his duty to empty the last drop. The hell that had been raging in his breast seemed all at once to be extinguished. He said to himself:

"Yes, I shall go back to the church, and to the spot where I made that awful vow; I shall implore the Holy Mother to allow me to take it back. I shall hurt no one; I shall take no revenge. Let the green grass grow again in the fields, and let her live in splendor in the smiles of the great ones. I shall not grudge her her happiness. This day, when she has received me so kindly, has banished from my memory the day upon which she left me. But I shall ask her for one kiss, so that I may remember nothing but that."

He delayed, however, too long in putting his desire into words. They were, indeed, hovering on his lips when the door suddenly opened, and a servant announced that his excellency was in the drawing-room.

(Now, Peter, God help you; you may go hence without your kiss!)

Eveline could hardly say good-bye; she had to change her dress. The footman showed him out at the secret door; there another footman led him down the back stairs, and, opening another door, left Peter in a narrow street, where he had never been before. While he made the best of his way to the hotel he had leisure to think over what he should say to Evila if he ever again had the chance of being alone with her in the round room. The recollection of how he had missed his opportunity roused the demon again in his mind. The burning lava of hell began once more to fill his veins, the stream of sulphur which the lost souls are ever drinking. He kept repeating to himself, "The grass shall not grow again!"

By the time he reached the inn he brought with him a goodly company—hatred, envy, rage at his own weakness, horror at his own wickedness, mixed with political fanaticism. A delightful gathering in one man's breast.

CHAPTER XXIII

FINANCIAL INTRIGUE

WE can give no authentic account of the interview between his excellency the minister and his beautiful hostess. We were not present, and neither had we a phonograph.

No doubt he complimented her upon her charming talent, and promised her his powerful interest, and as in this world nothing is given for nothing, there is every probability that his excellency, who was an undoubted scoundrel, hinted at the reward he would expect for using his powerful interest in her behalf; upon which Eveline, like a prudent woman, wishing to have everything in black and white, produced from the drawer of her writing-table the parchment which we have already heard of.

His excellency took the paper, probably believing it was a petition to grant her an engagement. He held it in his hand while he smilingly assured her that the matter was as good as concluded. It is, however, more than probable that when he gave a hurried glance at the contents his face assumed its official expression; he saw it did not refer to an operatic engagement, but to the grant for the Bondavara Railway. Seeing this, it is likely that his excellency got up at once, and, hat in hand, explained to his lovely hostess how distressed he felt not to be in a position to comply with her wishes, as there were insuperable objections in the way, great opposition from the legislative body, and yet greater opposition in the Upper House, where Prince Sondersheim was working heaven and earth against the Bondavara Railway, and, therefore, from political and financial reasons, from the condition of the country and many other causes, it would be impossible, or almost impossible, to hold out any hope of granting the Bondavara Railway a guarantee from the government. That then his excellency made a profound bow and left the room may be considered a fact. It is psychologically certain that he descended the staircase with a frown of vexation on his face, and that he murmured between his teeth:

"If I had known that I was going to talk to the *banker's wife* I should never have come here." As he got into his carriage—and this is historical—he banged the door with such violence that the glass window was shattered in pieces.

At the very hour when this interview was taking place a committee-meeting was being held in Prince Theobald's palace, which had for its object to lay before the shareholders the necessity of paying the third instalment—a critical operation, this attack upon the pockets of the public. The Bondavara Railway now played its part. Felix Kaulmann announced he had every confidence that in a couple of weeks it would be a fact. The deputation from Bondathal had caused a sensation, besides which the company had the interest of a very influential person, who could persuade his excellency to do anything, even give the grant for the railroad. The finely cut, aristocratic face of the president did not betray by a sign that he knew who this person was.

Kaulmann never for a moment suspected that Eveline told the prince the names of all the visitors who came to the palace during his absence, and that they were admitted through the little door. He would have called such stupidity by an ugly name.

While the meeting was sitting a note was brought to Kaulmann, who at once recognized Eveline's writing. He read the letter quickly, then laid it on the table with a discontented air.

"What is that?" asked the prince, pointing to a roll of paper.

It was the unsigned document which Eveline had returned.

Kaulmann wrote on a slip of paper, "Another hitch in that damned railway."

The prince said to himself, "Then his wife has again escaped." Then he bent over Kaulmann, and, laying his hand upon his shoulder, whispered to him:

"My dear friend, one doesn't get everything by a pair of black eyes."

Spitzhase was the secretary of the meeting. After this little scene he wrote upon a piece of paper, and, twisting it up, handed it to Kaulmann. Kaulmann read it; then tore it in small pieces and shrugged his shoulders.

"I know all *that*," he said, sulkily. "I don't want any advice."

The committee went away in bad humor with one another. The expense of bringing the deputation from Bondathal had been two thousand gulden, and this comedy had been of no use. The last stake should now be played. Csanta had determined not to pay the third instalment. He would sell all his shares at the price quoted and refill his casks with silver. On the day of the Proclamation, however, he received a letter from Spitzhase, which ran as follows:

"SIR,—To-morrow Herr Kaulmann is going to you to offer to buy all your shares at forty-five florins exchange. Be on your guard. I can assure you that the government has signed a grant for the Bondavara Railway, and so soon as this is public the shares will rise another twenty per cent."

Csanta believed in Spitzhase as in an oracle, and with reason. All happened as he said. Immediately upon the issue of the Proclamation, and when the shares were a little flat, Kaulmann appeared in X——, and offered him forty-five florins exchange upon his shares. But the old Greek was firm, not one would he part with; he would rather take his last cask to Vienna and empty its contents than part with one share.

He was rewarded for his firmness. Two days later he read in the newspaper how generously both Houses had voted a grant to the Bondavara Railway.

His excellency the prime-minister had himself pleaded for the cause in the Lords and Deputies House, and had proved conclusively that, from the political point of view, from the present favorable condition of the money market, as also from the side of the landed interest, from every point of view—strategical, financial, co-operative, and universal—the government guarantee for the Bondavara Railway was absolutely necessary, and, as a natural consequence, the motion was carried. Prince Waldemar, indeed, opposed it vigorously, but his following was small, so nobody minded him.

At the next audit of the Bondavara Company's accounts presented to the shareholders there appeared under the heading of expenditure this remarkable entry: "Expense of foundations, forty thousand gulden."

"What does this mean?" said the shareholders, with one voice.

Kaulmann whispered something to the man nearest him; he passed the whisper on, whereupon every one nodded his head, and tried to think it was all right. So it appeared to be, for after the government grant to the railway the Bondavara shares rose to seventy florins above par. Nothing could be more convincing. Csanta had punch at dinner, and got drunk for joy.

Some evenings later Eveline met his excellency in the green-room of the Treumann Theatre. The minister thought it was time to press for payment of his services.

"My dear lady," he said, "have I not obeyed your wishes in regard to the Bondavara Railway?"

Eveline made him a low courtesy. She wore the costume of the Duchess of Gerolstein.

"I am eternally indebted to your excellency," she said. "To-morrow evening I shall blow you *forty thousand* kisses."

At the words "forty thousand" his excellency grew red. He turned on his heel, and for the future Eveline was relieved from his attentions; but it was also quite certain that she had lost all chance of an engagement at the Opera-house. She might sing like a nightingale, but her petition would never be signed.

CHAPTER XXIV

THE BONDAVARA RAILWAY

The Bondavara Railway was begun. Prince Waldemar and his followers, the bears, were crushed—there *are* always people who die of hunger in the midst of a plenteous harvest.

Prince Waldemar met his noble relative, Prince Theobald, at the Jocky Club. Their encounter was hardly a friendly one, considering their close relationship.

Said Prince Waldemar: "You have chosen to put yourself at the head of my enemies. You have done your utmost to trump my best card. You have allied yourself with that man Kaulmann, with whom I am on bad terms. I sought your granddaughter in marriage; you promised she should be my wife, and then you sent her away from Vienna. You have invented all manner of pretexts to keep her at Pesth, and now the secret is out—she is betrothed to Salista. I had a fancy for a pretty little woman, and just to prevent my having her you invite her to your palace and forbid her to receive my visits. Worse than all, you have given over your only unmortgaged property, Bondavara, to a swindling company, who want to set themselves over me; and you have become their president. You have schemed and jockeyed the government into giving the guarantee for a railway that won't pay two per cent. You haven't an idea how you are implicated in these transactions.

I pity you—for I have always felt esteem for you—and I intend to set myself the task of regulating *your* affairs some day. Meantime take care, for if I succeed in upsetting the human pyramid upon whose shoulders you stand the greatest *fall* will be yours."

Of all this long harangue Prince Theobald only gathered the fact that Angela had chosen the Marquis Salista for her husband, and had never written to tell him. She let him hear it from another.

The Bondavara Railway was being pressed forward; it was nearly finished. There was no further need for a woman's black-diamond eyes. They had done their work. One day Eveline visited her husband. Felix received her with apparent satisfaction.

"I have come," she said, "to ask you a question. Prince Theobald has been for some days so sad; it is melancholy to see his distress. Have you any idea of its cause?"

"I have. His granddaughter, the Countess Angela, is married, and her husband, the Marquis Salista, is taking steps to put the prince under restraint, on account of the foolish manner in which he is squandering his fortune."

"And much of this foolish extravagance is spent on me."

"You are really wonderfully sharp, Eveline."

"I shall put an end to his spending his money on me. I shall tell the prince that I must leave his palace. I shall be always grateful to him; he has been a benefactor to me—and so have you. I ought to have mentioned you first. You have had me educated; you have taught me a great deal. I have to thank you for being what I am. I can earn my own living, thanks to you. I mean to become a real artist. But I must leave Vienna; I do not care to remain here any longer."

"I think, Eveline, you have decided well, and our minds have really a wonderful sympathy. I was about to advise the very course to you. By all means, leave Vienna; by all means, make use of your talents, and take up work seriously. I shall continue to do my duty as your husband. I shall take you to Paris; I shall settle myself in my house there on purpose to be of assistance to you. You will make a hit there, I know, and we shall be always good friends."

In spite of her previous experience of this man's character, Eveline was weak enough to be touched by his words and to blame herself for having done him injustice, for it was a great sacrifice on his part to leave Vienna for her sake. She could never have supposed that this sacrifice was part of his well-considered plan for ridding himself of her. She had played *her* part in making his fortune, and now she could go where she chose—to her native coal-pit if she liked. Once in Paris, he would be able to say, "Madam, you are here under the French law, and as no *civil ceremony* has passed between us, you are not my wife; you are at liberty to call yourself unmarried."

Felix had another reason for settling himself in Paris. It was here he counted on carrying out the second part of his programme. Now that the Bondavara Railway was nearly finished, the castles in the air of the Abbé Samuel were beginning to take shape; the next step should be a gigantic loan in the interest of the Church. This loan would be another means of aggrandizing the house of Kaulmann; its reputation would be worldwide. Already Kaulmann's name was of European celebrity; he belonged to the stars of the first order in the financial world. From being a *baron* of the stock-exchange he had become a prince. If he succeeded in effecting this loan he would be a *king* of the money-market, before whose name even that of Rothschild would pale.

A halo was also beginning to surround the name of the Abbé Samuel. The government had begun to see that this popular orator held the people in his hand, and could lead them as he chose. The people looked upon him as their benefactor, a man whose influence could get them benefits. Was not the Bondavara Railway a proof of this? The twelve Halinacoats were firmly persuaded that the abbé had carried back in his pocket the government grant. The clerical party acknowledged him as a new light. In Rome he was lauded for his zeal in the papal cause. If he was made bishop, which was almost a certainty, he would be the first Hungarian prelate who had taken his seat in the Austrian House of Lords. The minister would stare when he found his scheme for the secularization of Hungarian Church property met by another scheme from the new bishop, which, while proposing a gigantic loan upon these same Church lands, had for its object the elevation of the Holy See by these very means. The money-markets of France, Belgium, and the Roman States would vie with one another in promoting the loan, and the pontiff would look upon the man who had conceived such a project as the saviour of the pontificate; his name should be written in letters of gold. In Hungary, also, the scheme would be favorably received as a means of saving the church property already threatened, for the government dared not refuse this alternative.

Moreover, the primate was an old man; the pope was still older. All the wheels were in readiness; the machine could now be put in motion.

The day the first locomotive steamed out of the Bondavara station the Abbé Samuel might say to himself, "The way to Rome is clear." It would be also safe to prophesy that on this day Ivan Behrend's ruin would be complete.

This railroad would bring the goods of the Joint-Stock Company into the markets of the world, where they could compete with the coal of Prussia and the English coal. But, it will be said, Ivan had the same chance; his coals were equally good, and the giant with the seven-mile boots would carry his coal as well as his enemies'. But here was where the shoes pinched. What was of use to the company was destruction to him.

The railway was not to run through the valley where his mine was situated, although that line was the best and most natural course to take; instead of which mountains had to be made level, tunnels had to be bored through the hills, to avoid his colliery and to carry the rails close to the company's mine. In consequence of this, Ivan would be obliged to make a circuit of a half-day's journey to get to the railway, and so the freightage to the station made his goods five or six per cent. dearer than those of the company. For him, therefore, the railroad was a crushing blow.

In the meantime the end of the year drew near, the time when the miners were to receive their share from the profits. But profit there was none. Neither coal nor iron had any sale. The company's low prices had taken every customer from Ivan.

Any one who possesses ready money can always *say*, even if he loses, that he wins; the common people call this eating your own entrails. Ivan had a sum by him, which he had carefully gathered in better days. It amounted, all told, to several thousands, and he calculated he could hold his own against his giant rivals for at least ten years. He forgot that the giants were cunning as well as strong, and that they did not despise the smallest artifice.

When the railway directors issued their prospectus, inviting all contractors to send in contracts for iron rails, etc., Ivan thought to himself, "Now, I will have some fun. The shareholders of the Joint-Stock Company offer their iron six per cent. cheaper than it costs them. I will offer to the railway directors to deliver iron rails at ten per cent. cheaper than they cost *me*. I shall lose fifty thousand gulden, but I shall have the satisfaction of punishing my neighbors for their folly in lowering the price of the raw material."

Simple fool! Just as an honorable gentleman imagines that when a letter is sealed no one would venture to open it, so Ivan thought that all the offers were read together, and that the most advantageous to the company was accepted.

Good gracious! nothing of the kind.

It is always settled beforehand who is to have the contract. When the proposals come in it sometimes happens that some one makes a yet lower offer than that of the *protégé*, and this last is then told to take pen and ink and write an offer proposing to give the goods half per cent. lower than the offer made by the outsider.

This is a well-known trick, and it is only men like Ivan, whose minds are occupied with petrifactions and the stars, who are in ignorance that such things are done.

The contract offered by the shareholders was half per cent. lower than the one offered by Ivan.

But even this rebuff didn't daunt him. Two and two make four, and those who sin against multiplication must come to ruin sooner or later.

Ivan continued making in his workshop iron bars and rails. He accumulated a store in his magazines. Some time they would be wanted.

The Bondavara Railroad was to be made.

Csanta wanted to sell his houses in X——; the whole street was for sale. He said he was going to live in Vienna, and to fill his office of one of the directors to the company. He was to receive a large salary, and to have little or nothing to do. He had changed all his gold into papers—there is no use nowadays for houses or land or cattle or mines; nothing is good but paper. *It* wants neither groom nor manure nor pay nor machinery.

Therefore, he wished to sell the whole street. Fortunately, there was so little money in X—— that the inhabitants of the whole town put together couldn't produce enough money to buy a poor little street.

The Bondavara Railway was in progress. Along the line the navvies were working like a swarm of ants; they shoved wheelbarrows from morning until night; they dug the ground, blew up rocks, bored mountains, rammed plugs into water-sources, hewed stones, dammed rivers.

In the dark mouth of the Bondavara mine one man stood immovable. He was ever watching the work. His gloomy, threatening face was fixed steadily upon a windlass.

This man was Peter Saffran. He held in his hand a lump of coal, and as he looked back from the noisy landscape to the remnant of trees his eyes seemed to say, "Thou art the cause of all this tumult, this wealth, this splendor; thou art a living power—thou!" And he hurled the coal against the wall.

CHAPTER XXV

THE POOR DEAR PRINCE

"You have something to tell me: what is it?" asked Prince Theobald, as he entered Eveline's drawing-room in answer to a letter from her, written after her interview with her husband.

"I wish to leave Vienna."

"Ah! this is sudden. And where are you going?"

"My husband is obliged to go to Paris. I am going with him."

The prince looked inquiringly at her. "Have you, then, grown tired of being under my care?"

"I am afraid I cannot deny it. I am like a slave in a gilded cage. I am a sort of prisoner, and I want to see life."

"You repent, then, of the promise you made me? Well, then, I release you; but stay with me."

"I should be too proud to receive benefits from any one to whom I am ungrateful. Besides, it would be enough for me to know that you are the master of the palace to take all sense of freedom from me. I don't want to receive any more favors."

"You wish to become an actress?"

"I do wish that." Eveline laid a stress on the last word.

"From ambition?"

"I cannot say so. If I were ambitious I should be

more diligent. I want my freedom. I don't want my wings clipped. I like to feel I can use them as I choose."

"That is rather a dangerous experiment for any one so young and pretty as you are."

"One never falls so low that one cannot rise again."

"Where did you learn that?"

"From what I see every day."

"You are resolved to leave me?"

"I am—I am—I am!" Eveline repeated these words impatiently.

"Then I had better free you from my disagreeable society as soon as possible," said the prince, taking up his hat. Then, with an ironical bow, he added, "Forgive me, madam, for the weary hours I must have imposed upon you."

Eveline, with an impatient stamp of her foot, turned her back upon him. The prince, when he had got as far as the anteroom, found that he had forgotten his walking-stick in the drawing-room. It had been a Christmas present from Eveline, and he would not leave it with her. He went back to fetch it.

He opened the door gently, and he saw a sight that surprised him. Eveline still stood with her back to him. She had in her hands the stick he had come for, which she kissed two or three times, sobbing bitterly. The prince withdrew gently. Everything was made clear to him. Eveline quarrelled with him to make the separation less hard for him. She pretended to be mean and ungrateful in order that he might forget her more easily. Why did she do this?

The next day the prince found the solution of this riddle. His servant brought him the key of Eveline's apartments. The lady had left by the very earliest train. The prince hastened to the palace, and he then understood why it was that Eveline had left. She had taken nothing; everything was there. She was a pearl among women. A lock of her hair was wound round the handle of the walking-stick—her beautiful hair, which fell from the crown of her head to her feet.

Eveline arrived in Paris before Kaulmann. It had been settled between them that she should stop at a hotel until he arranged where she should live.

Some weeks later Felix came and said: "Your house is ready for you. Will you come and see it?"

Eveline drove with Felix to her new home, which was in the Rue Sebastopol, one of the best situations in Paris, the first floor. As she came into the apartment her heart beat. Everything was familiar to her eyes—the cherry-colored curtains, the carpets, the dove-colored panels, the black marble fireplace, the oval frames in china, the window looking into the garden—all as in Vienna. The same pictures, the same service of silver, the wardrobes, the jewel-cases, even to the glove which she had left upon the table.

The tears fell from her eyes as she murmured to herself, "The good, kind prince!"

Felix, however, with perfect *aplomb*, took all the credit to himself, and asked her, "Have I not arranged your apartment to your taste?"

Eveline made him no answer. Her thoughts were with the good, kind prince, her best friend. To him she owed her engagement at the Opera-house in Paris, the wreaths that were thrown to her on her first appearance, the carriage she drove in every day. All was due to the paternal interest of Prince Theobald, who, from the day he called her his daughter, had never ceased to care for her as his child.

CHAPTER XXVI

DIES IRÆ

ONE gloomy day in late autumn Ivan went from the forge to his mine, and upon the way his thoughts ran in a sad groove. "What a curious world we live in; everything goes wrong—at least, for most people. Bread is not for the wise man, nor success for the strong; it was so in the days of Solomon. One bad year follows the other, for even nature acts like a step-mother to men. The poor are hungry and beg for bread, and when they have eaten they forget from whom they received nourishment. All the great proprietors go to their graves without doing, either for their country or their neighbor, anything worth mentioning; all the burden of the present and the future seems to fall upon the less numerous and more exhausted class. The patriots are all hollow; they weep when they are in their cups; they show their fists, but no one dares to strike a blow. All manly strength is gone; there is not a man worth the name in the whole country. And the women—they are all the same, from the high-born dame to the peasant girl —false and heartless. Even in the bowels of the earth it is no better. For the last two days there has been choke-damp in the mine; the escape of gas has been so great that the men cannot work; it is as likely as not that there will be an explosion while I am in the pit."

You see, Ivan's thoughts were as black as the landscape, and suited to its gloom. His road from the forge to the mine led him past the workmen's houses, and as he passed one of these a miner came stumbling out of the door. The house was a wine-shop. The miner had his back towards Ivan, who did not recognize him, but he noticed that the man had great difficulty in walking straight.

"I wonder who it is that has got drunk so early in the day?" thought Ivan, and hastened after the man to find out who he was. When he got up with him he saw, to his surprise, that it was Peter Saffran. This struck Ivan unpleasantly; he recalled how, on the day when Evila had eloped, Saffran had sworn never again to touch brandy; he knew also that Peter had kept this oath. He recollected also, but imperfectly, that when he said that he wouldn't drink any more he had let fall some threat. Well, it didn't much matter; if he got drunk, that was his affair. But why did he come to Ivan's village to get drunk? Why didn't he go to the tavern in his own colony.

Ivan hailed the man. "Good-morning, Peter."

Peter did not return the greeting; he stared like a stupid dog who doesn't know his own master. He looked at Ivan with a wild eye, he pressed his lips together, and his nostrils extended. He drew his cap down over his eyes.

Ivan asked him, "Has the choke-damp got into your pit?"

No answer from Peter. He shoved his cap from off his forehead, and, opening his mouth to its full extent, bent his face to that of Ivan, and let his hot, spirit-laden breath blow over him. Then, without saying a syllable, he turned away, and set off running in the direction of the company's mine.

The heated breath of the man, with the sickening smell of bad brandy, sent a shudder through Ivan's frame. He stood still, staring after the runaway, who, when he had got a certain distance, stopped and looked back. Ivan could see his face distinctly. He looked like a madman; his lips hung apart, like those of a mad dog; his white teeth gleamed in contrast to his red gums. His whole appearance was so strange and desperate that Ivan laid hold of the revolver in his pocket. For one moment the thought passed through his mind that he would be doing a good work in freeing the world of such a creature, but on second thoughts he let him go unharmed, and continued his way to the mine to look after the ventilators.

In the vault the proportion between the hydrogen and the air was three to seven. Ivan forbade any work to be done in the mine, or any pumping out of the dangerous gas. He employed his men in the open air, removing the coal that was required, and only allowed those to remain below who had to look after the airpumps.

He remained the whole day on the spot, controlling everything and keeping a close watch. Towards evening he left the mine and returned to his house. Everything was apparently safe. It was a nasty, foggy, gloomy evening; the state of the atmosphere reacted upon the mind and body alike. When nature is out of sorts, man suffers; when the sky is overcast, he, too, is gloomy. And when the earth is sick, when worms and mould destroy the fruit, when the harvest is ruined by blight, and the cattle are decimated by pestilence—above all, when the noxious vapors from the coal-mines rise to the surface and poison the very air—then men sicken and die.

All through the day Ivan had felt cold shudders running over his whole body. His limbs were contracted by that unpleasant feeling called goose-skin, and when he got home he shivered, although his room was warm. He was restless, uneasy. He could occupy himself with nothing; everything palled upon him. The worst symptom of all, he could not even work.

When a man refuses food or drink, when he does not care for the company of a pretty woman, when his club wearies him, these are unhealthy signs; but when he turns away from work, and finds no longer any interest in his usual occupation, then it is time to send for the physician.

Ivan's head throbbed, yet he could not sleep, and to stay awake was torture. He lay down, and with a resolute effort closed his eyes. A panorama of past, present, and future kept dancing before him. Peter Saffran's hot, stinking breath seemed to breathe again in his nostrils, and the very horror brought back to his memory the man's long-forgotten words:

"No more during my life shall I drink brandy—*only once;* and when I do, and when you smell from my breath that I have been drinking, or see me coming out of the public-house, then take my advice and stop safe at home, for on that day no man shall know in what manner he shall die."

Who cares for the threat of a drunken man? Let me sleep. No, the drunken man would not allow Ivan to sleep; his breath was there. Faugh! it made him sick. His blear-eyed, pallid face was there bending over the bed, looking into Ivan's eyes with his blood-shot eyes; his open mouth and shut teeth came quite close to the sleeper, who, vainly beating his arms in the air, tried to drive away this horrid nightmare.

Ah, what is that sound? A crack like the crack of doom awoke Ivan; not alone awoke him, but threw him violently out of bed and on to the floor, where he lay stunned.

His first consecutive thoughts were, "The chokedamp has exploded! My mine is in ruins!" This was enough to get him on his legs and to send him out in the darkness—darkness, raven-black darkness, the stillness only broken by a whistling sound in the air. Ivan stood for a moment wondering. He felt the earth swaying under his feet; he heard a subterranean grumbling. There! the pitch-dark night was suddenly illumined; a bright pillar of fire rose out of the Bondavara Company's mine. At the same moment another fearful explosion was heard, worse than the last. The windows of the house were shattered in a thousand pieces, the chimneys, the roofs fell in. The pressure of the air forced Ivan back and threw him against the door of his own house. By the strong light of the demoniacal pillar he could see his own workmen all on their knees with a horrified expression upon their ghastly faces. Women and children were gathered at the doors of the houses, but the terror was so great that every one was speechless.

The entire valley glowed like the crater of a volcano. It vomited forth a rain of fire-sparks, as in Gomorrah. The flames reached almost to the clouds, and heaven sent forth clap upon clap of thunder, the like of which in the most terrible thunder-storm had never been heard.

Two minutes later the flames were extinguished. The whole valley was again enveloped in pitch-darkness, only over the company's mine floated a filmy white cloud.

"The neighboring mine has exploded!" shrieked Ivan. "Help! help!" He never remembered that it was his enemy's mine; he only thought that there, in the bowels of the earth, a fearful, indescribably fearful, calamity had happened. "Help! help!" he cried, and ran to the alarm-bell, at which he pulled with all the strength of his body.

His own men came rushing in hot haste, all repeating to one another, as if it were something new, "The neighboring mine has exploded!"

Then followed a significant pause. The men carrying lanterns surrounded Ivan, and looked at him questioningly, waiting for him to speak.

How had he guessed their thoughts?

Those who under God's free heavens drew their breath were bound to go to the rescue of those who lay buried underground, and who perchance still lived. Here it was no case of friend or foe. They were human beings; that was enough.

"We must get the ventilators, the well-buckets to work!" called Ivan. "Let each man bring a thick cloth to tie over his mouth. Bring crow-bars, cords, ladders, india-rubber tubes, hose-pipes. The women only are to remain behind. Forward, my men!"

He threw on an old coat, seized a strong iron bar, which he carried on his shoulder, placed himself at the head of his men, and led the way to the company's mine.

It was not easy to force an entrance into the works. The proprietors had set up all manner of barricades in order to prevent Ivan's carts from making any use of the new road. On the gates there were boards with "No trespassing. No one to pass this way without a written order."

No one now minded these orders. If a door or a gate impeded their progress, Ivan thrust his iron rod through it and soon made a passage, through which his men rushed pell-mell. The miners did not pause to harness any horses to the machines. They harnessed themselves, while others shoved behind, and drove them on over sticks and stones down to the mouth of the pit. Like an army of lunatics the party of rescuers rushed on through the night, making their way as best they could by means of the lanterns fastened to their waistbands. Soon, however, the darkness was again illumined. The forge nearest to the pit, and consequently the most exposed to the fiery heat, blew up suddenly, and the flames from the heating-oven filled the air with a red glow. The miners avoided, however, the direction in which it burned, as it would be impossible to predicate the direction which the molten metal would take.

When they reached the pit an awful spectacle presented itself. The ventilation-ovens which were placed over the shaft-mouth were gone. The bricks and tiles were scattered in a thousand directions all over the fields. The large windlass of cast-iron lay on the ground at a considerable distance from its former position, and of the conical, bell-shaped buildings hardly a stone was left. Only one wall was still standing; the iron fasteners hung from its side. The northern entrance to the pit had fallen in. The handsome stone gates lay in ruins. Stones, beams, iron bars, coals were all mixed up together in heterogeneous confusion, as if a volcano had vomited them out.

The air was filled with the cries of weeping women. Hundreds upon hundreds of women and children, probably widows and orphans, held up their hands to heaven and wept. Under their feet their husbands, their fathers, brothers, lovers lay buried, and no one could help them.

More from recklessness than from actual courage

some men had already attempted to go down into the pit. They had been at once stunned by the pressure of the gas, and now their comrades, at the risk of their own lives, were trying to drag them out by cords and slings. Already one lay on the grass, while the women stood round him wringing their hands.

Ivan now began to make his plans. "In the first place," he said, "no one is to venture near the pit. Let all wait until I return."

He took his way towards the house of the directors. He forgot that he had sworn never to hold any communication with Rauné. In any case, he was not to be found. In the next town there was high festival. The directors of the new railway had given a banquet in honor of the completion of the tunnel. Rauné was there. Ivan, however, met the second engineer coming out of his house. He was a cool, phlegmatic man, and consoled himself with the trite reflection that these things happened everywhere. "The gates must be rebuilt," he said. "The pit roads must again be re-made, and probably we shall have to sink another shaft. It will cost a lot of money. *Voila tout!*"

"How many men are below?" asked Ivan.

"Probably about a hundred and fifty."

"Only! And what is to be done for them?"

"It will be a hard job to get them out, for they were at work at the passage which we were making between the north pit and the east to improve the ventilation."

"Therefore there is no other entrance to the pit but the one which has fallen in?"

"No; and the eastern shaft is also in ruins. The flames came from there; you must have seen them."

"Yes; and I couldn't understand how it was that the

second explosion followed the first after an interval of a few minutes."

"That is easily explained. The communicating wall was already so thin that the explosion in the north pit blew it into fragments; the gas in the east pit undoubtedly was not kindled by the flames, for they had already gone out, but by the strong pressure of the air, which was heated to fever-heat by the accumulation of coal, and which, therefore, exploded through the shaft. So it is when you put sand into the barrel of a gun; the powder bursts the barrel before it throws out the sand."

It was plain that the engineer took a very cold-blooded view of the whole affair, and that the design for the new stone gate was a matter of more interest to him than the hundred and fifty lives which were in jeopardy. Ivan saw there was little assistance to be got from him.

"Before we can attempt the rescue of the men who are buried in the pit," he said, "we must pump the gas out of the opening of the cavern. Where is your air-pump?"

"Up there," returned the engineer, pointing to the sky; "that is to say, if it hasn't fallen down."

"You have no portable ventilator?"

"We never contemplated the necessity of having one."

"I have brought mine, if we can adjust it."

"I would gladly know how that can be done. If the ventilator has a copper tube, it would be impossible to introduce it through all the zigzag of the rubbish and general wreck; if it has an india-rubber pipe it would be too weak, and wouldn't stand being shoved forward."

"Some one must carry it into the pit."

"Some one?" repeated the engineer, with an air of amazement. "Look yonder; they are drawing up the third man who was foolish enough to venture down there; he is dead, like the other two!"

"No, none of them are dead; they will soon recover consciousness; they are stifled by the foul air."

"All the same, I can hardly believe that you will find a man mad enough to be the first to carry a tube fifty steps through all the wreckage."

"I have already found the man. I shall do it."

The engineer shrugged his shoulders, but he made no effort to dissuade him.

Ivan went back to the men, who meantime had been getting ready for work. He called the oldest miner on one side.

"Paul," he said, "some one must carry the india-rubber tube of the ventilator into the mouth of the pit."

"Good. Let us draw lots."

"We shall do nothing of the kind. I shall go. You are all husbands and fathers with families. You have wives and children to provide for. I have no one. How long can a man hold out in that foul air without drawing his breath?"

"A hundred beats of his pulse; no longer."

"Good. Fetch me the pipe. Bind a cord round my body and hold the other end. When you see that I no longer carry the pipe, draw the cord slowly back, but take care to draw slowly, in case that I should have fainted and that a sudden pull might strangle me."

Ivan loosened the woollen band from his waist, steeped it in a vessel of vinegar, and wrung it out and wrapped his face in it, so that his nose and mouth were covered. He then bound the cord firmly round his body, took the foremost end of the india-rubber pipe upon his shoulder, and began to make his way through the rubbish and *débris* at the pit's month.

The old miner called after him, in a broken voice: "Count the seconds. Fifty for going, fifty for coming back."

Ivan vanished behind the ruins. The miners took off their caps and folded their hands. The old man held the fingers of his right hand on the wrist of his left and counted his pulse. He had already counted over fifty and the other end of the pipe had not moved. It had passed sixty and was near seventy when suddenly it was pulled forward. Ivan had penetrated into the deadly atmosphere. The old miner wiped the perspiration from his brow. He counted eighty, ninety, a hundred seconds. They shall never see him again. Then the pipe remained steady.

Now they began to draw the rope. It was slack, and not tightened by any burden. Ivan was, therefore, so far safe; he was still walking, for the rope continued slack. Suddenly it got stiffer. Be careful now. The cord again slackened; the old miner counted a hundred and sixty seconds. Suddenly Ivan was seen coming out of the pit's mouth, supporting himself upon the fallen stones of the archway; but his strength failed, and as the men rushed to his assistance he tottered and fell into their arms. His face was like that of a dying man.

They rubbed him with vinegar, and the fresh air soon revived him. He sat up, and told them he was all right, but—

"The air down there is something awful," he said. "What is happening to those poor creatures who are buried below?"

It never occurred to him to remember that those poor creatures were the same ungrateful men who had deserted him, who had taken service with the men who had sworn to ruin him, who had formed a conspiracy against him, who were ready to murder him, who had sent a deputation to the enemies of their native land. Here they lay, buried in the depths of mother-earth, which thus revenged upon them their treachery. Ivan had forgotten their sin against him and their country, and his only thought was to save them if there was yet time.

Now that the ventilator had been set in motion, the work of rescue might begin; but all the same it was a terribly hard fight.

Ivan divided his band of men into two divisions. Each man was only to stay an hour at the dangerous work of clearing away the rubbish. Every one must have his face covered by a cloth steeped in vinegar. So soon as he began to feel faint he was to be carried away by his comrades.

When the day began to break the wreck of the fallen entrance had been moved to one side, but in the mouth of the pit the sun could not penetrate. The vault of slate-clay had fallen altogether to one side, so that Ivan, when he had carried the pipe into the pit, had found there was scarcely room to allow it to wind through the chasms. In the spot where he had placed the mouth of the pipe the vault was altogether destroyed.

It was an undertaking almost superhuman. What had been the work of weeks had to be done in so many days. And yet it must be done.

In their work of clearing away the rubbish Ivan's men had very little assistance from the company's men for this reason: the explosion had taken place at the time when the miners were relieved. When men are working in collieries it is usual to relieve them four times. It was the time of the midnight relief when the accident happened. One party of the miners had already gone down the shaft; they were undoubtedly suffocated. The other party were on their way out, and were killed at once by the explosion. There was another party who had only reached the resting-stage, where neither the flames nor the fragments could touch them. These men were buried alive. It therefore resulted that of all the company's miners only from twenty to thirty were available.

The men who worked the forge were forbidden by the director to give any help in the work of rescue. In all the ovens the metal was in a liquid state; if it was not attended to it would turn into rammers. The workmen give the name of *ram*, or *rammer*, to a solid mass of iron, which, in consequence of faulty melting, cannot be removed from the oven, and it and the oven have to be thrown away as useless lumber. The forge-work was urgently needed. The railway greaves had to be finished by a certain date, or a large fine would have to be paid. Ivan therefore had to set his men almost unaided to the task of clearing the pit. The women helped with all their strength. Their husbands, the bread-winners, were underneath the ruins.

What a terrible undertaking! In consequence of the falling in of the arches the roof had, at a distance of six feet, to be supported on plugs, and a sort of street made through the ruins, where at every corner a new enemy waited for the intrepid pioneers.

After the explosion the pit had been overflowed by water. The water-pipes had to be set to work, and where these were not sufficient the men were obliged to empty out the black slime in buckets, standing for hours in stinking mud, breathing foul air, threatened with death or mutilation from the constant falling of stones and wreckage. Undaunted by these obstacles, the men made their way step by step into the bowels of the earth.

In the afternoon Rauné arrived. In the middle of a convivial festival he had heard the news. He was raging. He came down the shaft and cursed all the dead men.

"The scoundrels! They have cost the company a million of money! What does it matter if they are all killed? Serves them right! Why should any of them be saved? Stuff and nonsense! Let them suffocate, the drunken dogs!"

The workers made him no answer. First, because they could not take up their time talking, and, secondly, because every man's mouth was covered. The clearing of a mine is very silent work.

But in the midst of his curses Rauné encountered one workman, who placed himself in front of him and confronted him with a steady look. This man was covered with mud and coal like the other laborers, his face was tied up with a cloth, and only the eyes were visible; they, too, were blackened with coal-dust, but Rauné knew by their expression that it was Ivan. No one who had ever looked into his eyes could forget him.

Rauné turned away without another word, and, in company with his engineer, left the pit. He interfered no further with Ivan's work.

Four days and four nights the men never ceased working. They triumphed over every obstacle and cut a pathway through every difficulty. During those four days Ivan never for one hour left the mine. He ate his meals sitting on a stone, and snatched an hour's sleep in some corner.

On the fourth day the workmen came upon one of the missing men. A man—no, but a mass, flattened against the wall, of flesh and bones, which had once been a man.

Some feet farther on there lay another body on the ground, but the head was nowhere to be seen. They tried to get him on one of the wheelbarrows which were for drawing coal, but he was all in fragments; splinters and shreds of that human body were sticking to everything.

Then they came upon the charred, blackened corpses of the men who had been burned. They were not recognizable.

Farther on there was a group of fifteen men crushed by a huge weight of slate stratum. This could not be moved, so they were left. It was more necessary to look after the living than the dead. Everywhere they found corpses; still the number of the missing was not complete.

The miners employed by the company told Ivan that if any of the men were still living they would be found at the resting-stage, where they left their coats before they began to work and fetched them again as they went up. In the passages, however, there had been such a total upset that the oldest hand could not find his way. In many places the explosion had torn down the partition wall, in other places the entrance was stopped up with rubbish, or the roof taken off some of the passages which led into the inner vaults. It was all in such utter confusion that no one could find out where the large vault lay.

At last it struck Ivan that underneath a mass of coal and slack he heard a faint, whimpering sound. He said to the men, "Dig this spot."

At once they set to work to clear away the rubbish, and as they cleared the company's men began to recognize different landmarks, which convinced them they were at the right place.

"Yes, here is the door which leads to the resting-stage." The pressure of the air had shut the door close, the side walls had fallen in, and so these, who had been safe from the conflagration, had been buried alive.

The whimpering cry for help, like that of an infant's wail, was heard now more distinctly. The door, too, was plainly visible, and as it was swung off its hinges Ivan took a light and peered into the dark cavern below.

No cry of joy reached him; the rescued men had not the strength to make a sound. They were about a hundred in all. They lay there still, speechless. Life had almost ebbed away, but not altogether. They had suffered the tortures of hunger and thirst, they had been suffocated by the foul air, broken-hearted, despairing. And now these human skeletons, when they saw the light, could hardly raise a finger to show they were alive. A heart-rending whimper, in which there was no human tone, rose from the hundred parched throats. When the explosion came they had been thrown upon their faces. Their lamps had gone out, and it would have been madness to relight them. They had remained in total darkness. After a little the danger of their situation increased. Soon they began to feel that the water was gradually— slowly at first—filling the space which served them as a refuge and a grave, and this space or vault was, they knew, a fathom deeper than the pit. They tried—for at first they were not so weak—to get hold of some boards and plugs that lay about, and out of these they made a sort of stage or platform, upon which they all clambered, and there waited for death—the death that might come either through hunger, foul air, or drowning. When their rescuers opened the door the water had reached the threshold and touched the bottom of the wooden stage.

Ivan directed that the poor creatures should be carried

carefully and silently out of their living grave. They did not press forward, for they could not stand. Each man lay where he was, and waited until his turn came. The foretaste of death made every one tranquil. Some of them could not at first open their eyes, but all were alive, and Ivan could not help thinking how wonderful is the strength of human nature.

He had saved them all, but the work was not yet finished. How if, beyond the breach of which the engineer had spoken, there were more men waiting for deliverance? One thing they must ascertain positively—if the explosion had finished the work begun by the engineer's men, and had carried away the wall which had divided one pit from the other. If this were so, it would considerably lighten the work of those who had come to seek for the victims. At the opening of the breach-tunnel lay a man's body; he was such a charred, burned mass that he was unrecognizable. The dead man held in his hand his safety-lamp. *It was open.*

So this was the accursed one who had done the hellish deed, and it was human folly that had caused this demoniacal explosion.

The corpse was not recognizable, the clothing was burned to ashes. In his girdle, however, they found a small steel casket, and in this casket a gold watch; upon the enamelled back was the portrait of a lovely woman.

When the watch was brought to Ivan he recognized the portrait. It was Eveline. With the watch there was also a bank-note for a hundred gulden. It was half burned. Upon the back was written:

"A year ago to-day I received this money; to-day I pay it back." What a fearful repayment!

Ivan was now able to grasp the connection between

the words and the acts of this terrible man, whose recollection of his own act of eating human flesh had prompted him to an unexampled and most horrid massacre. His threats after Evila's elopement, his entering into the company's service, the last occasion upon which he had drunk brandy, and the breath he had blown into Ivan's face. All was now explained. This was part of the drama. This man had a character such as Antichrist might be possessed of. His soul and body were full of concealed demons, who prompted him to take revenge of those who had offended him, ridiculed him, stolen from him, scorned him, treated him as a fool, insulted him with money, tempted him with luxuries, and taken advantage of his simplicity to pull him by the nose.

All of them should fall. He would pull the foundation-stone from under their feet, even if he dug his own grave in so doing. They should fall from their high estate — the banker, the pastor, the capitalist, the minister, and the actress.

In hell the demons could teach Peter nothing.

Ivan stood before the unsightly corpse deep in thought. In his heart there raged a wild conflict of passions. He also had been robbed, oppressed by the wealth of his enemies, his heart wounded by a hundred poisoned arrows, and this by the same men upon whom the revengeful hate of Peter Saffran had fallen. Ivan had come to their help. He had saved the lives and the property of his foes—at least, what they called their property; the monstrous treasure which lies in the very bowels of the earth does not, in truth, belong altogether to any man, but to all men; it is the treasure-trove of the state, destined to serve and minister to all ages.

And yet a great dread, an unconquerable fear, possessed Ivan. He dared not mention his fear to any one, for if he were to share his suspicion with any one of the workmen, who up to this had followed him obediently through every peril, they would, without another word, have turned their backs and fled for their lives.

The wire cylinder of Saffran's safety-lamp was filled to the very top with a red flame. This was a warning that the atmosphere was still charged with one-third of hydrogen gas, and that only two-thirds were of fresh air.

But there is an even greater danger to be feared than the pit-gas. Its fearful spirit had been laid; the victims lay silent upon the wheelbarrows. Yet another and a worse spirit lurks in ambush—a foe who goes about with closed eyes, whose presence is awful in its consequences: it is the carbon from the coals.

When the men had made the breach through the tunnel, they found, just as the engineer had said, that the explosion had burst through the partition wall, and that the *débris* had only to be removed, and the passage between the east and the north pits would be established. Not one of the workmen could remain long at this work. After some moments each one returned coughing, and complaining that in that place his safety-lamp would not burn.

In the pits the flame of the lamp filled the whole cylinder; this was not reassuring. But in the neighborhood of the ruins it would hardly burn; this was a far more serious sign.

The last miner who returned said that as he removed a large lump of coal such a terrible stench had penetrated through his mouth-protector that he had almost fainted. The smell was like that of putrid vegetable matter.

The old hands knew what this putrid stench signified. Paul suggested to Ivan that he should go and examine whence it came. Let him cover his mouth very carefully, and hasten back as soon as possible.

Ivan took his iron rod and his lamp, and went. Seizing hold of the rod with both hands, he struck it with all his strength into a mass of coal, upon which the lump rolled with a great noise into the adjoining space. He then fastened his lamp to the hook of his rod and pushed it into the hollow. The lamp went out at once, and as he looked from the darkness into the hollow, to his horror he saw in the next vault a red glow which lighted up the space. He knew at once there was no time to lose. He never paused to withdraw his rod, but rushed back to the men.

"The east pit is burning!" he cried.

No one answered, but the men seized hold of Ivan, and bore him with them out of the pit into the open air. Behind them followed the horrible stench—not merely that of foul air such as accompanies "bad weather," often with fatal effect; this was the more insidious carbon, that which kindles pit-fires, baffles the ingenuity of man, respects neither the brave nor the scientific, and which, when once it has begun, can never be turned back. There is nothing to do but to run for the bare life.

In a few minutes the pit was empty.

As they issued into the light of day they were surrounded by countless women and children, weeping and screaming in their joy at being reunited to their lost ones.

The engineer was also there. Ivan went straight to him. Taking the cloth from his mouth, he said:

"Do you know, sir, what is going on down there in your mine? Complete, utter ruin! The east pit is burning; it must have been alight some days, for the whole pit is red-hot. I shall never forget the sight. Now let me tell you what this means. It is not the hand of human wickedness, neither is it the avenging hand of God; it is altogether caused by the negligence of the overseer. You, who are a great scientist, know as well as I do that collieries take fire when sulphur gets mixed with coal-dust and is allowed to lie in a heap. It is always hot down there, and when the stuff is fanned by the air it lights of itself. Your pit is full of this dangerous burning mist. And now both your pit and my mine are finished. The colliery fire can never be extinguished. You have heard of the burning mountain of Dutweeler? A hundred and twenty years ago that coal-mine took fire; it is still burning. Here we shall experience another such tragedy. Good-morning."

The engineer only shrugged his shoulders; it was nothing to him.

Ivan shook the dust of the God-forsaken colony off his feet. He and his men returned to his own side of the mountain.

Meantime what had happened to his own mine? He had been absent four days and four nights, and had never given it a thought.

CHAPTER XXVII

FROM THE SUBLIME TO THE RIDICULOUS

Any one who wishes to understand the meaning of the proverb, "There is only one step from the sublime to the ridiculous," should gamble on the stock-exchange; there he will learn the full meaning of the words.

To-day you are a deity, to-morrow the meanest of street curs. To-day sixty agents shriek out the name of your speculation; you are a sort of king, and all the other kings on 'change study your countenance to see how the wind shifts. To-day, so soon as one o'clock strikes by the town clock, a swarm of buyers come round you. Your note-book is held up to the view of all the agents. It is handed from one to another; it is placed upon the back of an agent, and the competitors write the number of shares they want. To-day all hands point to the percentage, which is the proof of your high estate. To-day the crowd who are speculating on your credit fill all the passages; they scream out, "I sell!" "I buy!" Even outside the stock-exchange sweet creatures of the opposite sex, who like dabbling in stock quite as much as do the male creation, make their books. Women are prohibited from showing their faces on 'change; but they gamble all the same. Hundreds of ladies wait upon the stock-broker, with a copy of the exchange list in their hands; they have marked your shares. Still greater ladies sit outside the exchange in their grand carriages. In their eagerness they stretch their heads out of their carriage windows to know from the first-comer at what figure the shares—your shares—stand.

This is all to-day. To-morrow you are not to be found; your name is scratched out of the exchange list. Every one knows that your affair has "burst." You are nowhere. You are nobody. Your place is empty.

The firm of Kaulmann stood at the summit of its triumph. Felix and his bosom friend, the Abbé Samuel, were enjoying their afternoon siesta. The room was full of a cloud of smoke, and under its soothing influence the friends were building castles in the air.

"To-morrow," said Felix, "the pope's loan upon the Hungarian Church lands will be floated at the exchange."

"To-morrow I shall receive from Vienna my appointment as titular Bishop of the Siebenbürger."

"The silver kings are ready to plank down their millions on the loan."

"The pope gives it his blessing," murmured the abbé. "The cardinal's hat is ready for my head."

"The legitimist financiers have shown a decided objection to my wife appearing on the stage. This may injure the loan; therefore I intend to-morrow to explain to her that she is not legally my wife."

"Is it true that Prince Waldemar has arrived in Paris?"

"Yes, he has come after Eveline."

"But his presence here will be injurious to our speculation. He is our declared enemy."

"He cannot injure us now. Since he met such a total defeat in the matter of the Bondavara mine and the railway his teeth have been drawn. He and his bears have kept very quiet."

"Then it is Eveline who has brought him here?"

"He is mad about her; he follows her everywhere like a dog, and is only anxious to pick up any crumb she will give him."

"But she cannot endure him."

"That is the worse for her. It was greatly Prince Theobald's doing. That old fellow is mad."

"Is it not the case that the Countess Angela's husband wants to put the prince's affairs into the hands of trustees?"

"Before we left Vienna there was some talk of it."

"Will this affect in any way the Bondavara shares?"

"In no way. The only unmortgaged portion of his capital is absolutely made over to the company. I can assure you, the Bondavara speculation is built upon a rock of gold."

As he spoke three telegraphic despatches were brought in by the servant. One of these was addressed to the abbé, under cover to the firm of Kaulmann.

"Lupus in fabulâ," said Kaulmann, as he handed the first telegram to the abbé. The abbé read:

"The Prince Theobald has been declared incapable of managing his own affairs."

"Poor Eveline, she will have leisure to repent!" remarked Felix, with a cynical smile.

As he was speaking the abbé opened the telegram addressed to him. He handed it to Felix, saying:

"And I, too, shall have time to repent."

The telegram ran:

"The minister has resigned; the emperor has accepted his resignation; the whole system is to be changed."

"Good-bye to the bishop's mitre, to the cardinal's hat; good-bye to the velvet arm-chair in the House of Peers."

They read the third telegram together. It contained these words:

"Explosion in the Bondavara colliery. The whole mine is on fire."

"This is indeed a blow," said Felix, as he let the telegram fall from his hand. The three telegrams had come like three flashes of lightning. The last was the worst.

When the news reached Prince Waldemar he would let the bears loose with a vengeance. Something must be done to avert the imminent danger—but what?

If there was only time allowed to float the papal loan such small things as the Bondavara shares and the burning of mines would be of little consequence. But could the enemy be reduced to silence?

It was settled that the abbé should without delay repair to Eveline, and that Kaulmann should speak to Prince Waldemar.

The beaming faces of the two men now wore a sombre air. They had only one card to play—the smile of a woman was their only salvation.

CHAPTER XXVIII

TWO CHILDREN

EVELINE had arrived in Paris at a very important moment. Two great changes had been made in the world of fashion: the Empress Eugenie had decreed that the crinoline should be laid aside, and Cardinal Chigi, the papal nuncio, had pronounced that dresses closed to the throat should be worn at receptions. Piety had become the rage. It was considered good taste to go to church and to wait for the sermon.

Piety being, therefore, the fashion, no better moment could have been chosen by Kaulmann for floating the papal loan. He was well pleased to find that Eveline was as eager in the pursuit of piety as any of her fair sisters, the truth being that it harmonized with the poor child's frame of mind. A few days after her arrival in Paris her cripple brother had died. A celebrated surgeon had performed an operation which had put him out of pain forever. Eveline grieved over her loss; now she felt alone in the world, she had no one to love, no one to live for. She kept the boy's useless crutches in her room, one on each side of her dressing-table, and twice a week she went to the church-yard and put fresh flowers on the little grave. The penitential fashion just suited her. She preferred to sing Mozart and Handel in the church than Verdi at the opera.

One day she conceived the idea that she would have

a sacred concert in her own drawing-room; the price of the tickets should be high, and the proceeds would be for some good purpose—God knows what! perhaps to buy arms for the papal zouaves. She was busy making out her programme when the door opened; and Arpad Belenyi, unannounced, rushed in in his old unceremonious way.

Eveline was delighted to see her former friend. She threw down her pen, ran to meet him, holding out both her hands.

"Oh, you delightful person, what has brought you here?"

"My profession. I am looking for some place where I may strike the cymbals and give a concert."

"What a coincidence; you have come at the right moment. But how did you find me out?"

"Not much difficulty in that. If I didn't see your name in the list at the Opera, I couldn't avoid seeing it outside St. Eustache."

"Then you have heard me sing?"

"In both places—the theatre and the church. I must tell you I think the good fathers lay it on pretty strong. For twelve francs I heard you at the Opera, and had the play into the bargain; but I didn't get out of the church so cheap. A beautiful lady took twenty francs from me."

"You silly man! Well, I will pay it back to you. What are your terms?"

"May I ask your reason for the question?"

"How stupid you are! I am not going to engage you for a restaurant. What are your terms for playing the piano at an evening concert?"

"To you, merely thanks; to the public, five hundred francs."

"But if it is for a charitable purpose?"

"Then either not at all or for money."

"No, no. You are a cynical creature! Don't you feel sympathy for any one? Would you do nothing for the poor?"

"I know a poor woman to whom I owe everything; that is my mother. Every farthing which I give to another is taken from her. When the world has given back to her all that she has lost, then I shall give to the world all that I possess; but until then everything belongs to my mother."

"Very good; you shall pay your mother. You shall have the five hundred francs; but for this you must play something super-excellent—Liszt's Mass or one of Handel's oratorios."

"What is the concert got up for? Is it to help a religious object? or is it for the papal zouaves?"

"Yes. I am arranging it."

"Then I can do nothing."

"Why so?"

"Why, because I shall not play for Garibaldi's enemies!"

"Oh, what a goose you are, to be sure! Who asks you to play for Garibaldi's enemies? You play for my friends."

But the young man kept repeating no, no, he wouldn't, and in his excitement he got up from his seat, and, throwing back his waistcoat, showed her that he wore a red shirt.

Eveline laughed unrestrainedly. "A red shirt! So that means that you have enlisted as a Garibaldian?"

"I should have done so long ago only for my mother."

"And what would you do if your hand was shot off?"

"Then I should become a pensioner to some fine lady, who would, I know, support me."

Eveline burst into tears. His words had touched a chord in her tender heart. Arpad, however, could not imagine what he had said to grieve her; he tried to console her, and asked how he had offended her. Still sobbing, she said:

"My poor little brother is dead. There by my table I keep his crutches."

"I am sorry for you; with all my heart I sympathize in your grief. He and I were good friends; we had plenty of fun together."

"Yes; you liked him. The world is quite dead to me; everything is changed. I listen for the sound of his crutches scratching along the floor up the stairs. Ah, my little brother! I have no one now. I want some one to take care of. I should like to nurse some one—an artist who had lost his eyesight; a musician whose right hand had been shot off; or a political hero, who, being pursued, concealed himself in my room, and to whom I should be benefactress, protectress, breadwinner, everything."

"Why don't you go to Garibaldi?"

She was laughing now; her moods were as variable as an April day.

"You have heard me sing in public. What do you say of me?"

"I say you would be a great artist if you could sing for the devils as well as you do for the angels."

"I don't understand. What do you mean by the devils?"

"You surely have heard from the pulpit that the theatre is the devil's synagogue?"

"You rude man! Don't you know that I belong to the theatre?"

"I beg pardon a thousand times. I believed that in the daytime you were an abbess and at night you were an actress; that would be a fair bargain."

"You silly boy! Why do you think I am an abbess?"

"Because you are dressed as such."

"This is only a penitential dress. You godless creature, you are making fun of religion!"

"No, madame. I agree that it is a great mortification to wear gray silk, a great penance to play the coquette with downcast eyes, a real fast to eat crawfish at twenty francs the dish. I am also told that the reason the fashionable ladies of Paris have taken to wearing high dresses is that they discipline the flesh so severely that their shoulders and necks are one mass of scars, and therefore the effects of their flagellations must be concealed."

"That is not true. We don't do anything of the kind."

"The world says so. I don't want to inquire; it is your secret."

"It is not true," Eveline repeated. "We do not flagellate ourselves; look!" And kneeling down before Arpad she raised the lace collar which was round her neck and made him look at her fair skin.

They were a pair of children.

Arpad took his hat and his leave. He left a card with his address, but he would have no share in her concert.

Eveline, however, went on writing her programme.

CHAPTER XXIX

IMMACULATE

EVELINE was still writing her programme when the Abbé Samuel was announced. In Paris it is not thought out of the way for an abbé to visit an actress, and, for the rest, the abbé was an old friend, well known to both husband and wife. He was naturally very much interested in the concert, and read the programme most attentively.

"It would have been all so nice," said Eveline, in a vexed tone, "only for that stupid Arpad. See, father, just there, between my song and the violoncello solo, he would have come in so well."

"Is Arpad in town?"

"Yes, he has only just gone. I begged of him to help my concert; and my song from the Stabat Mater would have gone so much better to the harmonium, and he accompanies beautifully; but he has grown quite silly; he has become a heretic."

The priest shook his sides with laughter, and then a sudden idea struck him. It was plain Eveline liked Arpad, which was only natural, for they were about the same age. He was twenty, she nineteen—a pair of children, and children like to amuse themselves. They don't care for serious things; that comes later. What if he made use of Arpad to introduce Waldemar.

"I should like to take a bet with you that Arpad Belenyi will play the piano at your concert, and that, moreover, he will accompany your Stabat Mater on the harmonium. If he does so, what will you give me?"

"Oh, he won't do it; you may be sure of that! I know him well; he is very obstinate once he takes anything into his cockatoo's head, and if *I* have not been able to persuade him—"

Eveline had immense faith in the magic power of her black eyes.

"Well, you shall see. What will you give me if I succeed?" repeated the abbé.

Eveline replied to this question by another:

"How do you mean to get round him?" She said nothing of what she would give in case he succeeded.

"Oh, there are many ways; for instance, I might say to him that if he played in your drawing-room it is very likely he may be engaged by the empress, and that then his fortune was made—at least, for this season. An artist would at once see what a chance this would be. Then I would offer him money."

"I have done that already—five hundred francs."

"Well, although a young man may turn up his nose at five hundred francs, an old woman will appreciate a hundred Napoleons at their true value. Arpad must obey his mother's wishes, and what she promises for him he must do. I know the circumstances."

"You are a very sensible man. I should have begun with the mother, but it never occurred to me. Well, manage it all for me. If you only accomplish it I shall do whatever you ask me."

She was in such good-humor that the abbé saw he could ask her anything; still, it was with a slight hesitation that he said:

"I want you to give me an invitation for your charity concert for a friend of mine."

"You shall have ten," cried Eveline, joyfully.

"I only require one, but this invitation must be written with your own hand."

"Give me the name of your friend and I will write the card this moment."

As she spoke she seated herself at her writing-table, took an invitation-card from her drawer, and made all ready to begin.

"Now the name."

"Prince Waldemar Sondersheim."

When she heard the name Eveline threw down her pen and sprang hastily to her feet.

"No," she said, decidedly, "never!"

The abbé burst into a shrill laugh. "Your excitement is very becoming," he said. "You are a fine actress."

"I shall not invite Prince Sondersheim to my concert," returned Eveline, seating herself on the sofa with a defiant air.

"Is the prince disagreeable to you?"

"I loathe him."

"Do you imagine that the world contains nothing but simpletons like Arpad Belenyi?"

Eveline got up from the sofa, went to the writing-table, and tore the programme she had been writing into a hundred pieces.

"Arpad may stay at home, tied to his mother's apron-strings. I don't want him nor any one. I'll give up the concert;" and she threw the torn fragments of her programme into the fireplace.

The abbé rose from his seat and took the excited girl by the hand.

"Compose yourself, my dear young lady," he said. "I have come to you on a most urgent matter—a matter which is of serious consequence to you and your husband, and I do not deny that it is of great moment to me. I may, in fact, call it of vital importance to each one of us. If it should turn out as badly as it threatens your husband shall have to go to America, I must return to my monastery, and what will become of you I do not know."

Eveline sat down again on the sofa. She listened to him attentively.

"At all events, you will have to go out of this," went on the abbé, "and that without loss of time. You must know that the old Prince Theobald, after you had returned to him the palace in the Maximilian Strasse, which he had made a present to you, took shares in your name in the Bondavara Company to the amount of a million."

"I never knew it," said Eveline.

"That proves that you never thought of asking your husband what the expense of this splendid hotel was, to say nothing of your magnificent carriage and horses, your numerous servants, your conservatory—"

"I thought that my salary, added to what Herr Kaulmann—" She stopped suddenly; the incredulous smile on the abbé's lips made her silent. He continued:

"All this splendor is at an end. A telegram which came a few hours ago brings the news that, at the suit of his son-in-law, Prince Theobald's affairs have been placed in the hands of trustees; the trustees will, without any doubt, seize the shares taken for you."

"They may do as they like," returned the girl, indifferently.

"Oh, there may be a lawsuit! But there is worse to

come. Another telegram brings the news that last week there was a fearful explosion at the Bondavara colliery."

At this news Eveline gave a cry; then quickly asked:

"And Herr Behrend, has his mine also exploded?"

The abbé looked somewhat surprised, but continued, in his earnest manner:

"I believe not. The company's shares, however, have received a terrible blow. The more so, that one of the collieries is still burning, with no chance of being extinguished."

As he spoke he looked fixedly at her, and his penetration soon took in the truth: that her joy at the escape of Behrend's property outweighed her sorrow for her husband's loss.

"You can understand," continued the abbé, "in what danger we are of actual ruin; everything now depends upon one thing. Of course, you are aware that, in consequence of the Bondavara Company, Kaulmann's reputation is one of the highest in the financial world. Millions of money have actually been put into the affair, and ten times as much is floating in the air of the stock-exchange. Money is not a tangible quantity. This catastrophe—which, after all, may still be averted, for it is possible that the fire may be extinguished—will be a terrible engine in the hands of the enemies of the company, who want, above all things, to upset Kaulmann. The colliery explosion is a powder-mine in the hands of the bears. To-day he is a king, hands full of gold are stretched out to him, a hundred millions are eagerly offered to him; to-morrow these very people will surround him, clamoring to get back their money, which they have intrusted to him. Whether the cry is raised or not depends altogether on one man, and this man is Prince Waldemar Sondersheim. He is here; he arrived to-day. Probably he has had news of the explosion sooner than Kaulmann, whose director, Rauné, no doubt, hoped against hope to get the fire under. Kaulmann's fate lies in the hands of Prince Sondersheim, and so does my own. I do not conceal it. I was the pivot of an enormous, world-wide project. To-morrow Kaulmann's proposal for the Church loan was to be laid before the financial world of Paris and Brussels; it is an important crisis that may give to history a new page. If Prince Waldemar makes use of his knowledge of the collapse of the Bondavara Company to raise a cry against us, then the whole fabric upon which so much is built vanishes as a dream. If he or his bears call out on the exchange that the Bondavara shares are sixty per cent. below par we are lost. If he keeps silent the loan will float splendidly, and then the Bondavara misfortune will sink into a matter of small importance, such as constantly occurs in the money-market. Now you can understand what an effect a word from you may have, and what you can do if you speak this word."

Eveline shook her head, and laid her finger on her lips; she looked the very genius of silence.

"What!" cried the abbé, his anger getting the better of him, "you refuse? You think more of one word that can cost you nothing than of the consequences? The Holy See may be overthrown, the standard of infidelity may be unfurled, the saints torn from their shrines—and all for a woman's caprice."

Eveline spread out her arms as if she were engaged in a combat with a giant. She called out, in a resolute voice:

"No; I cannot speak to that man."

The abbé grew angry. He said to himself if he could

not persuade this vexatious woman, at least he would give himself the pleasure of wounding her in a tender point. He took his hat in his hand, and, holding it behind his back, said, in a cold, cutting voice:

"I neither understand your dislike to the prince nor your extreme delicacy. Prince Sondersheim is no way inferior to the men you have admitted to your intimacy."

At this insult Eveline seized the hand of the abbé, and cried, with a sudden abandonment of her usual reserve:

"Oh, father, I have never been a wife; I am still as innocent as a child!"

The abbé looked at her in unfeigned astonishment. He saw by her burning blushes, her modest, downcast eyes, her childish sobs, that she was speaking the truth. He sighed deeply; he could not help it. It was his last stake, and he had lost. Good-bye to glory, to greatness. All had vanished into thin air at Eveline's words; they had scattered his dreams. He recognized that all the great deeds which have made men famous were as dust and ashes in comparison with the real nobility of soul possessed by this peasant girl, this woman who, in obedience to her husband's infamous commands, and because she had sworn to obey him, had worn the mask of a Phryne while she preserved the purity of a saint. By no act of his should she descend from her pedestal.

"Eveline," he said, in a voice of deep emotion, "the words you have spoken banish me to my cell. My dreams of power and splendor lie in the dust—their fitting place. You said, 'I am still innocent'; my child, keep yourself so. The French law recognizes no marriage unless it has been contracted before the civil authorities. Your marriage with Felix Kaulmann is in this country null and void; you are here Mademoiselle Eva Dirkmal, nothing more. You can tell Kaulmann that I have told you this. I have given him the same information, as he wished to free himself from this nominal tie to you. And now, farewell; I return to my monastery, to reconcile myself with an offended God."

Eva Dirkmal threw herself at the feet of the priest, and covered his hands with tears and kisses.

"Put your hand upon my head," she sobbed, "and ask God to bless me."

"My daughter," said the abbé, "an invincible hand watches over you and protects you. May you ever be thus safely guarded."

With these words the priest left the room. He did as he said; he sought no further interview with Kaulmann, but went straight to the railway, and buried himself in his monastery. The world knew him no more.

CHAPTER XXX

MAN AND WIFE

FELIX lost no time in seeking an interview with Prince Waldemar. He preferred to look for him in his own house than to meet him accidentally on 'change.

Waldemar did not keep him long waiting, neither did he treat him to any display of his superior rank. He received him in his study.

"Ah, your highness is occupied with business," said Felix, with the airy manner of an intimate friend; but he was secretly astonished to see that a man of the prince's high position was actually cutting the pages of the pamphlet before him, and underlining with red and blue pencil-marks the passages that pleased him most.

The prince laid down the pamphlet, and asked Felix to take a chair.

"I have only this moment heard," continued the banker, "that your excellency had arrived in Paris, and I hastened to be the first to pay my respects."

"Strange! At this very moment, I, too, was occupying myself with your affairs," returned the prince, with a peculiar smile, which Felix noted and thought he understood. He tried to put on a jaunty air as he made answer:

"I have come as an envoy under the protection of a flag of truce into the enemy's country."

The prince thought to himself, "The fellow's flag of truce is a handkerchief worked with the letter E."

"Even greater powers than we," went on Felix, twirling his hat in his fingers with some embarrassment, "have in sudden emergencies co-operated, and from being enemies have become fast friends, recognizing that to bury the hatchet was for their mutual advantage."

"And may I inquire what is for our mutual advantage?"

"My projected loan."

The prince said nothing, but the smile that played upon his thin lips was a sufficient and most irritating answer. Felix began to lose his calmness. He rose from his chair, and in his earnestness leaned over the table at which the prince was sitting.

"Prince," he said, "this loan is for the benefit of the Holy See. You are, I know, a good Catholic."

"Who has betrayed my secret?"

"Besides, you are a thorough aristocrat. It must go against your highness's feelings to see that while in Hungary a bureaucratic minister pillages the Church and puts its revenues in his pocket, a band of freebooters throws the patrimony of St. Peter to the mob. All this can be prevented by our striking one blow. You will strike it, for you are a nobleman in the best sense of the word."

"What else am I?"

"Above all, you are a financier. It cannot escape your keen eye that this loan is one of the greatest, the soundest of speculations; for you are a prudent man, and you know how to add two and two."

"Have I any other qualifications?"

Waldemar's cold, sarcastic rejoinders did not put Felix out of countenance. His face assumed a still more amiable expression as he offered his hand to the prince, saying, in a cordial manner:

"I trust you will be the honored friend of the house of Kaulmann."

These words would be met either by a warm shake of the hand or by a box on the ear. He ran the risk, waiting breathlessly for the answer, which was different from, and yet worse than, that he expected. The prince took up the pamphlet which he had been busy underlining with red and blue pencil.

"Now, my excellent brother in the faith, my fellow aristocrat, my comrade in finance, and my best friend, just you throw your eye over this little brochure, for there you will find my answer. I beg that you will take your time."

He handed the pamphlet to Felix, and while that gentleman cast his eye over it the prince pared his nails carefully.

Felix laid down the pamphlet. "This purports to be my biography."

"As I think the title-page mentions."

"Your highness is, I presume, the writer?"

"I have given the heads."

"There are all manner of affairs mentioned here in which I have played a sorry part by throwing dust in the eyes of the public, principally, however, in the Bondavara speculation, in which, it seems, I have announced a false balance and a feigned bonus, drawn ten millions out of the capital, which capital is now irrecoverably lost by the late catastrophe in the mine. It is a terrible indictment against me."

"Perhaps it is not true?"

"*It is true!* Your highness is my faithful biographer; but allow me to fill up the details of the memoir.

The unlooked-for misfortune of yesterday can be repaired to-morrow; the unlucky speculation may be glossed over if a better takes its place; a small defeat is compensated by a great victory. What use does your highness intend to make of this brochure?"

"Frankly, I intend, as soon as you declare your new loan, to circulate this pamphlet freely on 'change. I shall then set the bears to work, so that in no time your shares shall be driven out of the market."

"I guessed as much, and, to be frank, it was on this very account that I have come here, to prevent, if I can, such ruin to myself."

Felix tried by continuous winking of his eyes to express his despair. He put his right hand into his vest, and in a low voice added:

"Perhaps when you see me stretched dead before you your aim will then be accomplished."

Prince Waldemar broke into an irrepressible fit of laughter and clapped Kaulmann on the shoulder.

"I beg of you not to act a farce for my benefit. You did not come here to blow your brains out. Nothing of the sort; you came to sell me something. You are a ruined speculator, but you still possess one jewel of value, a wonderful black carbuncle which you found in the coal-mine and got smoothly cut, which you have already sold at a great profit, but which is now back on your hands. You are perfectly aware that I desire to get this jewel if I can, that I am willing to offer all I have for it; and this is why you have come here to-day. Let us understand one another. I will treat with you. What is your price?"

The prince threw himself back in his chair, but he let Kaulmann stand without again asking him to be seated.

The banker gave up his tragic manner, and resumed his customary cool, hard, matter-of-fact voice.

"First of all, this;" and he laid his hand upon the pamphlet.

"Good! You shall have it—a thousand copies and the manuscript. You can burn it, unless you care to keep it as a souvenir."

"Secondly," went on Felix, "you must abandon your conspiracy against me. During the three days of raising the loan your bears are to keep quiet; there are to be no manœuvres. Thirdly, your name must appear in the list of subscribers with a good sum after it."

"Good! We shall understand one another. Now listen to my modifications of your proposal. On the first day when the shares of the new loan are drawn I undertake to keep the bears quiet, but I shall take no shares. On the second day I shall also keep quiet, but I shall not give you a shove. On the third day I shall take one million shares, and from that time I undertake to push your speculation as if I were your best friend."

"And why not on the first two days?"

"I will tell you what is to happen on those days. This very day you must go to madame and tell her that Prince Theobald's fortune is sequestrated and that she can no longer occupy his hotel. Madame was once generous enough to return to the prince his palace in the Maximilian Strasse, together with all it contained. She will have to repeat this act of renunciation and return to her husband's roof. Her husband must celebrate this happy event by a splendid entertainment, to which he will, as a matter of course, invite his best friend." Here the prince laid, with a significant gesture, his little finger on his breast. "The friend will take this opportunity to show madame a photograph of his summer palace, which is situated on the Lake of Constance, and only waits for the presence of its mistress to be perfection, while she stands in great need of the lovely breezes of the lake to restore her."

"You are really very thoughtful."

"Do not praise me too soon. On the second day you must have an explanation with madame. You will tell her that in France a marriage, to be legal, must be contracted before the civil magistrate; therefore you will go with her before the registrar and have yourself legally married."

"But, prince," cried Felix, with a horrified expression upon his face, "why should I do that?"

"Why?" returned the prince, standing up in his turn, so as to be able the better to overwhelm his victim. "Because I wish to defeat your little game. You took to yourself a wife in another country, knowing you could repudiate her here. It is my wish that madame shall bear your name always; otherwise you would have it in your power on the fourth day to say to me, 'I gave you what was not mine to give.' I shall have the diamond in its proper setting. I shall not remove the centre-stone from your wedding-ring; but I shall wear it on *my* finger."

Kaulmann could not conceal his embarrassment. "This whim is incomprehensible," he said.

"On the contrary," returned the other, with a devilish sneer, "it is quite clear; it simply means that *I know you au fond*. And now to my own affairs. I am desperately in love with one woman, and she detests me. She will not even look at me. But she little thinks I know the reason of her abhorrence. Your wife is a virtuous woman. You look surprised—naturally. It is no merit of yours that she has remained so. Oh, you need not protest! Prince Theobald has told me the whole history. Among other things, he made her swear that she would never receive me. Poor old fool! He did not act with much knowledge of human nature. If he had not interfered it's very likely I should have tired of pursuing a woman who did not care for me; but the mystery that surrounded her has added to my interest. I adore her, not alone for her beauty, her charm, but for her innocence, her goodness. She requires nothing to raise her in my estimation; but before the world she must take her fitting place. She must have the shield of her husband's name, the right to his protection. Now you understand what I require of you."

"Prince, your ideas are demoniacal. You wish to bind me to my dishonor."

"To your dishonor!" and the prince laughed scornfully. "My good Kaulmann, who asked you to come here and sell your honor? Ah, you cannot answer that! Never mind, we shall keep our secret; the world shall know nothing. In society the head of the house of Kaulmann shall be considered an honorable gentleman, an excellent husband, a good family man. In the commercial world he will be looked upon as a sound financier. Honors will crowd upon him; he will go far. . . . His real position will be known to only three people. There, my good friend, don't feign so much virtuous indignation. You are overacting, which always spoils the effect. I will take it all for granted. Time is short; it will be better to make use of it."

This was true. Every moment was precious. Felix abandoned all attempts at outraged feelings of honor and the like, and, composing his agitated features, held out his hand to the prince. The latter, however, did not take it.

"There's no need to shake hands over our honorable compact. Take your note-book and write down the conditions, and be sure you put the dates correctly. To-morrow, if I receive by one o'clock the card of invitation to your entertainment, I shall remain away from the exchange. The next day I do the same; that is, if I receive *before* one o'clock the official notification that your civil marriage has taken place. On the *fourth* day, if *before* one o'clock your solicitor brings me the news that you have set off to Brussels to negotiate the papal loan, and that he hands me the key of your house, with the request that I will look after the business in your absence, then I shall go down to the exchange, and push your affair as if it were my own. Now you may go, sir, and indulge your outraged feelings in private."

CHAPTER XXXI

EVA DIRKMAL

FELIX KAULMANN felt that he had made good use of his opportunity. All would now go well. The prince would no longer avail himself of the Bondavara catastrophe to ruin him; on the contrary, his influence would stem the panic which the news had, no doubt, already caused in the Vienna money-market, and when the papal loan was concluded all would be smooth. There was Eveline, of course; but a man such as Kaulmann, whose conscience had long since been as withered as was his heart, soon found excuses for any ill-doing. No one could blame him for the prince's infatuation; it would be only a fool who wouldn't take advantage of it, especially one in his situation. A drowning man catches at any plank; and as for Eveline, she owed him a debt of gratitude. Had he not raised her from the very dust of the coal-pit to her present situation, saved her from a brutal husband like the savage Saffran, educated her, made her a fit companion for a prince? Better women than she would be glad of the elevation that was awaiting her; and this reminded him that the Abbé Samuel's interview must have opened the matter, so he went in search of him. The priest, however, was not to be found at any of his usual haunts. Felix, therefore, repaired to Eveline's hotel; neither was she at home. She had gone to the theatre; it was one of her acting nights.

Felix drove to the Opera-house. He went first to his wife's box, where there was no one but her companion. He took a view of the house. In the pit there were numerous *claquers*. In one of the front boxes he saw Prince Waldemar. Then he went behind the scenes, for he was known as the husband of the prima donna and was allowed access to her dressing-room.

Eveline was dressed for her part and waiting to go on. When she saw Kaulmann she turned away angrily. Why did he disturb her when she was busy with her calling?

"I have only come to wish you good-evening," he said.

"You might have waited until to-morrow."

"To wish you good-evening? Ha! ha!"

"No; but you know I am always so nervous before I go on—"

"I only wished to tell you that the cream of Parisian society are fighting to get tickets for your concert. Have you reserved one for me?" Felix was full of amiability and admiration.

"I have reserved none."

"Ah! And why not?" He said this in a soft, complaining voice.

"Because I have given up the concert. It shall not take place."

The face of her husband suddenly lengthened. "Will you kindly tell me the reason of this change?"

"After I have come off. My scene has come. I must go." So saying, she left the room and went to the wings.

Felix followed to a point from which he could see his wife on the stage and have a general view of the house.

Eveline played badly and sang worse. Her voice

trembled, she was out of tune, and her runs and *roulades* were imperfect. She was evidently nervous. Nevertheless, she was applauded to the echo, the *claque* worked hard; and Prince Waldemar, from his box, clapped as if he had been paid for it. When she had finished her last song a shower of bouquets and wreaths came from the prince's box and fell at her feet.

Eveline left them on the stage and hurried away to her dressing-room. Kaulmann followed her.

"Why didn't you pick up those lovely bouquets?" he asked, carelessly.

"I felt I didn't deserve any. I know I did badly tonight."

"But surely for the sake of the giver you should have taken one of the bouquets."

"Ah, you would like that."

"I?"

"Yes. All those flowers came from you—at least, so I have always understood."

"Pardon me, *ma chère*. Didn't you notice that they all came from the side box? Didn't you recognize who was in that box?"

"I never looked."

"It was Prince Waldemar."

"The man who is your enemy—who wants to ruin you?"

"Oh, that is not so! He has quite changed. He is now *our* best friend."

"*Our* friend? Whom do you include in 'our'?"

"You, as well as myself."

"Thanks; but I decline my share."

"I am afraid you will find it difficult to stand aloof, for I consider Prince Waldemar as my best friend, and henceforth my house is open to him as to a brother."

"As you please. My house shall be shut in his face."

"I am sorry, but your words oblige me to break a disagreeable piece of news to you. But I see you are busy; you don't take any interest—"

"Go on talking," returned Eveline, who was standing before the looking-glass washing the paint off her face. "I am listening."

"For the future, I regret to say, you will not have a house of your own. The affairs of your friend, Prince Theobald, have been sequestrated; his property is now in the hands of trustees. I need not tell you, for I am sure you have known all along, that the hotel you occupy, together with all your expenses, has been paid for by him. This, naturally, is at an end. In my circumstances I could not afford to give you a separate establishment; we will, therefore, be obliged to live together, and it follows naturally that I shall expect my wife to receive as her guests *my friends*, and to make them welcome."

Eveline had laid aside her queenly robes; she now took off her diadem, and as she slowly unfastened her bracelets she turned and faced Felix.

"And do you think," she said, "that when I leave my hotel I cannot get for myself a garret somewhere, where there will be a door with a strong bolt, with which I can bar the entrance of any unpleasant visitors?"

Felix looked at her in amazement; he constrained himself to take a more friendly tone.

"I must call your attention to one fact. We are in Paris, and the French marital law is strict. A wife must dwell under her husband's roof. She must go where he goes. She must obey him."

Eveline was now busy undoing the gold sandals which bound her feet. She looked steadily at Kaulmann, with her eyes glowing like lamps.

"I must call your attention," she said, "to one fact. We are in Paris, and according to the French law those persons who have been married before the altar, and not before the civil authorities, are not considered legally married, and that, therefore, our marriage is null and void."

Kaulmann sprang to his feet as if he had been bitten by a tarantula.

"What are you saying?" he cried, in a voice that was almost a shriek.

Eveline had loosened the golden sandals. She stood before Felix in her bare feet, and threw him the sandals.

"These belong to you. I am once more Eva Dirkmal. I belong to myself."

"Who has told you this?" stammered the banker, pale with rage.

"The Abbé Samuel, who advised you to treat me in the same manner."

Kaulmann felt the room going round.

"And now," continued Eveline, with a dignified motion of her hand, "I must remind you that this is the dressing-room of a young girl."

Felix did not wait to have his dismissal repeated; he took his hat and went without another word. He ran away, and he ran so fast that he took no heed where he was going till he stumbled and fell.

All was over; he had played his last card and lost. Everything was gone; there was no more help. He had two courses open to him: he might put a pistol to his head, and so end the drama, or he might take all the money in his counting-house and fly. He chose the last.

CHAPTER XXXII

CRUSHED

EVELINE felt as if she had been given new life. She was no longer married, and yet she was not a widow. She had to shed no tears over happiness that had vanished, no regrets for domestic joys. Her heart was full of newly awakened desires, hopes she hardly dared to confess to herself, dreams that delighted while they embarrassed her—a delicious riddle that she feared to guess. Next day, however, when she heard that Kaulmann had absconded and would never return, she recognized fully that her chains had fallen off.

When the caged bird has escaped into the open air of heaven, does he ever regret his gilded cage and all its luxurious comforts or the tender endearments of his owner? The bird enjoys his freedom, and rejoices he is no longer a slave. It may be that wilder and stronger birds tear him in pieces; that the frost and rain may chill his body, unused to exposure. He cares not. He wings his flight still higher; he seeks for a branch; he cooes to his lady-love; he is happy.

Eveline never for one moment reflected that she was in any way implicated in the fall of Kaulmann and the shame that attended his ruin. She had no idea that her name was bandied about. She who had been as a queen, who had been so admired, had such a *succès!* What was to become of her now? She belongs to no one. No one knows anything of her past; but it is pretty safe to prophesy her future. She will have another protector. Of course; but who will he be? Which of her many admirers? She has a legion of adorers from which to choose.

This was the talk of the clubs and the gossip of society. While Eveline sat in her room, rejoicing at her new life of freedom, an idea suddenly came into her head. She looked for Arpad's visiting-card, ordered her carriage, and drove out to visit the Belenyis. They lived some little way from Paris, in the suburbs, where houses can still be had with rooms on the ground floor. Madame Belenyi liked to live on the ground floor. The house she had lost was of this sort, and it had the advantage that, having her own kitchen, she could cook for her son, and feel sure he was not dining at some tavern in bad company. Unless on special occasions Arpad invariably came home to dine with his mother; he would not have missed doing so for a splendid feast. He thought there was nothing to compare with her dishes of pig's ear and delicately cooked vegetables.

Eveline's coachman found it hard to make out the narrow little street in the neighborhood of Montmartre, where the Belenyis had established themselves. Eveline would not let the carriage go farther than the corner; there she got out, and, accompanied by her footman, walked up the street, looking for the right house. It was an old-fashioned cottage, in which Madame Belenyi had hired two rooms divided by a kitchen. A girl who was working in the garden showed Eveline where the young gentleman lived. As Eveline pushed open the kitchen-door very gently she noticed that the door of the inner room opened suddenly and a woman looked out. This was undoubtedly Arpad's mother, who was curious to see who had come to visit her son.

Eveline went on her toes to the door of the opposite apartment, and noiselessly turned the handle; she wanted to surprise Arpad.

His room was the picture of comfort and order. It was easy to see how carefully it was kept by his mother. The table, the walls, were crowded with handsome pictures and ornaments, the gift of different persons—cups, wood-carvings, antique weapons, classical paintings; the windows were supplied with plants in bloom; there were bookcases full of books. Everything was well arranged; there was taste and comfort, and Arpad liked to be at home better than anywhere else. The hired piano was from Erard's manufactory, and was now open. Arpad was sitting with his back to it, brush in hand; he was painting. The pianoforte-player was also a painter. Artists, many of them, indulge in these freaks. One of our most distinguished portrait-painters loves to torture his neighbors by scratching like a cat upon the strings of a violin; so also a well-known musician spends his time writing feeble verses; and a third, who is a real poet, produces unsightly excrescences in marble and terra-cotta.

What was Arpad painting?

Eveline stepped softly behind his back, but the rustle of her silk dress betrayed her presence.

Arpad turned scarlet, shoved the picture into a drawer, and, getting up quickly, confronted his visitor, who had only time to see that it was a portrait he was painting.

"Ah, it is you," he stammered, in an embarrassed voice. "I thought it was my mother."

"Aha, you are doing something you should not! Your mother does not allow you to paint; isn't that it? Well, it is a silly thing, I must say, for a pianoforte-player to spend his time painting; and what is the subject?"

"Oh, nothing—a flower!"

("What a lie!" thought Eveline; "it was a portrait.")

"Then if it is a flower, give it to me."

"I should rather not."

"But if it is only a flower?"

"I am not going to give it to you."

"Don't be so cross. Won't you ask me to sit down?"

Arpad was really vexed. Why had she come to disturb him just at this moment? Any other time she would have been welcome. This beginning spoiled the happy hour; for the picture was not Eveline's portrait.

"Sit near me, else I shall think you are afraid of me. I expected that you would have come to see me, to find fault with me for my performance yesterday evening. Tell me frankly—didn't I sing badly?"

"Very badly," returned Arpad, discontentedly. "You are going back instead of forward; and you seem to forget all you learn. I was quite ashamed of you. And your acting! I thought I was looking at an automaton."

"To tell you the truth, I was in a miserable state of mind; I had several domestic troubles. I am separated from Kaulmann."

"That was no reason to sing false; he wasn't worth risking your engagement for, and playing in such a perfunctory manner—singing, too, all out of tune. You never troubled yourself much about him." (Arpad knew nothing of what had happened to Kaulmann; the news had not penetrated to Montmartre.) "And, at all events, you should have had the discretion not to order a shower of bouquets when you were doing so badly; it doesn't look well."

Eveline was very much wounded at this unjust accusation. She answered, almost crying:

"I beg to assure you I have never ordered bouquets to be thrown to me."

"Well, it was one of your adorers, that crazy prince. It is all the same thing. To be handsome, to sing badly, and to receive wreaths, those are three sins rolled into one. The world cannot distinguish between them."

"Very well; go on finding fault, go on scolding, my excellent old master. What else have I done that is displeasing to you?"

Arpad began to laugh, and held out his hand to Eveline.

"Forgive me," he said. "My roughness is only the grumble of the preceptor; it is over. Now we shall be young again and chat. Shall I fetch the draught-board? Shall we play for love or for nothing?"

This tone warmed Eveline's heart. She laughed, and slapped Arpad's hand, which he did not like.

"What are you going to do now you have got rid of Kaulmann?" he said. "Will you marry again? Is another man ready for the yoke? Men are as plentiful as blackberries. Or are you going to preserve the autonomy of the actress?"

Eveline cast down her eyes and grew suddenly grave.

"I have no one," she said, sorrowfully.

"Ah, that does not mean that there are not plenty you can have if you like."

"It means the same thing. I shall belong to no one. I shall never take a husband who is above me in station. Do you see, the girl who went barefoot in the coal-mine must stay in her own class. If I could give any one a place in my heart, it would be to one who was as free and independent as I am. He should owe nothing to great people; he should depend absolutely on his own genius; live absolutely by his own work. He should be esteemed not for his money nor his rank, but for his talent; he should glory in being an artist."

This was a frank confession for any one who understood. Arpad understood; he became more discontented.

"H'm! Then I am afraid you are walking in a path that leads you away from such a man as you describe."

"What *do you* mean?"

Arpad got up from his chair. "Artists have many strange ideas; these are inseparable from the artistic temperament. Do you see that antique goblet there in the centre of the table? It was a present to me from Count Demidoff on the occasion of a concert. It was an heirloom in his family. It is a wonderful relic; a classsical work. Princes, generals, rulers have drunk out of it. I have a great respect for it, and I keep my visitors' cards in it. But I never drink out of it; I prefer a common glass, for which I have paid fifteen pence, but out of which no one has drunk but myself."

Eveline flushed deeply at this cruel speech.

Arpad had, however, resolved to make the matter still clearer.

"You say," he went on, "that you would like to find an artist, a genius, a proud, independent man; him you would choose for your husband! And you imagine that a man of this type would submit to sit by your side as you drove in the Champs Élysées, knowing that the people driving behind in other carriages or walking along the path were saying, 'There is the curled and scented Hyperion, but the steeds that draw him are not paid for by *his* muse, they are the blood-horses of Prince X——; and his wife is not content with the glory of *his* name, she wears the diamonds provided by Marquis G——.' Do you think you will easily find such a husband?"

Poor Eveline! She tried to defend herself against this cruel boy.

"But I am ready to throw away all splendor—everything that is not earned by my honest labor. I wish to live by my art, to be what I am—an actress. I would work night and day to perfect myself. I do not want any other distinction but that of an artist."

Arpad then told her what she had never heard until now. Children and fools speak the truth, and in Arpad there was a mixture of both; he was a child in years, and a fool as regarded the claims of art.

"My dear Eveline, you are not an artist; you will never be an actress; you are one of the step-daughters of the muses. There are many such, to whom have been given great capabilities; one only is wanting—courage. You sing wonderfully well, you act with feeling, with humor —*at home*, before three people; but so soon as the lights of the proscenium are lit your voice grows weak, you sing false, you see and hear nothing, and you act like a wooden doll. This is called stage-fright, and it is *never cured;* it has ruined more brilliant careers than the critics have. You shake your head and appeal to your former triumphs. Don't deceive yourself; I know the machinery of the stage well, and how artificial thunder and lightning are manufactured. At every performance you gain a triumph; you receive thunders of applause, mountains of flowers. The morning after your performance your breakfast-table is covered with newspapers teeming with laudatory criticisms. This is all gold-dust, and will only last as long as some rich admirer pays the piper. But try the experiment of closing your doors to your wealthy patrons, and step on the boards with no help but your own talents; ask to be applauded for your own sake. Then you will learn the price of the entertainment, and that the critic's praise is only to be bought."

Eveline's head sank. She knew that every word he said was true. Arpad viewed the matter not so much from the artistic side as from his youthful, ardent nature. He was indignant against the fashions of the world; he was indignant that Eveline should have lent herself to these low intrigues, and so taken the place of better artists, better musicians, better actresses; but in his heart he was sorry for her. She had been kind to him; she had never offended him. Why was he so cruel to her? It was due to the petulance of his boy's nature. Why had *she* disturbed him when he was happy at his painting? Why had she asked him questions? What was it to her whether it were a flower, and, if it were a flower, why should she want it? And when he put out his hand, why should she tap it in that intimate manner? The picture was not painted for her.

"What shall I do? What am I fit for?" asked Eveline, with a downcast air. Her beautiful eyes were full of tears; she was crushed to the earth.

The young man considered a few minutes what he should answer. As she had asked to drink the chalice she should do so to the dregs.

"You have two courses open to you, for I would not advise you to take a third and return to your husband. If I were a woman I would prefer to lie stretched out at the morgue than be the joint possessor of that man's ill-gotten wealth. We therefore have only the two courses to consider. Either you continue on the stage as before, take the bought applause and the flowers paid for by your noble patrons, or return from whence you came, and be content to shove wheelbarrows for the rest of your life."

Eveline rose from her seat, drew her wrap round her shoulders, and, with a low, constrained voice, murmured:

"Thank you." Then she silently left the room.

Tears came into Arpad's eyes. But why had she come here? Why had she disturbed him when he was happy painting? The moment she had closed the door he returned to the table and took from the drawer *his flower*, to see if it had sustained any injury. It was in one sense a flower—a fair child with blue eyes!

The door opened again; the picture was hastily concealed. No one, however, came in. Arpad's mother spoke through the half-opened door.

"Arpad, my son, who was that beautiful lady who was here just now? A princess, was she not?"

"She was a poor woman who came to beg from me."

"H'm! Surprising! What extraordinary beggars there are in this city—beggars dressed in silk, with a Persian shawl for a wrap. Did you give her anything, Arpad?"

"Mother, I had nothing to give her."

"You have done well, my boy." And she shut the door and went back to her own room to finish stitching at her son's shirt-collar.

CHAPTER XXXIII

CHARCOAL

EVELINE had resolved to make a great effort. She recognized that there was truth in what Arpad had said; only in one particular he was wrong: he had not measured the gulf between "can" and "must."

She felt herself possessed by sudden energy; her resolution to succeed grew in proportion as her chance of success was less. Many people have found strength in the thought, "If I have no one to care for me, I, at least, am master of myself." She would carve her own future; she *would* be an actress. She would show the world what was in her. She would nerve herself to courage before the footlights. The very circumstances which had deprived her of all courage would now give her strength; she would sing to the public as if she were alone. The crowd should go for nothing, except in being sharers in her triumph.

She spent a miserable night. The luxury which surrounded her, the works of art which lay upon her tables, in her cabinets, the costly vases, seemed silently to reproach her; the cups set with precious stones recalled Arpad's words. Better to be a glass of fifteen sous than a goblet of silver!

At last sleep fell upon her tired eyelids, and in the morning she awoke refreshed and full of fresh energy.

This day the opera in which she had sung the day before yesterday was to be repeated. The rehearsal was to take place in the morning. At this rehearsal, then, she would show what she could do; she would look at no one; she would sing like a blind nightingale.

She ordered her carriage. When she reached the theatre she told the servants to return for her in two hours.

As she entered the vestibule the stage-manager came to meet her, and told her that her part had been given to another singer.

Eveline flew into a passion. Why had it been taken away from her, and in such a manner, without asking her permission? Such a want of proper deference towards her!

The man regretted the circumstance, but either could not or would not offer any explanation. Would she like to see the manager?

Eveline, in a very excited frame of mind, went to look for him; but he was not in his office. His secretary, however, handed her a letter, which the manager had desired him to send to her address.

Eveline took the letter, and when she was in the hall she broke the seal and read it. It was a dismissal, immediate, discourteous, on the grounds that she was quite unequal to fill the position of prima donna.

How she got out of the theatre and into the street she did not know; she came to herself when she saw the crowd of passers-by staring at her. She felt that it was no wonder they looked at her. She was walking like one who was dead; her body moved forward, but her mind was lifeless. It was strange to feel one's self thus annihilated.

Then it was true; the cruel boy was right. The clouds were golden only so long as the sun shone. All her splendor had been on the outside. There was nothing tangible; nothing came from herself. The whole thing had been a *fata morgana;* it had now vanished forever.

Eveline wandered, she didn't know where. Suddenly she found herself opposite her own house. She would not have thought it strange if some one had told her at the door of the hotel that no one of her name lived there, that she had been dead and buried years ago. She thought she was too stunned to feel either astonishment or pain, but her composure soon gave way under a new trial.

She walked up-stairs, still in a dream, and through her apartment until she reached her dressing-room. When she entered it she saw, stretched in an arm-chair, Prince Waldemar.

He was faultlessly attired, with a most elegant *tournure*, carefully arranged hair, and fair whiskers, hanging down on both sides in what were then called "cutlets"; his mustache was pointed and waxed.

Eveline called out, in a voice of fear, mixed with anger:

"May I ask, sir, what you want here?"

"I was waiting to see you," said the prince, with well-bred nonchalance; but he never rose from the seat in which he lounged so comfortably.

"Who gave you permission to enter my room?"

"I asked for no permission."

"What right have you to intrude yourself here?"

With a lazy air the prince put his hand into the pocket of his coat and drew out a red paper like a bill; this he handed to Eveline with a slight motion of his head, which conveyed, "This is the cause of my presence here."

Eveline took the paper, which trembled in her hand.

"What is it? I do not understand it."

"It is, however, very intelligible," said the prince, at last getting out of the chair. "The creditors of Kaulmann have seized your things. Kaulmann was careless or thoughtless enough—I really cannot say which—to announce that what belonged to his wife was *his*, and therefore his creditors have seized everything here, believing it is his. During your absence this morning they got the law officers to break open your door and to take possession. They affixed a notice outside, inviting all passers-by to come in and inspect the things for sale. In consequence of this invitation I am here. I came in to look about me. You will observe that there are government seals upon everything. I am here in the right of purchaser."

Eveline looked round, and saw that what he said was true.

"But, sir, it is impossible. Kaulmann knew perfectly that nothing here was his property."

"I am sure of that. It was gross negligence on your lawyer's side; he should have protected your interests better. Every one knows that Kaulmann brought the goods here; it was supposed that he bought them. In any case, he cannot testify in your favor. A misfortune has happened to him. When he saw that the police were after him he jumped out of the railway-carriage he was in. Unfortunately, he broke his neck and died immediately."

Eveline fell back upon the sofa and hid her face in her hands.

"If you wish to shed a few tears to the memory of Kaulmann I will retire to the window," remarked Prince Waldemar, with ironical courtesy.

Eveline made him no answer. In her mind everything was in confusion; she could think of nothing. Let everything go; what did it matter? Should she institute a law-suit to recover her property? Should she bring witnesses to prove that this ornament, these costly hangings, these rich carpets were not the property of her husband, but the gifts to her from a graybeard — the most upright, the dearest of men, a Hungarian magnate, who had adopted her, an actress, to be his own child, with no self-seeking, no sinful gratification, but out of pure affection? No one would credit her story. She would tell it to no one. She would not subject the name of her benefactor to the jeers and laughter of the incredulous. Sooner let everything go.

"I am not weeping, sir," she said to the prince. "If you have anything further to tell me I am ready to listen."

"I could tell you many other unfortunate circumstances," returned Waldemar, leaning against the fireplace with the silver grate. "For one thing, Prince Theobald, your former patron, has been placed by his family under legal restraint, and cannot take any active part in the affairs of this world."

"I know that."

"The shares which he took as a provision for you in the Bondavara Company have been also sequestrated by law."

"That has been told to me already."

"This loss, however, has a compensation: those shares are now almost worthless. Since the colliery explosion, and the impossibility of extinguishing the fire in the mine, they have fallen to nothing."

"That does not concern me."

"I have not quite finished. The clergyman who was

your friend, whose dreams were of a bishop's mitre, has returned to his monastery."

"I have known that some time."

"You seem to have learned everything. Perhaps you know also that your manager has cancelled your engagement and given your part to another actress?"

"Here is the letter," answered Eveline, drawing a crumpled paper from her pocket. And then she looked at the prince with proud contempt. She was wondrously beautiful. "Have you taken the trouble to come here to tell me all this?" she asked, her eyes gleaming not through tears but with indignation.

"I did not come here on that account," answered the prince, sitting down on the sofa and bending over her. "I came to speak to you frankly. Do you not see that the whole fabric upon which your golden dreams were built has crumbled? The Bondavara mine is on fire; the shares are falling; the prime-minister is disgraced; the prince is under restraint; your husband is dead; your property will be sold by auction; you are dismissed from the theatre. The five acts of the drama are played out. Let us applaud the finish, if we are so minded, and let us begin again. I can give you back your shares. I can get you a palace in the Maximilian Strasse. I can buy back for you all your seized goods—your furniture, your diamonds, your horses. I can arrange matters with the manager of the theatre; you shall be reinstated as prima donna on better terms than before. I can give you a far greater position than you have ever enjoyed, and I can offer you a truer, more self-sacrificing, more adoring lover than you have possessed. His name is Waldemar Sondersheim." He bowed low before her.

Eveline looked with intense gravity at the top of his boots.

Waldemar was now certain that he was master of the situation. He took from his waistcoat-pocket a watch, and pressed it into her hand.

"My sweetest love, my time is precious. I am expected at the stock-exchange. The Kaulmann speculation has to be crushed. It is just twelve o'clock. I give you one hour to think over what I have said and to decide your own fate. I am content to wait until then; it is only one word I ask for—yes or no."

Eveline gave him a yet shorter answer. She dashed the timepiece which he had put into her hand with such force on the floor that it flew into a hundred pieces. That was her answer!

Prince Waldemar laughed, put his hand in his left-hand waistcoat-pocket, took out another watch, and said, dryly:

"I expected just such an answer, and therefore I brought with me another watch. I beg of you to break this one also. I shall be only too happy to provide you with a third."

This time, however, Eveline did not take the timepiece in her hand. She sprang to her feet, and, pointing with her hand towards the door, cried out:

"If you have bought my things, take everything away; but the apartment is still mine. *Go!*"

Prince Waldemar looked at her haughtily, although he was still smiling.

"My dear lady, this is easily said; but reflect a moment. What will become of you if you reject me? You have no other expedient."

"I have a shelter," returned the girl, bitterly, "to which I can turn, and that is charcoal."

Prince Waldemar made her a low bow, and, without uttering another word, took his hat and left her.

A woman who appeals to charcoal needs no man's friendship. In the metropolis of fashion many poor wretches have found their last refuge there.

That evening Eveline paid a visit to her jeweller. She brought him a pair of diamond ear-rings. They were all she had; her ornaments had been seized by the law officers. She sold these to the jeweller, and left the purchase-money in his care, to be spent in a yearly sum on her little brother's grave in Père la Chaise, to have sods of green grass round it, and have fresh flowers placed there on All-Souls' Day. The jeweller promised, for she had been a good customer. She told him she was going to travel. Apparently it was a long journey, for the next morning a bundle was found by the police on the banks of the Seine. It was tied up in a cashmere shawl, which her maid recognized as belonging to the lost actress.

Prince Waldemar offered a large reward to whoever found the body. But it was never found, for the bundle laid at the water-side was only a pretence; and while every one was dragging the river, Eveline had kept her word and sought refuge in the charcoal pit.

Prince Waldemar never heard of her again. He and his household wore mourning in memory of her for six weeks.

CHAPTER XXXIV

CSANTA'S LAST WILL AND TESTAMENT

WE have now to go back to the Bondavara Company before the crash came, and when the shares stood at sixty over par, and looked as if they would go even higher. But Csanta was satisfied to sell at sixty. There could be too much of even a good thing. One should not be too grasping, and sixty thousand gulden is a nice profit in one year. He thought he would act as Spitzhase had often recommended, and sell out his shares in small quantities until they were all gone. It would add to the pleasure not to do it all at once.

For some time the quotations had been stationary. He was accustomed to go every morning to the café and read the exchange column, and had always seen the same quotation—" Bondavara, sixty above par."

On the morning of the day upon which Csanta had arranged to send the first instalment of his shares to Vienna he went to his café, and, while waiting to be served, took up the first newspaper that came to hand. As usual he commenced by reading it backwards, beginning at the exchange column. The first thing that caught his eye was, " Bondavara, sixty *below par.*"

A printer's error; and a very serious one! The printer was drunk when he printed it. The fellow ought to be put in prison. If there is any police in Vienna, or justice in the government, such a thing should not pass unpunished; it is enough to shake the nerves of any man not made of iron. If this is not a disturbance of the peace, I don't know what you can call it.

Then he took another paper. The same mistake! He went through the round of the daily papers, and found that all the printers must have chosen this day for a drinking-bout, as each one made the same error between *above* and *below* par.

Csanta was convinced that some great mistake had been made; but as he could not rest until it was cleared up, he telegraphed to Spitzhase.

A telegram from Spitzhase crossed his. It ran:

"Great misfortune. The Bondavara mine is on fire. Great panic. The shares are sixty below par. Every one is selling."

Csanta cursed and swore with rage. "The devil take him! Sixty below par; a loss of sixty thousand gulden! That means for me extinction. Where is the cord and the nail? Let me hang myself! Six casks full of silver gone! I shall murder some one! I must go to Vienna. I shall knock the whole place about their ears like a card house if I don't get back my silver. I didn't take my money to Vienna to leave it there."

He foamed like a madman, dragged his bonds out of his safe, threw them on the floor and stamped upon them.

"Villains! knaves! paper beggars! It is you who have eaten up my silver crowns! You have swallowed my sixty thousand silver crowns! I will tear you in pieces! I will cut my crowns out of your stomachs! I will kill you dead!"

The upsetting of his safe had disturbed his papers.

He suddenly caught sight of a deed. He looked at it closely. His mood changed.

"What a fool I have been. I don't lose as much as my finger-nail. Here is my young friend's signature. How lucky I didn't destroy this, or light my pipe with it. He binds himself *at any time*, subject to my desire, to take over a thousand shares *at par*. Ah, well done, Csanta! You are an old bird not easily caught with chaff. I am saved, thanks to my own sagacity, to my prudent, far-seeing nose that smells danger ahead. This letter covers all loss. So far as I am concerned, stones may fall from the sky. I am safe."

He folded the shares tenderly, and locked them and the precious letter safely up in his safe. He then sat down and wrote to his dear young friend in Paris. Fortunately he had the address. He asked him politely—seeing how the matter stood—to send at once some accredited person to take over the bonds, according to their previous agreement, and to arrange in what manner the money should be paid. As for the outstanding interest, some compromise or arrangement could be made.

A week passed, and no answer came; but, after all, it is more than a cat's jump from X—— to Paris.

During the week he received twice every day, morning and evening, a telegram from Spitzhase pressing him to part with his shares, for every day they were falling ten per cent. lower. At the end of the week they had gone down still more. The bears had won the day.

Csanta never moved a finger. He hugged himself in his own safety; and as for the others, their shares might go to the bottom of the sea for all he cared. He had no shares. They were all Kaulmann's. "Take them away, and give me back my silver!" This was his cry. "Rogue! villain! I have you by the neck!"

The accounts that he read of the sudden collapse of the company and the ruin of the shareholders did not in the least disturb him. The losses of others could not affect him. On the ninth day, however, he began to tremble. The morning's paper contained an account, telegraphed from Paris, of the flight of the banker, Felix Kaulmann, leaving his affairs in the uttermost confusion. This was succeeded by a second telegram, announcing that the banker, Kaulmann, seeing that the officers of police were on his track, had thrown himself from the window of the railway-carriage, and had been killed instantaneously.

Csanta narrowly missed an apoplectic stroke. When he came to he telegraphed to Spitzhase to sell all his shares for what they would fetch.

Spitzhase answered by return:

"Too late; they are quoted at *seventy*, but this is only nominal. There are neither buyers nor sellers. The mine is gone; the railway is gone; everything is gone. Why didn't you part with them a week ago, when I advised you? Now you can put your shares in the fire, and cook chestnuts at the blaze."

"All is over with me!" sobbed Csanta. "Let me get home; let me lie down and die! I cannot live! I shall not be alive in three days!"

He took leave of his acquaintances; he had no friends. He told them they need not be afraid, he would do himself no injury. He was simply dying of grief, just as a man might die of sickness.

All gone!

Some compassionate souls had pity on the old man and took him home. If he had been alone he had never found his own house. Once arrived there, he insisted on going down to his cellar, to see with his own eyes if it were not some hideous dream, from which he would wake and find his beloved casks in their old places. When he saw all were gone, he set up a fearful cry, "Fool! fool! fool!" and fell forward on his face.

They carried him up-stairs, tenderly undressed him as if he were a child, and put him to bed. He shrieked for a priest, so they fetched him one. He made his confession, and received the sacrament.

His lawyer then appeared on the scene, and his last will was written out and duly signed. He had still something to leave. There were his houses, the whole street front; the church into which no one came, on whose threshold between the stones the grass grew thick, in whose court-yard the school-boys played ball on Thursday half-holidays.

The church, notwithstanding, was endowed with a priest, a verger, and a bell-ringer. The priest should say mass, the bell-ringer should ring the bell, the verger should open the door *every day;* just as a hundred years ago, when through the open church doors a stream of men passed, with silver buttons on their jackets, and women with long silk veils. The old man now dying is the last descendant left on this earth of the old Greek traders. The church shall remain standing in memory of them.

The house next door to his own he bequeathed to the widow, who was the daughter of the last Greek. This woman and he had quarrelled long ago. God alone can decide the justice of a quarrel that has to do with paper money, which to-day is worth a great deal and to-morrow not a penny. Therefore, he bequeathed to her and her son the heap of cursed, worthless papers called shares in the Bondavara Company, which have caused his unexpected death. They shall have these papers, whether for good or ill.

After he had made these depositions and arranged his affairs his will was sealed and inscribed by himself. He divided among his neighbors and servants his few remaining possessions. He called the bell-ringer, and enjoined him to toll the bell three times every two hours, and if any one asked the reason why, he should answer, "The Greek, Csanta, is dead." Then he sent every one out of the room.

When next morning they returned he was dead. He had died of grief, just as an aged husband will not survive the loss of his wife with whom he had grown old. So a man with a strong will dies when he has said that he can no longer support life.

CHAPTER XXXV

THE GROUND BURNS UNDER HIS FEET

PETER SAFFRAN's curse seemed likely to be fulfilled: "Upon this field no grass shall grow for evermore."

It was true the green grass grew still upon the field, but who could tell what was seething underneath, in the bosom of the earth?

The directors of the company's mine believed that when they closed all the entrances and openings to the shafts and vaults, they had given, by so doing, a check to the conflagration; by preventing the current of the outer air from getting in, they felt sure the fire must in a short time be extinguished.

On the other hand, there was the irremediable evil that the supply of coal gradually diminished; even the necessary material for keeping the forge heated was wanting. They tried to heat it with wood—there were plenty of trees in the forest—but without coal the heater would not work, and much iron was lost in consequence. Instead of iron bars, a great quantity of "rammers" lay scattered about. It was soon patent that, from all these causes combined, the company were not in a condition to fulfil their contract for supplying the railway contractors with iron rails. The guarantee was in danger, as was also that of the railway company, in case the railway could not be opened for traffic at the time promised in their agreement.

The Bondavara Mine Company and Railway Company were, so to speak, glued to one another; one could hardly take a step without dragging the other down the dangerous path on which both were going headlong to ruin.

Being in such evil straits, the directors began to look for help to the other mine. Coal they must have. In Ivan Behrend's colliery there must be a large supply. For a whole year he had sold none. They must buy from him, even at an advanced price.

Rauné also bethought himself of begging for coal from the same source. Surely no one could refuse to oblige an old friend and neighbor.

His letter, however, came back to him with the seal unbroken. At this moment Rauné was terribly hard pressed. He resolved to wait upon Ivan, and make his request in person.

His visit was a short one. He was in all less than two seconds in Ivan's room, from which the first thing that issued was his hat, which he followed promptly. After this Ivan's voice was heard.

"I hold no conversation with spies."

Rauné wrote the directors a long letter, in which he said that Behrend was a boorish, selfish man, who was determined to profit by the misfortune which had happened to the Bondavara mine, and would not give his coal at *any* price; instead of selling, he was using it in the manufacture of a quantity of iron rails, and speculating on the chance that the company would be forced to buy at any sum he chose to ask.

The result of his letter was very different from what he had looked for. The railway directors wrote at once to Ivan, and made him an advantageous offer for his iron rails; and if he had asked fifty per cent. more they were prepared to accede to his demand.

The profit for Ivan's faithful workmen was a very full harvest. The deserters to the enemies' camp now implored to be taken on again; they had no work. But they were not received by their former comrades; a committee of the men decided, without a dissentient voice, against taking on one of the deserters, but took on a total stranger. This decision settled the matter, and Ivan was forced to acknowledge it was just. The new member was bound to work for a year as a common laborer, and the committee were not to decide whether he should be admitted to the rights of the existing colony, and entitled to his share of the profit; this should be put to the vote.

Meantime the work was splendidly done. Each man looked upon the mine as his own property; there were few blunders, and the success was remarkable; neither labor nor time was spared. Order was preserved, discipline maintained, and there was no necessity for harsh measures, nor for overseers.

Under all this fine weather, however, there lurked clouds. In the far distance storms were gathering, evident to an experienced eye.

Ivan noted the coming danger, but he did not let it escape his lips. It could not be averted. His mine was threatened; the fire that was consuming the neighboring colliery might spread to his. This thought filled his mind by day and by night. From the situation of the coal-stratum he could draw the conclusion that the conflagration must spread to Bondathal. It might take years, but in the end the Bondathal mine would share the same fate as its neighbor of Bondavara, and be reduced to ashes.

The earth has buried many such wrecks in its bosom. But not alone below, but on the earth itself this Bondavara misfortune had ruined a multitude of people.

In the beginning the board of directors, who administered the affairs of the shareholders, hit upon the idea that with the ready money at their command they would buy up all the shares in the market, and in this way serve a double purpose. In the first place, they would secure for themselves the shares which had been issued at par at a price far below par, and in the next they would check any further fall.

The board, however, by this manœuvre only effected a more rapid smash; the money in the treasury dwindled away until at last for the necessary expenses there was nothing left.

Prince Waldemar knew how to make use of the daily papers. He was always ready, and the shares having, through him, fallen thirty per cent. lower, he was resolved to send them still further down. The time was at hand when they would stand at *nil*, and then the owner of these miserable shares would be glad to *offer* one per cent. to any one who would take them off his hands.

It was a wicked game to play. Thousands were made beggars. The poorer people suffered most—those who a short year ago came with their little savings in their hands, crying to take shares. Poor souls! the high interest had tempted them to their ruin. Ah, it is an old story this, that repeats itself with periodic fidelity; the clerk, the old man, the widow, the old maid, the governess or teacher—these are the victims of this cruel Juggernaut. The cashier who has gambled with his master's money fills in the picture. But there are not wanting others who suffer, but are not reduced altogether to want. Solid tradesmen are crippled, people who drove their carriages have to walk, lovers whose wedding-day was fixed have to wait, and sometimes pine away in single blessedness. Woe! woe! on every side.

But the Bondavara catastrophe had ruined not alone poor and well-to-do people; it had dragged down in its fall the high and powerful family of Bondavary, one of the most ancient in Hungary. The Marquis Salista had learned a severe lesson; he found that you cannot take away the centrepiece of a building without endangering the whole edifice. The sequestration of the prince's property had drawn the whole body of creditors upon him. And so it came to pass that the large property of a great nobleman, a reigning prince, fell under the administration of his creditors; the heirs had really burned the ground under their own feet.

If the stewards and agents in the prince's time had been thieves, the administration of the property by the creditors was the very realization of plunder on all sides.

The result was disastrous so far as the Countess Theudelinde was in question; there was no one responsible, so it appeared, for her forty thousand pounds. All the family charges and mortgages came first on the list of payments. Let her grasp hers—if she could.

The one who suffered most was the Countess Angela. Her husband, Marquis Salista, had from the first lived in the extravagant manner befitting a man who has come into a fortune of twenty millions. It was impossible to induce him to change his ideas. This led to sharp conflicts between the married pair.

On the other side, Angela showed him plainly that she had married him not from liking, but out of pique.

The marquis knew it—and so did Ivan; but he had something else to think of. The ground was burning under *his* feet.

CHAPTER XXXVI

CHILD'S PLAY

The concert season was in full swing when the Belenyis received the news that Csanta was dead and had bequeathed to them their former house. If Arpad had been engaged to play a quartet with Beethoven, Mozart, and Haydn he would have thrown up his engagement and flown back with railway speed to his old home. His mother was just as eager to be gone as he was. Not a day did they stay; they were off the very same evening.

On their arrival at X—— the magistrate unlocked the door of their old home and gave Madame Belenyi possession. Everything was exactly as they had left it, only the dust of years covered all the pretty things.

Arpad's first thought was to run down to the garden. The magistrate, however, detained him. He had another legacy to make over to him, a large iron case fastened with three iron locks. It contained the Bondavara shares.

"The devil take his shares!" cried Arpad, laughing. "Unluckily it is summer, so we don't want to make a fire."

"They are down to nothing," said the magistrate. "They are quoted to-day at ten guldens. They killed poor Csanta."

They had to take the shares all the same. You must not look a gift-horse in the mouth.

Arpad slipped out of the room and ran down to the garden. The fruit-trees were untouched, and all in full bloom. The cherry-tree was one mass of rosy blossom. He remembered well how he daren't touch a blossom under pain of a good whipping. And the forget-me-nots on the bank of the stream, which flowed past the end of the garden, and the May bells were ringing in a chorus, to which no one listened.

Everything was just as it had been, only grown. The trees had such long branches that they were entangled with those on the opposite shore.

He laid himself down in the green grass, all dotted over with yellow cowslips. No one could beat him now. He might waste his time and drink his fill of lazy enjoyment. Fame, the chatter of the newspapers over his sudden disappearance, the ladies who would regret him —what were they all in comparison with this? In a hiding-place on the river-bank he sought for the little flute he had secretly made in those old days. To his great joy it was there, just as he had left it.

Arpad took from his pocket a newspaper full of his Parisian triumphs, an announcement of his next appearance. Where is Paris now? Out of the sheet he made a large boat with sails, that it might take a cargo on board. He pulled a bunch of the cherry blossom; he set the tiny vessel on the water, and while it danced over the little bubbles in the stream he laid down again among the forget-me-nots and played upon his flute the national air, "Repülj fecském."

At the sound of the flute another child appeared. She came from the house opposite: a young girl about fifteen. She had a round, fair, laughing face and beautiful blue eyes. Timidly, like a frightened fawn, she made a few steps, then stopped and listened. By-and-by she drew nearer, then stood still again. She did not see the flute-player; she noticed nothing but his flute and his boat with the cherry blossoms.

The girl had come quite close to the bank without Arpad having seen her approach. He was made aware of her presence by hearing her laugh. The laugh of a child is as clear as a bell. Arpad looked up, surprised.

"Ah, is that you, Sophie? How pretty you have grown! I beg you will send me back my boat."

Sophie did not want to be asked twice. She held up her frock with one hand, tucked it between her knees, and after she had replaced the red cherry blossoms by some white flowers, she gave the little boat such a hearty shove that it came back to the opposite side. Then the game began again. It was so amusing!

Madame Belenyi saw the pair from the window. She didn't disturb them, but let them amuse themselves until the sun went down and the air began to get chill. Then the most prudent of the two children—it was the girl, no doubt—suggested to the other that the grass was wet with dew, and that it would be well to go back to the house.

Arpad took his boat out of the water, and put it and the flute back in their hiding-place, and returned to his mother.

Madame Belenyi did not scold him. She did not, however, kiss him on his forehead, as she was wont to do. She showed him all she had done to settle the house while he had been amusing himself in the garden.

Arpad was very much pleased to find it so comfortable.

"Mother," he said, "we will live here always."

"I don't object to our living here, Arpad; only there is one condition. You must marry a good girl, and bring her here to help me."

"I, mother?" returned Arpad, half pleased and yet astonished.

"Yes, you. Why not? You are a young man. I cannot look after you always."

Arpad laughed again. "So, because I have grown a young man, and that you cannot keep me any longer at your apron-string, I must take a wife who will keep me in better order than you can. Is that it, mother?"

"My son, it is in the natural order," returned Madame Belenyi, gravely, and as if there were no other course for a young man but to have either a mother or a wife to look after him. It did not enter into her imagination that he could look after himself.

"Sooner or later I shall obey your wishes; but just now, as we have got a house, I shall have enough to do to provide the house-keeping, and I could not take a wife with me here and there when I have to fulfil my professional engagements. For this sort of Bohemian life, vagabondizing from Paris to London, Petersburg to Vienna, is a bad thing for a woman, whether she goes with her husband or is left behind."

"But we have something to live on, Arpad. I have been very lucky with your earnings, and there is a nice nest-egg in the bank. Besides, there are the shares. Don't laugh, you silly boy! Although they are only worth ten gulden, yet there are a thousand of them. If we realize them, that would be ten thousand gulden. In a small town like this that sum would be a fortune, and with it you need not scruple to take a wife."

"Mamma, you don't understand about these shares. *One* could easily be realized, but if the next day I were to go to the same place with another for sale they would kick me out. Any one who would offer a thousand Bondavara shares in the money-market would be sent to the mad-house. Put the shares away with those other important papers Csanta gave you, and, if you like, treasure the hope that one day they may be worth as much as the paper they are printed on."

"Well, stranger things have happened. Did you ever think we would come back to this house? I am very sorry I did not keep the other papers. I burned them. Who knows what luck we may have with those bonds? If, one day, they rise again to par, we shall realize twice two hundred thousand gulden—"

"I don't count on such strokes of luck as that, mamma. The worst compliment Providence can pay a man is to let him win in a lottery. It is just as if God said to him, 'You ass! I cannot keep you in any other manner.' God would not allow a man who has any intellect to win in a lottery. To such a one he would say, 'Wilt thou cease to beg alms of Me in such a shameless manner? Is it not sufficient that I have endowed thee with talent? My consolation prizes are reserved for the dunderheads.'" Then he added, "Mother, don't be afraid, we shall live from my art. Wait a little and you shall see; only give me time. Meantime I shall buy for the little girl a doll with a china head as a plaything. You must take care of me for a little longer."

At these words the widow embraced her boy tenderly. She was happy; but that evening Arpad, when it was moonlight, went out and sat under the weeping-willow and played a melancholy air on his flute. Sometimes he stopped to listen to a soft silvery voice singing a national air on the other side of the stream. The singer, however, when she heard the flute no more, knew that he was listening, and stopped her song. It is so sweet to be young!

CHAPTER XXXVII

EUREKA

IVAN's fears as to the safety of his own colliery were growing day by day. One morning he found that the amount of hydrogen was scarcely perceptible; still there was water in the pit. This discovery made him thoughtful; he could not understand it. He descended into the cavern where the pond was. Not one drop of water!

Ivan remained for three hours, watching anxiously to see would the water rise; but none came.

At the end of three hours he was relieved by the men, and it was then arranged that during the night they would take turns in watching the tank. As soon as the water began to rise they were to call him. Ivan went home, lay down, and fell into a deep sleep, from which he did not awake until the sun was high in the heavens. He wondered that no one had called him, as had been agreed.

It might be that the men had also been overcome by sleep. Poor wretches, they also were exhausted. He hastened to the pit. The men told him they had watched all night, but there had been no sign of water in the tank. He waited patiently for twenty-four hours. Not a sign of water!

Ivan thought he could explain the absence of the water by the theory of the periodic springs—a theory too complicated to enter upon here. It is sufficient to say that the water-supply of the mine was worked by the pressure of the air upon these springs. If the water did not now return, it would be attributable to one of two causes: either the pipe which conducted the water from the larger basin had suddenly closed, and was no longer subject to atmospherical pressure, on which it depended to keep open; or some split or crevice had come in the stone masonry which protected the basins, and the force of the air had driven the water down farther into the bowels of the earth, where, no doubt, another basin was ready for its reception. We will remember that from the first Ivan had the idea that some such reservoir existed. But where? — that was the problem; and if the reservoirs were not found, what then?

The cavern where Ivan stood was empty. The black portals which guarded the subterranean kingdom of death stood open to him. He could enter the labyrinth; he could discover what he had long sought, the communication between the upper and the lower water basins. One difficulty lay in his way. He should take a workman with him. He called the old miner, Paul.

"Paul, how old are you?"

"Sixty-nine."

"You would like, no doubt, to complete your seventieth year."

"I should like to see the gold wedding of this pit. Next year it will be just fifty years since it was opened."

"And if you die before then?"

"I should say, 'The name of the Lord be blessed.'"

"Are your sons grown to man's estate?"

"My grandson is able to keep himself."

"Would you be ready to accompany me on a dangerous

expedition—one where the chances are we might never return?"

"I think I have run that chance before now."

"You must understand, Paul, the whole risk before you agree. We are going to look for the water that has left the tank. It is a matter of life and death to every one of us, and, therefore, I think God will help us'; but it may not be so. The Almighty may say, 'Why should you mere worms of the earth dare to interfere between me and the sentence I have passed against you and yours? I did not listen to the entreaties of Lot, and now the Dead Sea covers the ruins of the city. You men of Bondathal are not better than the men of Gomorrah.' Do you understand me? I have often sought for the source of the spring through the narrow winding paths of this cavern. These windings are so narrow that one must sometimes press through them by mere force, at other times creep along upon one's stomach. Great abysses yawn under the feet; a fall down one of these would be fatal; we will have to cling to the wall as we creep along. Again, we will pass through stinking sewers, up to our elbows in putrid filth. All these clefts and fissures have been made some time— God knows when—by an earthquake which has caused the uprooting of the coal stratum. Now it is quite possible that this last explosion has closed again many of these clefts and opened others. If it has happened, as I surmise, that the aperture has been shut which communicated between the pit beneath us and the one above—if this has taken place, then we have a tank full of water over our heads. If we, in our search through the bowels of the earth, come upon this aperture, and accidentally break the smallest hole, not the size of a pin's point, the water in the basin over our heads will burst through and annihilate us; if we hear it roaring we are already lost. But, on the other hand, it may be that the explosion caused a rent in the upper cleft, and if so the water has rushed through it to the lower basin under our feet. What we have to do, whether we die in the search or not, is to find out where the water is."

"I have no idea what you mean; all I know is that I am ready to go with you."

"Then go home and take leave of your family, as if you were going a long journey. Go to your priest and make your peace with God. Then come back, and tell no one where we are going."

Ivan now made his own preparations. From this adventure he might never return. He made his will. He bequeathed his mine to his workmen, his money to Paul's family. This was an act of justice. If the old man were killed, it was in a measure his, Ivan's, doing.

When this was all done he went out and took his leave of light and air before going into the blackness of everlasting night. It was well under the free air of heaven. The sky might be bluer elsewhere, the grass greener; still, it was not eternal darkness.

The post brought him a letter. It was from Arpad Belenyi. It told him all that we already know—the fall of Kaulmann, the disappearance of Eveline, whom every one thought had drowned herself. Ivan's heart was stirred by deep sorrow. The sky lost its brightness; the meadow was no longer green; the blackness of the pit would be welcome to him. This news acted upon him as a tonic; he felt braced; his fears vanished. Life was now more worthless than before.

He set about the necessary preparations with calmness. He collected the instruments which would be needed for this strange search—the levelling instrument, the circumferentor, the plumb-line. He put them in a bag, which he tied round his neck. Paul carried the pick, the iron rod, and a strong cord.

With this equipment they descended into the cavern, and vanished through the windings of the water-course. After six hours they reappeared. This went on day after day.

Ivan took the measurements of all the windings of the labyrinth, and when he was at home compared them carefully. It took him hours. At night he retired into his laboratory, heated deadly gases in his retorts, and forced the mysterious elements to surrender their long-concealed secrets. He fought with demons who refused to obey him.

"Which of you is the spirit that can extinguish fire? Appear! appear! Not with Alpha and Omega, not with Solomon's Seal, not in the name of Abraxas and Mithras do I conjure you, but by the force of all-powerful science I order you appear!"

But no spirit appeared.

This double battle, the one under the earth, the one in the air above it, this fight with the two great demons of the world's creation, went on day by day, in daylight and darkness. Ivan had no rest.

One morning he was told that the water in the castle well was hot, and it had a decided taste of sulphur. He began now to despair. The subterranean conflagration was closing round him sooner than he had looked for it. The situation was lost; one year, and the whole place would be consumed.

Rauné, when this fact became known, threw up his appointment and openly took service with Prince Waldemar. He was commissioned by his employer to write —as an authentic witness—the accounts of the catastrophe, which appeared constantly in the Vienna papers.

Ivan threw himself with the energy of despair into the search; he penetrated farther into the subterranean labyrinth. Paul was like a ghost; his very soul was steeped in terror, but he held bravely to his master.

One day, amidst the confusion of the different winding passages in the rock, they came to a place out of which there seemed to be no exit. They struck the wall. It returned a hollow sound, so that they drew the conclusion that on the other side there was a large cavern, or space of some sort. The tumbled masses of slate-stratum fallen over one another was a proof that the blockade had been recently made.

"We must clear a passage here," said Ivan, taking the pick in his hand.

Paul cowered down, clinging to the wall. He trembled at every blow of the pick given by the vigorous arm of Ivan, who worked with terrible earnestness. So might a despairing soul beat against the gates of hell and summon the devil to single combat.

At last the pick made a small hole, through which Ivan passed the iron rod, and raised a whole mass of slates.

"Now, if the water is overhead the crack of doom has come."

The old man crossed himself, and recommended his soul to God.

Ivan, however, shouted with all the joy of a discoverer: "Do you hear? The rubbish as it falls makes a splash. The lower basin I am in search of *is here*, underneath us!"

But what if the one above is full? They had still to wait while they counted a hundred beats of the pulse.

Never was a pulse felt under such terrible circumstances, not even when Ivan had gone down into the burning mine. Not a sound was heard. In the bosom of the earth all is quiet. Ivan was trembling with joyful excitement.

"Found at last!" he cried. "Now bind the cord round me, and lower me into the well cavern."

It was done. The old miner, as he held the rope, prayed fervently to the Blessed Mother that she would forgive this heretic, who did not know what he was doing. Meantime the lamp sank deeper and deeper.

Suddenly Ivan cried out, "Pull me up!"

His old comrade drew him slowly out of the depths of the earth. As he held out his hand to help him, Ivan suddenly threw his arms round him and embraced him.

"We have reached our goal," he said. "The plumb-line shows a monstrous depth of water."

Paul's brain began to clear. For the first time he had a dim idea of the aims of their labors.

"Now let us get into daylight."

As soon as Ivan got out of the pit he ran home as fast as he could. He compared his measurements, and was well content with the result. At night he shut himself in his laboratory. He was flushed with triumph; another victory would be his. He would also conquer the demon that had hitherto resisted his will. He had the proud feeling of a victorious general who demands the last stronghold to surrender.

"I have already conquered," he said. "You are the next to submit. God sometimes lends to his creature immortal gifts, moments of creative power, when the infinite takes, as it were, shape, and the finite cries to the infinite, 'Eureka!'"

Ivan poured out ten drops of the water he had brought from the well. There was not more than would be held in the point of a pen. The laboratory became suddenly dark. The strong heat of the burning coal in the oven went out as if by magic. All was dark; black as night. This darkness was the light for which Ivan had been seeking.

"I have found it!" he cried aloud. "I have found it!" he cried to his workmen, among whom he rushed, half undressed, with his hat off, like a lunatic.

They did not know what he had found, but they felt certain the discovery which was considered so important by their guide and master must be a matter of rejoicing, in proof of which the miners cheered lustily.

CHAPTER XXXVIII

AT PAR

THE devil's comedy was being played daily on the stock-exchange. The Bondavara Company's shares, the Bondavara Railway shares were tossed here and there, from one hand to another. The tragedy had turned to comedy—that is, for some people, who found the game very humorous. The very word Bondavara made the stockbrokers laugh. When it happened that some fool bought a share, no one could help laughing. The shares, in fact, were given in exchange for anything of little value — for instance, as make-weight with an old umbrella for a new one. They were also presented to charitable institutions.

One witty man went to a fancy ball in a coat made of the shares. This conceit was thought diverting. The exchange, however, was still the field where a desultory fight was kept up by the shareholders. These poor wretches fought for the last flicker of the lamp, which the bears wanted to extinguish altogether.

Prince Waldemar, the leader of the conspiracy, forced the shares day by day lower and lower. At last they fell to one and a half per cent., then to one and a quarter, and this quarter was to go lower, the prince wanting to banish the shares from the quotation list. The owners were making a fight to prevent this—an ineffectual one, it seemed to be. They were almost agreed to give up the fight as a forlorn hope. How could they make head against such odds? The day upon which Rauné's report was in the newspapers they resolved to lay down their arms; there seemed no good in protracting the struggle. The report in question was the one which stated what was the nature of the elements that, since the fire in the Bondavara mine, had been found mixed with the water on the lake of the castle; this caused a great "sensation," and was the last straw upon the back of the unfortunate shareholders.

Prince Waldemar had the news proclaimed on 'change that on the last day of the month he would sell his Bondavara Company shares at ten florins. Some people took up the gauntlet he had thrown down. These were shareholders who knew that they would lose by taking this wager, but at the same time hoped by this stroke of policy to prevent the shares from disappearing altogether from the share list. If, therefore, at the end of the month the shares went down to six gulden, they must pay the other side twenty thousand gulden difference; if the shares went up, the other side must do the same.

About noon a broker came to the bank, and said, loud enough for all bystanders to hear, that a gentleman was present who would take five hundred Bondavara shares at par.

If some one had struck a hammer upon the open keys of a piano no greater whir and whiz could have been heard than now ran through the hall. Screams of laughter, exclamations of astonishment, howls of joy, curses, and ejaculations of incredulity were raised in every corner. Who is he? Is he a lunatic? At par! Bondavara shares! Where is the man?

The broker pointed him out. He was evidently a provincial gentleman, very unassuming in his appearance.

He was leaning against a pillar, calmly surveying the Olympian games.

"He is evidently a silly knave who wants to have a joke," scoffed Prince Waldemar. "Go to him," he went on to the agent, "and ask him for his name. We must know what is the name of any one who treats with us."

The broker returned in a few minutes with the news that the gentleman gave his name as a Hundred Thousand Gulden, saying that money was the best surname. He showed his hands full of bank-notes, which he received from the stranger.

"Who sells five hundred Bondavara shares at par?"

This cry caused a revolution on 'change. Tranquillity was at an end; tumult took its place; uproar and confusion reigned. Credulous and incredulous people surrounded the stranger; they pressed upon him, overwhelming him with questions, stretching over one another to thrust their note-books into his hands. The unknown met all this noise with cool indifference, merely pointing out to his broker the crowd who were ready to do business with him.

Prince Waldemar now made his way through the mob to where the new-comer stood. With the most refined impertinence he drew the brim of his hat over his eyes and stuck his hand into his waistcoat pockets as he surveyed the other.

"Sir, your appearance has caused a sudden revolution. May I ask your name?"

"My name is Ivan Behrend," returned the stranger, without changing his negligent attitude.

"Ah," said the prince, suddenly taking off his hat and bowing low. "I have had the honor of hearing of you. Are you not the renowned pistol-shot, who can shoot a cigar out of a man's mouth? I am a nobody in comparison; I am only Prince Waldemar Sondersheim. I cannot shoot as you do. But let us talk sensibly. You want to buy Bondavara shares at par? Have you inherited suddenly the fortune of an Indian nabob, who made it a condition that you should buy the shares at par?"

"No. I buy them because they are worth that price."

"Don't you know that the Bondavara mine is on fire?"

"I happen to own the adjoining one, therefore I am quite aware that such is the fact."

"Then your mine will be on fire next."

"Not so. I extinguished the fire in mine a fortnight ago."

At these words the noise rose to a regular tumult; the shareholders pressed round Ivan, and nearly suffocated him. The man is there who can extinguish the fire. The mine will soon be again in working order. Bondavara stands once more at par.

The bears had to retire. The joyful shareholders surrounded Ivan and carried him in triumph out of the hall.

That same evening a large meeting was held, at which Ivan, before an enormous audience, filling the room to suffocation, declared authoritatively that he had an infallible plan, which had, in fact, been tried on the Bondavara mine, and had put out the conflagration. He invited every one present to see the experiment tested next day in the open air, when it would be distinctly proved that his words were no idle boast.

The following morning, in presence of a large crowd, he fulfilled his promise, succeeding admirably in the demonstration. A funeral pile of coal and turf, over which petroleum had been poured, was set fire to, and when blazing to its greatest height was put out in a few minutes by some drops from a small bottle.

The jubilant public conducted Ivan back to the town

in triumph, and at the next general meeting of shareholders it was resolved to offer him a remuneration of six hundred thousand gulden if he would undertake to bring the Bondavara mine into working order.

There were not wanting, however, plenty of opponents. Foremost there was Prince Waldemar, who possessed the largest proportion of shares, and who, nevertheless, offered the most determined opposition. He did everything to embarrass and obstruct Ivan's scientific propositions.

"I grant," he said, "that you may be able to put out with one bucket of fluid six cubit feet of burning coals; but consider for a moment that in the Bondavara pit, reckoning from the place where the explosion took place to the castle, there must be at least sixty thousand cubit feet of burning stratum. You must have, to meet this, ten thousand buckets of fluid ready to shoot over the mass. What machine have you that would be able for such an operation as this?"

"I have not forgotten that such a machine would be necessary," returned Ivan, quietly.

"Let us suppose," continued the prince, "that you do succeed in getting a sufficient quantity of fluid to bear upon the burning mass. Don't you perceive that this very supply will develop a monstrous amount of gas, which would permeate the pit from top to bottom, and cause another and still worse explosion?"

"I have foreseen this danger."

"And, finally, if you possess any idea, which you evidently do, of the mechanism of machines and the expenditure necessary to procure the best, you must face the problem that a million of money will not be sufficient to procure the necessary materials which would be wanting to make the experiment successful."

"I have drawn up an estimate of probable outlay."

The shareholders here shouted out to him that they undertook all expenses, even if they amounted to a million, and on the spot it was agreed that Ivan should receive full powers to do for the Bondavara mine what he considered necessary, let the cost be what it might.

Prince Sondersheim saw that he could not stem the course of Ivan's popularity; it must have its way. While the assembled shareholders were signing the deed of authorization, he took Ivan aside, and said to him:

"Ivan Behrend, whether the undertaking you have engaged in succeeds or not—I do not believe that it will succeed—you will have taken out of my pocket a million—a million net. Besides this, you have squandered five hundred gulden of your own money, without reckoning what is yet to be spent. Let that be. You have done this by fixing the quotations at par. It is true that the shares will neither be bought nor sold, for both sides will be afraid, and will hold back; nevertheless, the quotation will stand at par, and I am obliged to pay the difference on this—that will cost me a million. But that is nothing; I have lost as much before now, and recovered it again. One has only to play the waiting game. If, however, in a fortnight's time you find that you miscalculated your powers, and that your experiment fails, you have only to let it be known, and I shall pay one million into your hand."

Ivan answered this contemptible proposal with business-like composure.

"Prince Sondersheim, the stock-exchange is, as I am well aware, a privileged place. Here a man can say things without having any fear of consequences. What a man says or does, what proposals he makes—everything is, in a sense, allowable, and the ordinary rules which govern the outside world do not apply. Here one man may ask the other, 'How much do you ask for selling the honor of your company?' and if the answer is, 'It is not for sale,' that is enough. Here there is plain speaking; no one is offended at being asked to be an accomplice in a robbery. It would be no reflection on his character; he would assume no airs of righteousness, but simply answer, 'I really haven't time.' If men quarrel, if they spit at one another, tear the hats off one another's heads, that is nothing; it goes no further; no one turns round to look at them. They wipe the spittle off their faces, pick up their hats, and after half an hour walk about arm in arm. No one remembers that they were fighting; it was only a little 'difference,' which led to an animated scene. Therefore, to the proposal made by Sondersheim, the Bondavara coal-merchant, to Behrend, the Bondavara coal-trader, there is but one answer, 'Sir, I cannot entertain your offer.' Prince Waldemar Sondersheim will, however, do well to remember not to repeat outside the stock-exchange such a proposal to Ivan Behrend."

The prince laughed. "I guessed as much. I have often heard of you, and if you behave well you shall hear how it came to pass that I know so much about you. Once upon a time you took my part in a very energetic manner; and to a very pretty woman. I do not know why you should have done so; it is sufficient for me that you did. Also, you withdrew your own claim to the favor of this very pretty woman. But it was no good, she is now the wife of an unworthy fellow; but your unexplained intervention in my favor, which could not have been a business manœuvre, but must have sprung from almost a chivalrous Puritanism, has placed me under a debt of gratitude towards you. It that lady had listened to your advice, things would have been very different. No sulphur deposit would have been found in the castle lake; the whole speculation, in fact, would have had no existence. Outside the exchange we will not recur to the subject. I have mentioned it from a sense of gratitude, and I shall note it in my book. If you succeed in extinguishing the fire you are to receive six hundred thousand gulden from the company; if you fail you shall have a million from me."

This long conversation between Ivan and the prince excited some alarm among the shareholders; they tried to interrupt it.

"No tampering, prince. Let our man alone." They were afraid he would turn round.

"Don't be afraid," returned the prince; "we are talking of a lady whom we both admired."

But the shareholders' suspicions were not allayed by these words. They chose from among themselves a commission of three members, who should accompany Ivan in every step he took, never leave him, eat with him, sleep outside his door, keep watch under his window, so that their enemy should not approach him without their knowledge. This was all done under the pretence of giving him assistance, and for the purpose of keeping him supplied with money.

Ivan procured the necessary machines and workmen, and travelled back with them and his three companions to Bondavara.

His three commissioners were likewise to furnish the company with a daily report of the progress of the work. One of the three was the clerk Spitzhase, who had the reputation of being the most circumspect, careful, and impudent servant of the company. This last epithet is not meant in the worst sense of the word. In money matters modesty and meekness are oftentimes great faults, and the contrary qualities are of infinite use. The word is therefore meant in praise. Ivan many times chucked Spitzhase out at the door, but the clerk always returned by the window.

CHAPTER XXXIX

THE UNDERGROUND WORLD

THE three commissioners for the first fortnight had little to say; their report was meagre of incident. Behrend came morning and evening to dine and sup with them in the little village inn; the rest of the day and of the night he spent continuously underground. When they asked him what he was doing, he said, shortly, that everything was going on well.

Things might be going well, but there was nothing visible to the commissioners. And, moreover, there was *one* very suspicious circumstance which struck Spitzhase especially, and this was that Behrend spent his time in his *own colliery*. It was there that all the expensive machines had been set up and all the chemical stuffs had been taken. Not a single thing had been done to the company's mine; not a bit of rubbish had been cleared away, not one of the entrances had been opened; in fact, a fortnight had slipped away, and no work had been undertaken. It was undoubtedly true that the machines were always at work, and cart-loads of clay and stones were perpetually being wheeled away.

The whole thing was incomprehensible, and Behrend would not give the slightest explanation.

At the beginning of the following week Spitzhase lost all patience.

"Sir," he said to Ivan, with suppressed irritation,

"you promised that in a fortnight the conflagration in our mine would be extinguished. The time is up, and I have not seen that anything has been even attempted."

"That is very probable," returned Ivan, quietly.

"Do you maintain still that everything is progressing satisfactorily?"

"I do."

"Can I see for myself what has been done?"

"Where you are standing it would be impossible for you to judge."

"Well, let me go where I can see something."

"Do you really wish to go below? It is not a pleasant place."

"Where you go, so can I; for my part, I don't care if it was hell itself."

"It is not unlike what hell must be."

"Well, I am resolved to pay it a visit. I want to make the acquaintance of the devil; perhaps I could make an arrangement with him to supply us with coal."

"You may come on one condition: if you accompany me you must understand that I cannot let you stand gaping about. There is not room in the place for more than two people, and they must both work."

"I am not afraid of work. I am the devil for work."

"Very good, then, come along," said Ivan; "and if the other gentlemen would like to accompany us to where the machines are working they can follow us."

The others seized the opportunity.

Ivan made them put on miners' dress. They were then hoisted into the crane, and descended into the shaft. Each one had a safety-lamp fastened to his belt and wore a thick felt hat.

Ivan led them through the different windings of the pit until they came to the iron door of the cavern in which, not long since, the pond used periodically to come and go. The middle of this space was now filled by a large mill-like machine, which was kept in motion by an endless strap worked from above. In this mill some substance was being ground, and, when reduced to fine powder, was carried, by means of certain mechanical contrivances, through a pipe and over a bridge, where it disappeared from view.

Ivan led his guests through still more tortuous ways. Once they descended the shaft of a well; once they mounted high ladders, finding themselves when they had done so in a small chamber, not measuring six feet in circumference, in which two miners were waiting—an old and a young man.

"Now," said Ivan to Spitzhase, "here is our dressing-room; we must put on our costume."

"What! have we another change of clothes?"

"Yes, we have to don a coat of mail in the tournament in which we are going to take part; we require armor."

At a sign from him the miners came forward and began to prepare the two gentlemen. The equipment was something similar to that of a fireman—a coat and stockings, the outer stuff being made of asbestos, while the space between that and the lining was filled with pulverized charcoal; the hands and arms were also covered with long gloves made of asbestos, the fingers being air-proof.

"We could pass for knights," said Spitzhase, jestingly.

"Wait until you see our helmets," returned Ivan.

The miners brought two helmets made of glass, each of which had a hollow space with twelve joints and three apertures. Ivan explained the use of these.

"The place into which we are about to descend is full of coal-gas. We must have an apparatus which will enable us to pass through fire and to dive under water."

Spitzhase began to repent that he had been so venturesome, but he was ashamed to turn back now, and he had a certain amount of pluck.

"We need," continued Ivan, "an apparatus which is a combination of the diver's and the fireman's dress. To the glass helmet, which will be attached to the coat-collar by means of air-proof caoutchouc, there will be fastened two tubes, through one of which the necessary amount of air will be conveyed to us, and through the other the bad air will be expelled. The ends of both the tubes will remain here, while we drag them after us in the same manner as does the diver. Although all bad air escapes from our helmets, still we shall find the air rather warmer than it is up here, and it will smell like vulcanized india-rubber; still we cannot suffocate. To this third aperture an elastic tube will be fixed, which unites both helmets; through this tube each will hear what the other says, for the glass is so thick that no sound penetrates it, and when you have it on your head you will with difficulty hear what is said by me."

Spitzhase had begun to feel very uncomfortable, for now the miner proceeded to adjust the glass helmet to his head. When the tubes were being fixed into the three apertures he perceived that he had become suddenly stone deaf. He saw the lips of the two commissioners moving, but not one word could he hear. He no longer belonged to the world. Only one sound reached him, and that was the voice of the man to whose head he was fastened.

"Take one end of the hose upon your arm," shouted

the voice into his helmet; yet the sound seemed to come from a long way off, or as if out of a tunnel.

Mechanically he took the coil on his shoulder.

"Let us go," shouted Ivan, taking the other end of the coil on his shoulder, and, opening a thick oak door, which had hitherto escaped Spitzhase's observation, they passed through.

The two commissioners had heard nothing that had passed between the two "knights"; but when they saw the oak door open they hurriedly asked the miners whether the foul air did not come in. The older workman reassured them; the carbon was much heavier than oxygen, and even thicker than hydrogen. The foul air remained below, where the two divers had gone. They might have every confidence so long as the safety-lamps burned. Meantime, the others had penetrated into a roomy cavern, the walls of which proved it had not been made by the hands of men, but was a natural formation. Each partition of the wall fitted into another, like the blocks of a puzzle, and each block was as smooth as a steel mirror. They were masses of coal set obliquely one upon another. The cavern was bridged over with thick, strong wooden planks. The gearing strap, which had made its way from the cavern in serpent-like fashion, had set a wheel in motion, and the noise of the clapper resounded under the bridge, and made a sound as if it were working in deep water. From this bridge a narrow path led obliquely into the stone layers. Once beyond the entrance into this dark path the lamps ceased to burn; the coal-gas had begun its sway. Upon the bridge an electric machine was placed, whose brilliant light was shaded by a wire screen.

The old miner set the machine working, and the light flashed into every nook and cranny of the subterranean cavern. It lighted up the narrow tunnel which, for the last month, Ivan had been boring from his own mine to that of his neighbor. He had told no one what he had been doing, but now the work was almost finished; it only required to be broken through. This work, which would take another week to complete, needed to be done in a diver's equipment. The length of the narrow tunnel was perfectly illumined by the electric machine, as if in the broad light of the sun. Where it turned out of its course high looking-glasses of polished steel were placed in positions which reflected the light itself until it faded away to a faint glimmer. The two divers could now hardly discern an object.

"We shall soon be in darkness," said Spitzhase to Ivan.

"We shall have light enough," returned Ivan; and he led the way farther into the tunnel.

Spitzhase was forced to follow, for his head was fastened to Ivan's head. Wonderful pair of Siamese twins! If the pipe that bound them together were to break, both were dead men.

"Halt!" cried Ivan. "Here is the pump. Give me the pipe."

In the half-darkness a little machine three feet high was discernible; it was provided with a spring wheel. This suction-pipe had been brought here only the day before. Ivan took the caoutchouc coil from his companion's shoulder, and screwed the pipe to the aperture of the machine; then he set the wheel in motion, and in a few seconds it, with the heavy balls attached, was revolving with velocity. Then he took the end of the pipe and gave the coil back to Spitzhase with this difference: instead of putting it over his arm he hung the hose over his neck. Spitzhase felt as if the pipe were about a hundredweight heavier, and that it had grown suddenly stiff.

"Forward! quick march!" shouted Ivan into his helmet.

"It begins to be hot as hell itself," grumbled Spitzhase, who was suffering horribly.

"Because we are in a part of the mine where the fire has been put out."

Both the men wore on their feet glass slippers, otherwise they would have felt that the ashes through which they were wading were glowing with heat.

The india-rubber hose hung round Spitzhase's neck. It grew darker and darker, until at last it was as dark as Erebus.

"I can see nothing," shouted Spitzhase.

"You are safe if you follow me," returned Ivan.

It began to grow somewhat lighter. The light, however, was rose color; there was twilight, then, in the bowels of the earth.

Spitzhase complained he could hardly draw his breath.

"That will get better presently," said Ivan, encouraging him.

They had now turned the corner of the road, and the terrible tragedy of hell itself lay before them. Yes, hell itself was there. A burning labyrinth, in whose glowing passages the prismatic colors changed every moment. The blue-green flames leaped from the ground and blended with the flames of brilliant scarlet which played upon the burning wall, and again faded in the far distance into a deep purple color. It was like a fairy transparency at a pantomime. Through the fissures and crevices sheets of white sun-rays poured like molten silver. Amid the glowing coals there seemed to rise shapes as of demons dancing, creatures with green hair and red beards, and from the red sulphate of the vaulting there fell slowly a golden shower, a melting rain of sparks. From the clefts in the side walls the gas, let loose from all restraint, hissed like so many demoniacal serpents, and kindled a subterranean flame of its own. Out of the depths of the pit a waterspout of fire shot suddenly, sending in every direction a shower of sparks. Over the whole floated a milk-colored cloud, which filled the vault with a nebulous vapor, wandering as a will-o'-the-wisp here and there, and threatening every moment to envelop the rash visitors to hell in its chill embrace. Spitzhase, alarmed out of all control, pressed closer to the wall; fright was overcoming him.

"Let go the hose!" shouted Ivan. The hose fell like a serpent unchained, wriggling backward and forward. "Now follow me. Hold the pipe on your arm;" and he drew Spitzhase after him.

He was constrained to follow, although his heart was in his mouth; their heads were fastened to each other. If he had had sufficient strength to free himself from this terrible companionship, it would have in no way helped him, for the carbon would have killed him instantaneously.

Mechanically he allowed himself to be drawn on. Hell with all its horrors disclosed itself to his affrighted gaze. His companion seemed to fear nothing. Was he a human being, or a fiend, who was in reality possessed of power over the demons of hell? He dragged him to the very border of the fiery lake; then he took from his shoulder the hose, which lay in rings and coils, and, opening the mouth of the stop-cock, directed its force at the bosom of hell. The hose shot forth a flash like a diamond; the water-spirit fell into the glowing Gehenna.

"Hold tight!" shouted Ivan.

And from the force which the stream from the pipe exercised upon the burning mass the air was filled with dark clouds of smoke, which peopled the still brilliantly lighted cavern with strange, unearthly, spectral-like shadows, which, dissolving suddenly into steam, covered the two adventurous visitors with a damp moisture. One of them tottered.

"Fear nothing," calls out the other; "we are quite safe here."

"It is suffocating; I am burning!" cried Spitzhase.

"Do not be afraid; follow me," said Ivan, and drew his trembling comrade after him over the wet rocks, over the charred, burning mounds. Every spot where he saw the flames rising he directed the hose, and a shower of cool, refreshing water fell from the india-rubber pipe upon the burning, seething demoniacal flames. The gas hissed, the hot steam boiled round them, the flames, beaten down in one place, sprang up in another, but on they went. He was afraid of nothing. "Forward! go on! forward!" The mysterious clouds hovered over him.

"We are lost!" moaned the other poor mortal, whose fear began to be uncontrollable. He fell on his knees.

"You of little faith," said the conqueror of hell, "get up. Let us go back." And he lifted him up, as the Redeemer did Peter on the stormy Sea of Galilee.

Then he rolled the hose once more round his neck, and took it back to the suction-pump; this he closed, and then led his comrade again to the little room where they had put on their equipment.

Spitzhase sank back when he reached this haven. When his helmet was taken off he panted like a man who was suffocating for want of air. Ivan looked at him compassionately.

The miners gave each of them a glass of fresh lemonade to drink, and rubbed their temples with vinegar. They then undressed them to the skin, put them into a tub of cold water, took them out in two seconds, and rubbed them with coarse towels. Spitzhase began to recover his senses.

As they put on their usual clothes Ivan said to him, "Well, sir, how did you like being below?"

Spitzhase was no fool, but he answered, good-humoredly, "I wouldn't have missed going down for a hundred gulden, but I would pay twice that sum rather than go there again."

"Now you know what to write to your board of directors. Paul, take this gentleman home. I remain here to continue the work."

Spitzhase wrote a glowing account of what he called "the fight with the world of spirits" to the Vienna papers.

The next day Ivan said to the commissioners, "We have now laid pipes four inches in diameter to work upon the very heart of the fire. So soon as I am ready we shall set the high-pressure machine at work. This will empty in four hours ten thousand buckets of fluid on the burning mass."

"The devil take it!" cried Spitzhase. "Will this farce never have an end until the escaped gas blows up the colliery, and makes of it and of us a new Pompeii?"

"Do not be afraid. I have thought of this danger. We have taken care to stop all the outlets to the quarry gallery with sand-bags. We have walled up every possible fissure, crevice, and exit. The entrance to the well-shaft has been provided with a strong iron door, over which we have fastened a thick bed of clay. If, therefore, it should happen that in the gallery, where the conflagration is at its worst, and where the fluid must be poured freely, the mass of gas should develop in such force that it must explode, then the iron door will prove our salvation. It will resist all attack, and the force of the gas will be broken."

The members of the commission shook with fright. Here was a pleasant prospect! Ivan, however, had no time to spare on reassuring them; the crisis was at hand, and he had still much to do. Prudence, foresight was necessary. At mid-day he returned to the quarry gallery.

As the clock struck twelve he gave the signal at which the large suction-pump was to be set in motion. He remained from this time at his post, never leaving the machine until the work was finished. To their honor be it spoken, the three commissioners remained with him; they kept their places without moving, never speaking a word. During the awful time that followed no voice was heard but that of Ivan. Soon after the signal was given a rushing sound was heard underground, faint at first, but growing louder. It sounded as if in the distance water was pouring from an open sluice.

At first the machine was worked at only half its strength. After half an hour or so there mingled with the rushing sound a great tumult, as if many bells were vibrating in the air. The noise did not die away; on the contrary, the vibration grew every moment stronger.

The earth was in labor; the ground heaved and trembled, and those who felt its throes trembled also. The earth's sufferings were shared by her children. Only one man was calm; the master-spirit was not afraid.

With close attention Ivan watched the pendulum and the thermometer of the machine; he marked the variations in the condition of the barometer, the ozonometer, and electrometer, writing his observations in his notebook. After another hour he made a sign to the man working the machine to put on more pressure.

Thereupon arose from below a terrible uproar; it was the battle of the Cyclops. The bowels of the earth sent up a dull roar like the rolling of thunder; occasionally came a shock as of an earthquake. The houses began to rock, the tops of the tall trees and the cross upon the tower tottered, and its fall added to the anxiety felt by the entire valley. The underground fight grew every moment fiercer; the giants joined issue with their foes. They howled in rage; they put their gigantic shoulders together and tried to upset the earth. To their cries was added the bellowing of the hurricane confined in the cave, and the tumult was indescribable.

The listeners to this fearful scene looked with a stony stare of horror; they were speechless, but their look seemed to say, "What rash act have you done? Are you inciting the spirits who dwell under the earth to war against one another?"

Ivan answered with another look of calm superiority. "Fear nothing; I have my foot upon the head of the giant."

The underground battle had lasted three hours. The people were beside themselves with fright; they turned upon Ivan and cursed him.

"Do you think you are a God," they cried, "and can create an earthquake?"

Ivan paid no attention either to their fears or their curses; he gave another signal to the men at the machine—

"With the whole power!"

The machine, the outcome of the wonderful inventive

genius of man, stormed the very gates of hell itself. The underground tremblings followed one another rapidly, growing stronger and stronger; the deep groaning rose to a stentorian, deafening roar.

"It is all over!" shrieked the people in the valley, and fell upon their knees.

In the air a shrill, whistling sound was now heard, as if an engine had suddenly let off steam, and out of the shaft of the company's mine there arose rapidly a white column of steam, which, as soon as it encountered the cold regions of space, shot up into the sky, where it formed itself into a white cloud, which cloud suddenly broke into a deluge of rain. At once the underground convulsion ceased, and the shrill whistling died away in the distance.

Ivan, looking round, said, quickly, "Paul, collect the rain-water; I must know what it is made of." Upon this he gave the machinist the signal to stop the machine. There was not even a drop of perspiration upon his forehead. He took the bottle of rain-water that Paul brought him and put it in his pocket. "Now, gentlemen," he said, "you can go to supper. The work is accomplished."

"Is the fire extinguished?" asked Spitzhase.

"Absolutely."

"And the pillar of steam yonder?"

"Will remain in the sky until midnight and then slowly damp away. Go to supper. I have something of importance to do at home."

Who cared to eat supper?

The pillar of steam still continued to rise from the shaft, and to form a cloud from which a steady downpour of rain fell continuously, occasionally interspersed by flashes of lightning; but no one thought of going indoors. The richer members of society wrapped themselves in mackintoshes, the workmen in their cloaks, and all continued to watch the strange appearance, until at last, towards ten o'clock, it began to grow smaller. The whistling sound was interrupted now and again by a piercing shriek, and sometimes a flash of lightning illumined the shadow of the pillar—the white cloud.

The steam giant then sank back; not all at once, but by degrees, into the pit from which it had arisen. Only occasionally, from time to time, its head reappeared for a second, but the whistling ceased altogether; so, too, did the heaving of the earth. The unearthly tumult was silenced. In the church the sound of the organ was heard, and voices intoning "Alleluia! Alleluia!" The people walked in procession, carrying lanterns and banners.

The commissioners made their way to the inn, where they found Ivan eating his supper. He could eat now; it struck him that he was mortal and wanted food.

"I have finished the chemical examination," he said to the other three with polite indifference, "and I can give you the satisfactory news that in the residue 0.75 of carbonic acid is to be found."

Spitzhase did not understand. "What good is it," he asked, "if seventy-five parts of carbonic acid are in the residuum?"

"To-morrow we can open both entrances to the colliery, and after the air-pumps have been settled the work can be resumed."

Alleluia! Alleluia!

CHAPTER XL

ANGELA IS EVEN WITH IVAN

SUCCESS brings with it fame, fortune, and universal esteem. Men worship success, and with justice.

He who has saved a great treasure, who has restored to thousands of people their country, their industry; he who has overcome a universal calamity which threatened an entire province; he who has given to thousands on the verge of beggary their livelihood, who has dried the tears of the widow and the orphan—he is near to God himself.

Honors and rewards were showered upon Ivan. The government gave him for all time the patent for his discovery. By the Joint-Stock Mining Company he was handsomely remunerated. A monster deputation obliged him to accept the place of director. Scientific societies at home and abroad elected him member. His picture and biography appeared in all the illustrated papers of Europe and America. The simple villagers in Bondathal prayed for him night and morning; and when the first train steamed out of the Bondavara station, the locomotive bore the name of "Behrend." It was only God's providence that preserved him from receiving "an order."

Perhaps the most interesting testimony, and the one most valued by Ivan, was a letter which the Countess Angela wrote to him with her own hand.

The countess told him frankly all that had happened to her since they had met; how she had married the Marquis Salista; how unhappy he had made her by the pressure he brought to bear upon her grandfather, Prince Theobald, which ended in his property being sequestrated, to the ruin of the whole family of Bondavary. She had suffered greatly in consequence, and had known what privation meant; also the income of the Countess Theudelinde had been considerably diminished, and the old lady had been forced to reduce her household. This condition of affairs had shown them their former friends in their true light—among others, Salista, her husband, who had gone to Mexico, and left her to shift for herself. Then Ivan had come to the rescue. Prince Waldemar's triumphal progress had been effectually checked. The million of money placed by Prince Theobald in the Bondavara Company had regained its value. The prince had arranged with his creditors, and his affairs were once more settled. She had been reconciled to him, and lived with him. Countess Theudelinde likewise had recovered her rents. The great family of Bondavary, which had been so near ruin, was reinstated in its former position. And for its new lease of life it had to thank a certain beneficent, clever—

Here Countess Angela's letter broke off. There was, however, a postscript:

"Answer this letter. I beg for one word. Write 'I forgive you.'"

Ivan answered her immediately. He expressed his gratitude for her kind remembrance of him, but he could not imagine what he had to forgive. On the contrary, he had a lively recollection of the many kindnesses he had received from the Countess Angela Salista.

The letter was evidently written with an effort to be cold and polite. It was followed by a second letter from Angela, which ran thus:

"Do not answer me in that way. I have sinned against you. You do not reproach me, but my own heart and conscience do. To quiet these tormentors I need your pardon. Answer me sincerely. Can you ever forgive me? I should not have treated you as I did—"

Ivan answered this by a long, confidential letter. He confessed to her secrets of his heart, made to her confessions which never before passed his lips. The countess might be confident that she had never offended him. She had never forfeited the place she held in his respect."

A third letter came from Angela.

"If you can do so from your heart, write upon a piece of paper, 'Angela Bondavary, I forgive you, from my heart.'"

Ivan wrote these words and nothing else.

One evening two carriages drove into the court-yard of Ivan's house. He lived now in the handsome residence provided by the company for the director of the mines. The porter exchanged some words with the person who sat in the first carriage, and then came to Ivan with two visiting-cards.

Ivan, to his surprise, read the names—

Countess Theudelinde Bondavary.

Countess Angela Bondavary.

These names caused a great disturbance in Ivan's mind. What did they want? Why did they come to him? He told the porter to show the ladies in, and then, taking up the cards again, it struck him as odd that the Countess Angela's did not bear the name of her husband.

The door opened, and only one lady entered. She was dressed in mourning, and her face was covered by a thick veil, the thick crape concealing her features. It was the Countess Theudelinde. She had on a long black travelling-cloak with two capes. She came to Ivan and held out to him the finger-tips of her black glove, which he carried to his lips, while she murmured some words of greeting.

"Where is the marquise?" asked Ivan, anxiously.

"She will be here immediately; but it is very difficult to bring her in."

Ivan conducted the lady to a sofa and asked her to be seated.

"Do not go to meet her," continued the countess. "She will find her way. You will receive her kindly, won't you?"

"Oh, countess," Ivan began; but Theudelinde interrupted impatiently.

"No phrases, please. We have not come here for polite words or to exchange compliments. We come to make a request; the answer is simple. Yes or no. Angela wants to remain here."

"Here!" repeated Ivan, horrified.

"Yes, here! Do not be afraid; not in this house, but in the neighborhood. She wishes to remain near you—never to leave you—that is her desire; and she has a right to have her wishes granted."

Ivan began to think he must be dreaming; he did not know what to say, but his thoughts were distracted by a strange noise outside. Along the passage came the heavy tread of several men. The door opened and four miners came in, carrying between them a metal coffin, on the lid of which lay a white wreath of *repoussé* silver.

The wreath surrounded the arms of the Bondavary family, and underneath was carved in gold letters—

ANGELA BONDAVARY.

The coffin was placed upon the oak table. Ivan stood as if he were turned into a statue, his eyes fixed upon the wreath and the name underneath.

Theudelinde got up and seized his hand, saying, in a low, agitated voice:

"This is the Countess Angela Bondavary, who begs of you, as the master here in Bondavara, to find for her a small place in the family vault of the castle, where she may lie among her own people, waiting for the coming of Jesus Christ — the Bridegroom of all poor women whose lives have been desolated."

"How is it possible that she is dead?" said Ivan, who was deeply moved.

"How? Very easily! When you throw a rose into the fire, in two minutes you will only find its ashes. I had just heard her laugh; she was quite gay. Then she went too near the stove; the next moment she screamed, and I saw her enveloped in flames!"

"She was burned to death!" cried Ivan, covering his face with his hands. Then, after a pause, "Was there no one near to save her?"

"Was there no one?" answered Theudelinde. "Were you, then, asleep at midnight? Did you not hear her call, 'Ivan, help me!'? Did you not see her standing beside your bed in flames — an angel with hell in her heart? Why were you not by her side to hold her in your arms, to stifle the flames, to snatch her from the jaws of death? Where were you, who should have saved her? Now she is here, and says to you, 'I am gone. I am no one. Let us be united.'"

Ivan felt as if an iron band had been laid upon his heart.

"She lived," continued Theudelinde, "for two days. She suffered the most terrible pain. When I think of all she went through I feel as if my senses were leaving me. To the last she was conscious. She spoke— But no—why should I tell you what she said? Just before she died she asked for a pencil, and wrote a few words to you. Here they are in this envelope. Do not break the seal, do not read them, so long as I am here. I would rather give you no explanation. If you have anything to ask, ask it from her. Here is the key of the coffin; I give it to you."

Ivan recoiled from receiving such a present.

"Why should you be afraid? Why do you object to opening the coffin? There is nothing to fear. The body is embalmed, and the flames did not touch her face. You will see that she smiles."

Ivan forced himself to raise the coffin-lid and to look on the face of the dead. There was no smile on her lips. She was calm and cold; as when she lay insensible in the wood, with her head upon a cushion of moss, so now she lay upon her white satin cushion. Ivan felt that if she could open her eyes for one minute she would look at him proudly and say, "I want nothing," and close them again. How beautiful she was, with her still, marble face, her immovable eyebrows. Ivan would not disturb its calm loveliness by even one kiss. He would have felt it to be dishonorable, and yet, if she could have come to life again, who knows—? As on the day when he had closed her dress with his breastpin, so now he shrouded her secret with the coffin-lid. Her secret was safe with him.

"Keep the key," said Theudelinde. "The coffin, its key, and the treasure it holds are yours; that is settled. You are the master of the vault; it is your duty to take her there. You cannot escape it."

With eyes that were hot and tearless, Theudelinde looked through her veil at Ivan. He returned the glance. If either had shed a tear, or even let a sob escape, both would have burst into passionate weeping, for grief is infectious; but each one of them was resolved to show mental strength in the presence of the other. They could even command their emotions.

"Do you undertake the duty?"

Ivan bowed his head.

"Then you will perform it alone. Alive I shall never enter the family vault. You know why."

Both were silent. Then Theudelinde burst out:

"Why was I not left in my castle? Why was I undeceived when I imagined that my ancestors visited me? If I had not been shaken in my delusions I should still have been happy. I should never have gone into the world, where I have only found misery; Angela would not have come to me; my brother Theobald would not have been ruined; hell would not have been let loose in the Bondavara mines; I should have never known you; all — all would have been different!" Then, after a pause, she went on: "There is no need of a clergyman; there is no need of any ceremony. You can say some prayers. You are a Protestant—so was Angela. She became one that she might get a separation from her unworthy husband. Let them carry the coffin quietly and reverently to the family vault. There I shall leave you and it, for I shall not go inside —never, until I am dead. You will put the coffin in its place, and then I return whence I came, where I am wanted by no one."

Ivan called the miners to take the coffin again upon their shoulders, and told them to carry it through the vestibule to the private door which led into the park. The park separated the director's house from the castle.

As they walked through the winding paths of the park the trees shed their golden leaves upon the coffin and the titmice in the brushwood chanted the dirge.

Ivan walked bareheaded behind the coffin, and behind him came Countess Theudelinde.

When they reached the entrance of the vault Ivan told the bearers to put the coffin down, and, kneeling down beside it, he remained for a long time praying. God hears us if we speak to Him in a whisper; nay, He hears us, even although we do not speak, but feel.

Theudelinde bent over Ivan and kissed his forehead.

"I thank you. You walked behind her with your head uncovered. Now she is all yours." Then she returned by the winding path, as if she were afraid that Ivan would make her take away what she had brought.

Ivan placed the coffin in its resting-place and sent away the bearers; then he remained for many hours beside it. By the light of the torches he read Angela's last words to him—

"For whom shall I wait on the shore of the new world?"

Ivan sighed deeply. "Who will wait for me on the shore of the new world?"

Then he made his way back to the house. There was no trace of either the countess's travelling carriage or Angela's hearse.

CHAPTER XLI

HOW IVAN MOURNED

THEY were both gone, the high-born lady and the peasant girl—gone where there is no sorrow and no more sin. One had lost her life by charcoal, the other by fire—two vengeful spirits.

Ivan thought of both with bitter regret. He felt now that he was alone in the world. He would have given all the fame he had acquired, the money he had earned, the good he had done, to have been able to save even one of these women. He mourned for them not in black, not with crape on his hat. What good are these signs of grief?

The European mourns in black, the Chinese in yellow, the Mussulman in green; in the classical age they mourned in white; the former generation of Hungarians in violet; the Jews in rags; the philosopher in his heart. The wise man never shares his grief, but he does his joys.

Meantime, in the Bondavara Valley there reigned peace and plenty; where there had been a half-savage race there was a happy people. The worst characters had settled down, morality had grown popular.

Ivan sent the young men at his own expense to factories abroad, where they learned the arts of civilization. He brought wood-carvers from Switzerland and lace-workers from Holstein to teach their trades to the women and children, so that they might unite artistic labor with increase of wages. For a population where every one, big and little, works either from necessity or for amusement—a people who look upon work as pleasure and who feel it no privation to be employed—such a people are ennobled by their toil.

Ivan looked after the schools. He emancipated the national teachers from the misery of their national tyrants; he rewarded the student with scholarships, the school-boy with useful prizes; in every parish he established a library and reading-room. He accustomed the people to put by the pence they could spare; he taught them how to help one another; he established in Bondavara a savings-bank and a hospital.

His own colliery was a model. The miners and himself were the joint owners, and shared the profit. Whoever was taken on in this colliery should pass an examination and work one year on trial. This rule applied to women and men alike. This trial year was not easy, particularly for the girls.

Nowhere was a girl so looked after; not in her mother's house or in a convent or state institution was there more particularity as to manners and morals than in Ivan Behrend's colliery. Every word, every act was watched. If any one failed to be up to the mark during his year of probation, no one taunted him, nor was he despised. He was simply told to go and work in the company's colliery, where there was better pay; and the workman or workwoman imagined this was an advance, not a degradation. In the company's colliery there was certainly more freedom, the rules being less strict.

If, however, at the end of the trial year the applicant had fulfilled all requirements, he or she was received into the colony and became a shareholder, so far as the profit was in question. Besides this, a prize for virtue was given once a year, on the anniversary of the great pit-burning, to the most modest, well-conducted girl in the colony.

Ivan spent on this prize fifty ducats, and the miners on their side promised the winner a handsome wedding present.

It was, of course, an understood thing that no one went in for the prize. No one knew who was likely to get it. The elders took notes; it was their secret.

The giving of this prize was not to be attended with any ceremonial. It would take place on an ordinary working day, when all the miners would have picks and shovels in their hands, so that every one could see that the reward was not for a pretty face, but for a good heart and industrious fingers. It was to be a day of general rejoicing.

This was how Ivan mourned.

CHAPTER XLII

EVILA

It was the anniversary of the great pit fire. Old Paul had gone to look for Ivan at his house in the principal colony, but Ivan had already started for the smaller colliery. He saw Paul on the road, and, stopping his carriage, took the miner up.

"This day last year was a memorable day," said Paul.

"I recollect it well," returned Ivan; "but to-day we have to give the prize for virtue. Have the jury settled to whom it is to be given?"

"They are agreed. A girl who has been little less than a year in the colliery."

"And she has fulfilled all conditions?"

"In every way. The child is most industrious. She is every morning the first to come and the last to leave. She never complains of the work, as many of them do; she treats it as if it were a pleasure to her. If her wheelbarrow is overloaded, she encourages the digger to put on still more; then she runs away gayly with her burden, and comes back singing as if she had been amusing herself. At the end of the recreation she drives the other girls back to their work."

"Is she vain?"

"No; she wears the same holiday clothes in which she was dressed when she came a year ago; naturally they are not quite as fresh as they were. She has a little string of beads round her throat, and in her hair a narrow ribbon. At night she washes her clothes in the stream, for she has one peculiarity—she wears fresh linen every day; but she makes it up herself, so she alone has the trouble."

"Is she saving?"

"She has more in our savings-bank than any one of the girls. She would have still more, only that on Sundays she gives a whole day's wages to the beggar who sits at the church door."

"Does she go to church regularly?"

"Every Sunday she comes with us, but she never sits with the other girls; she kneels before a side-altar, covers her face with her hands, and prays all through mass."

"Is she good-tempered?"

"She has offended no one and has never been angry. Once a woman said something very offensive to her, for which we gave her a heavy fine. The woman was ready to pay it, but the girl denied that she had been offended. Soon after the woman got ill; she had no one to nurse her, because she is a solitary widow, and this girl nursed her every night, and fetched the medicine from the apothecary for her."

"Do you think she is a hypocrite?"

"She is too merry for that, and ready for a joke. Hypocrites are gloomy folk. Our people would soon find her out if she wasn't on the square; but she is a prime favorite with every one. We don't choose our words exactly, but we can make a fair guess at the girl who respects herself. We like one that gives a good box on the ear to a fellow who would make too free. Sharp with the hand, but soft with her tongue; that's our sort. And still, sometimes I have watched her when she was in quite another mood; for instance, on Sunday afternoons, when we sit under the mulberry-trees, they all get round me and make me tell them—God knows how often!—the story of how you carried the pipe of the air-pump into the gallery of the Bondavara mine, and how we all thought you were a dead man. Women and children hold their breath while I tell it. I believe I do tell that story well, for they know it by heart, and yet they cannot but listen. They take it in different ways; but this girl, I have noticed her, she covers up her face and cries the whole time."

"And is she a modest girl?"

"To ascertain this point we had to call a jury of married women. They couldn't bring forward a single charge against her. Then we got the girls together, and we pressed them very close, if there was anything with the young men, but they all said—no. And there was no need for them to deny, for a peasant girl is fitly mated with a miner, and if he wants her he can have her."

They had now reached the colliery, and went into the station-house, which stood at the corner of the branch railroad. There was now another line, which ran underground and connected the two collieries. Here Ivan found a great many of the miners. He sent for the rest, and told them work was over for the day. Men and women assembled by degrees, and only one group of girls still remained working. These had agreed not to leave off until they had driven their load of coals to the coal-hill, which lay between the entrance to the quarry gallery and the station-house where Ivan sat waiting. He could not see the girls; he could only hear their clear voices as they called to one another to make haste and get the work finished.

Some one began to sing. The melody was familiar

to Ivan—one of those sad Slav airs in which the singer seems on the brink of tears; and the voice was sweet and tuneful as a bell, full, too, of feeling.

> "Say when I smoothed thy hair,
> Showed I not tender care?
> Say when I dressed my child,
> Was I not fond and mild?"

Ivan's face clouded. "Why do they sing that air? Why should it be on the lips of any one? Why not let it fall into oblivion?"

"The girl is coming," said old Paul. "I hear her singing; she is now coming down the hill with her wheelbarrow."

The next moment the girl appeared upon the summit of the coal-hill. With a run she had shoved her wheelbarrow forward and emptied the contents with extraordinary dexterity; the big lumps of coal rolled down the hill. She was a young, well-developed girl in a blue jacket and a short petticoat; but this red petticoat was not tucked up—it fell over her ankles, and only showed her feet. The colored handkerchief on her head had fallen backward, and the rich plaits wound round her small head could be seen. Her face was smudged with coal-dust and was beaming with good-humor—earthly dirt, supernatural glory. But what the coal-dust could not conceal were the two large black eyes shining like two brilliants—the darkness illumined by dazzling stars.

The girl stood immovable on the summit of the coal-hill, then looked down with some surprise on the crowd gathered in and around the station-house.

The next moment Ivan was beside her. In his joy he had made one bound from the station-house across the rails and had rushed up the coal-hill.

"Eveline!" he cried, clasping the girl's hand in his.

She shook her head, smiling at him. "No, sir," she said, "Evila."

"You here! You have come back here!"

"I have been in your colliery, sir, for a year, and if you will keep me on I should like to stay."

"You shall stay only on one condition — as my wife," cried Ivan, pressing her hand to his heart.

All who were at the foot of the hill saw this action; they could almost hear his words.

Evila shook her head and drew away her hand. "No, no. Allow me to be your servant, a maid in your house, the maid of your wife. I shall be quite happy; I expect nothing more."

"But I wish it. You have come back to me; you are mine. How could you be so cruel as to be a year so near me and never to tell me?"

"Oh, sir, you cannot raise me to your position!" said Evila, with a sad yet dignified expression. "If you knew all you would never forgive me."

"I know everything, and forgive everything."

These words proved that Ivan knew nothing. If he had known the truth he would have been aware there was absolutely nothing to forgive. As it was, he pressed his young love close to his heart, while she murmured:

"You may forgive me, but the world will never pardon *you*."

"The world!" cried Ivan, raising his head proudly. "My world is *here*"—laying his hand on his breast. "The world! Look round you from this hill. Everything that lives in this valley owes its breath to me; every blade of grass has to thank *me* that it is now green. Hill and valley know that, under God, I have saved them from destruction. I have acquired a million, and I have not despoiled any one. With every penny I receive a blessing. In the palace of the prince and in the cottage of the widow I have dried the tears of despair; I have delivered my enemies from a living grave, and I have saved their wives and children from the misfortune of being widows and orphans. My name is spoken of with admiration all over the globe, and yet I have hid myself *here*, not to be troubled with their praises; I do not care for praise. The most lovely of women has smiled on me and loved me, but she was not of *my* world. She is dead, and the key of her coffin is a perpetual reminder to me that her world has passed away. My world is within me, and into that inner world of mine no one has ever entered, no one *will* ever enter, *but you!* Speak, Evila; answer me. Will you try to love me?"

The girl's eyes sank before the ardent gaze of her lover. Many men had made love to her, but none like this man, whose face shone like Jupiter's when, with a look, he killed Semele.

"Oh, sir," she murmured, "if I do not die I shall love you always; but my mind misgives me that I shall die."

As she spoke she fell back fainting, her brilliant color faded to a waxen pallor, the flashing eyes closed; her body, which a moment before was like a blooming rose, was now as lifeless as a withered leaf.

Ivan held her motionless form in his arms. The woman whom he had so loved, for whom he had suffered so much, was his, just as her pulse ceased to beat, just as she had said, "I shall love you always, but I know that I shall die."

But she did not die.

CHAPTER XLIII

THE DIAMOND REMAINED ALWAYS A DIAMOND

THE END

www.ingramcontent.com/pod-product-compliance
Lightning Source LLC
Chambersburg PA
CBHW022109300426
44117CB00007B/650